Andrew Jackson

THE GREAT GENERALS SERIES

This distinguished new series features the lives of eminent military leaders who changed history in the United States and abroad. Top military historians write concise but comprehensive biographies including the personal lives, battles, strategies, and legacies of these great generals, with the aim to provide background and insight into today's armies and wars. These books are of interest to the military history buff, and, thanks to fast-paced narratives and references to current affairs, they are also accessible to the general reader.

Patton by Alan Axelrod

Grant by John Mosier

Eisenhower by John Wukovits

LeMay by Barrett Tillman

MacArthur by Richard B. Frank

Stonewall Jackson by Donald A. Davis

Bradley by Alan Axelrod

Pershing by Jim Lacey

Sherman by Steven E. Woodworth

Andrew Jackson

Robert V. Remini

palgrave
macmillan

First published in 2008 by PALGRAVE MACMILLAN® in the
US–a division of St. Martin's Press LLC, 175 Fifth Avenue, New
York, NY 10010.

Where this book is distributed in the UK, Europe and the rest of the
world, this is by Palgrave Macmillan, a division of Macmillan
Publishers Limited, registered in England, company number 785998,
of Houndmills, Basingstoke, Hampshire RG21 6XS.

Palgrave Macmillan is the global academic imprint of the above
companies and has companies and representatives throughout the
world.

Palgrave® and Macmillan® are registered trademarks in the United
States, the United Kingdom, Europe and other countries.

ISBN-13: 978-0-230-60015-7
ISBN-10: 0-230-60015-8

Library of Congress Cataloging-in-Publication Data
Remini, Robert Vincent, 1921–
    Andrew Jackson / Robert V. Remini ; foreword by General Wesley
K. Clark.
        p.   cm.
    ISBN 0-230-60015-8
    1. Jackson, Andrew, 1767–1845—Military leadership.
2. Generals—United States—Biography.   3. Command of
troops—Case studies.   4. United States. Army—Biography.
5. Tennessee. Militia—Biography.   6. Indians of North America—
Wars.   7. United States—History, Military.   8. Presidents—
United States—Biography.   I. Title.
E382.R415   2008
973.5'6092—dc22
[B]

                                                2008000394

A catalogue record of the book is available from the British Library.

Design by Letra Libre

First edition: September 2008
10   9   8   7   6   5   4   3   2   1
Printed in the United States of America.

For Ruth

Contents

Foreword—General Wesley K. Clark   ix

Introduction   1
Chapter 1. The Indian Fighter   5
Chapter 2. The Creek War   41
Chapter 3. The Battle of New Orleans   79
Chapter 4. The First Seminole War   123
Chapter 5. The End of Military Service   165
Chapter 6. The Military Legacy   175

Notes   183
Index   197

The photosection appears between pages 122 and 123

Foreword

EVERY YEAR IN MOST STATES, DEMOCRATS FLOCK TO THEIR annual Jefferson-Jackson dinners. The emphasis is on Thomas Jefferson, of course, considered the founding father of the Democratic Party. Almost forgotten is the military record and legacy of Andrew Jackson, America's seventh president and perhaps greatest military hero before to the American Civil War.

Robert Remini's sparkling biography of Andrew Jackson helps set the record straight and reinvigorate Jackson's military legacy for modern Americans. More than anyone else, it was Jackson, through a combination of military leadership, inspired vision, and strong personality, who insured that America retained its independence, drove out European rivals. Under his leadership, America's influence grew to eventually span the entire continent.

Jackson's was a classic American success story: a young man born into poverty, orphaned, struggling against severe tribulations, and ultimately rising to the highest levels of success. As a youngster during the Revolutionary War, Jackson lost his mother and two brothers. His father had died just before he was born. Like other lads, he worked as a messenger around the American troops, was captured by the Brits, and "bladed" by a British officer for refusing to polish his boots. It was probably a defining moment in his life. Though lacking a proper education, he was determined to gain the military skills that would allow him to strike back against the British.

Jackson moved to Nashville, Tennessee, and took on the mantle of leadership as a young civic leader, lawyer, and militiaman. But his principal aspiration was military leadership. A rising star in the political arena on the frontier, he parlayed his connections into an appointment as a leader in the Tennessee militia, and all else followed.

Jackson had seen war as a child; he was steeped in the lore and practice of Indian fighting, an all-too-common circumstance on the frontier. He'd learned the tricks of moving through the woods, of before-dawn stand-to, and early morning readiness, and he'd learned to encircle a foe. It was a standard repertoire. But Jackson brought to this three unique qualities: first, he was a keen judge of strategies and intent; second, he had an indomitable will; and third, he had a real thirst to be in charge. These qualities shone through, effort after effort.

Under Jackson, the United States defeated a superior British force at the Battle of New Orleans. It was his greatest victory; it made him a household name and it cleared a path for the United States to dominate North America.

From today's perspective, the battle looks tactical and almost feeble: a few thousand American troops defending a barricade behind a ditch along the Mississippi River south of New Orleans, with a weak and under-protected flank guard across the river. The outcome almost seemed to turn on luck—fog, clumsy, ill-timed British attacks, ponderous movements—and a poorly executed final assault which led to the slaughter of the British troops attempting to breach the ditch and storm the barricade. It would be easy to mistake the battle as more of a British defeat than an American victory. But that would be to underestimate the incredible strength and resourcefulness which Jackson brought to the campaign, and to disregard the months of maneuver and conflict which culminated in the battle. Jackson was not only a strong tactician; he was a master strategist, operating at the highest levels of the military art.

Over a period of more than a year preceding the battle, Jackson raised a force of several thousand men, marched them overland and moved by river from Nashville to Natchez, returned his force to Tennessee, reformed and refitted a new force, marched south into Alabama, wiped out an Indian force aided and abetted by the British, drove off a British force in the Florida panhandle and around Mobile Bay, countermarched to New Orleans, took control of the city (under martial law), and bent the city's resources to its own defense, including even the local band of pirates under the Lafitte brothers. In the course of these maneuvers he dealt with severe shortages of supplies, an absence of effective strategic direction from higher authority, and repeated disobedience, rebellion and desertion from within his command. At one point he faced down mutinous troops with a musket and his steely gaze; at another he actually trained his cannon on a mutinous brigade, stood in the line of fire, and invited the men to decide their fate, acknowledging that if they broke he would open fire and be among the first casualties.

Jackson was a man with a steel will. He persevered in command despite illness and personal suffering. He demanded the same level of hardiness from his troops, even as he took care of those who were ill and injured. And, ultimately, they came to love him for it.

New Orleans was a victory which set bells pealing across America. Despite defeat after defeat in the War of 1812, the Battle of New Orleans proved that the United States could beat the best that Britain could field. Jackson's victory confirmed America's independence.

In the years subsequent to the battle, Jackson went on to drive the Spanish out of Florida and became America's president. In that position he encouraged further settlement of the west, and was instrumental in pushing the American effort in Texas.

By twenty-first-century standards Jackson appears as a deeply flawed personality—a slave-owning, hot-tempered duelist, quick to anger and never able to forget a slight. He was quarrelsome, egocentric, and utterly demanding. His leadership as President was marked by deep controversy. But Andrew Jackson's military prowess, proved on half a dozen battlefields, makes him one of our greatest generals and a strategic force in the shaping of modern America. His is a legacy that must be remembered.

—*General Wesley K. Clark*

Introduction

ANDREW JACKSON HAS THE UNIQUE DISTINCTION OF FIGHTING those nations that, at one time or another, claimed possession of part or all of the continental United States. He fought the British as a soldier boy during the American Revolution and again during the War of 1812. He fought the Spanish when he invaded and seized Florida from them in 1818. And during much of his life, from his early years into maturity, he fought Native Americans.

Jackson had a vision. National security was central to his thinking about the destiny of this country. He felt that national security dictated the occupation of North America by citizens of the United States. And he was motivated by an intense love of country. He did not talk about Canada very much but concentrated on the lower half of the continent, especially the Southwest, along the Gulf of Mexico. It was dangerous, he declared, "to leave a foreign power in possession of heads of our leading branches of the great mississippi [*sic*]." Expansion was "necessary for the security of the great emporium of the west, Neworleans [*sic*]." Besides, he went on, "the god of the universe had intended this great valley to one nation." And that nation—obviously—was the United States. For that reason, he regarded the presence of the British, Spanish, and Native Americans to be a constant threat to the safety of the American people and why he was determined to get rid of them. One by one he had defeated all of them militarily. But that was not enough. Jackson was simply repeating what he had said just prior to the War of 1812. In a letter to General James Winchester, he said that with "less than two million [dollars we] can conquer not only the Floridas but all Spanish North America."

All Spanish North America! "I have a hope," Jackson continued, "that at least two thousand Volunteers can be led into the field at a short notice—That number commanded by firm officers and men of enterprise—I think could look into Santa Fe and Mexico—give freedom and commerce to those provinces and establish peace, and a permanent barrier against the inroads and attacks of foreign powers on our interior—which will be the case so long as Spain holds that large country on our borders."

That large country on our borders must be surrendered to us, he said. And it will be—from the Floridas to Mexico.[1]

A dream of empire—and, to a very large extent, General Andrew Jackson converted it into a reality.

What makes it all so intriguing is that this conqueror had almost no training in the art of war. He did, in fact, participate in military action as a youth, but what he learned resulted from observing leaders whom he admired. His development into a superb military general came about mainly because of his ability to inspire troops by his obvious talents as a commander. They had confidence in him, they trusted him, and they were devoted to him.

One example of the intense relationship between Jackson and his soldiers occurred during the War of 1812 when he escorted his men through a wilderness back to Nashville. He surrendered his horses so that the sick would not be left behind and would have transport to bring them safely home. As the army marched, he walked alongside his troops, urging them on, appealing to their love of country, and assuring them of his pride in their bravery. They knew he cared for them and would do everything in his power to get them safely home. And it was that overwhelming sense of his affection for his troops that helped him to win victory over his country's enemies and lifted him into the ranks of great American generals.

CHAPTER 1

The Indian Fighter

ANDREW JACKSON WAS BORN TO A SCOTS-IRISH FAMILY THAT came to this country from Castlereagh on the east coast of Northern Ireland in 1765 and settled in the Waxhaw district, which straddles an area between North and South Carolina. General Jackson always claimed that he was born in South Carolina, but he may have been mistaken, for many North Carolinians, even today, believe he was born in their state. The problem arose because his mother, Elizabeth Hutchison Jackson, visited two of her sisters after her husband died, one living in North Carolina, the other in South Carolina. Presumably she was visiting Jane Crawford, her sister in South Carolina, when on March 15, 1767, she gave birth to a son and named him after his late father, Andrew. We do know that she took up residence in Jane's house and remained there for several years, serving as housekeeper and nurse to her ailing sister. So it is most likely that General Jackson was indeed a South Carolinian by birth.

There were two older brothers in the family, Hugh, the eldest, and Robert. When they were old enough, they, along with Andrew, attended an academy operated by Dr. William Humphries. Because Elizabeth was a very pious Presbyterian, she hoped that her youngest son would become a minister. To attain this goal, Andrew later attended a school run by a distinguished Presbyterian minister James White Stephenson, but he never demonstrated any interest or talent for the church. Quite the contrary. Lacking a father to properly guide him, young Andrew developed habits of speech to convey his anger or disappointment that no God-fearing person would tolerate. And his education was most deficient. He did learn to read and write and do simple problems of arithmetic, but he never received an education that prepared him for the great office he later achieved.

It was therefore up to Elizabeth to assist the boy in his character development, and being a strong woman herself, she contributed a great deal to the man he became. According to tradition, she taught him not to steal, lie, or sue for slander or assault. The dueling ground was the place to resolve personal grievances, she lectured. "Sustain your manhood always. . . . Never wound the feelings of others. Never brook wanton outrage upon your own feelings." Apparently these instructions had a great impact on General Jackson. After he defeated the British in New Orleans in January 1815, he reportedly said to a group of friends standing nearby: "Gentlemen, I wish she could have lived to see this day. There never was a woman like her. She was gentle as a dove and as brave as a lioness."[1]

Elizabeth also taught Andrew to fear and hate Indians. According to a neighbor, Susan Alexander—Aunt Betty, as Elizabeth was known to family and friends—was a "fresh-looking, fair-haired, very conservative, old Irish lady, at dreadful enmity with the Indians." Alexander claimed in what was pure speculation that Elizabeth's eldest son, but not Hugh or Robert, was killed by the Indians. The family, Alexander remarked, "did lament about their eldest son and brother. They took great spells of mourning about him." Now Hugh, the eldest living child, died while fighting in the American Revolution, most probably of heat stroke, and Robert died shortly after his release from British captivity during that same war. And there is no evidence of any other son of the Jackson family. Still, Susan Alexander insisted that Elizabeth's fierce hatred of the Indians resulted from the killing of a kinsman.

"Mrs. Jackson and her son, Andrew, came to our house," Alexander continued; but not Hugh or Robert. "Nor do I recollect hearing them mention any other brother than the one that was killed. I only recollect about the death of that one brother, and I had it as a perfect belief, that he was killed by the Indians—for they often mourned him, and they were inveterate haters of the Indians, on account of their barbarities—both he and his mother.

"Oh," said Alexander, "we all suffered by those horrid Indians, and the remembrance of it has not gone out of me yet."[2]

Although the local Indian tribe in the Waxhaw region was the Catawbas, who had long since learned to live peacefully with the white community there was always the danger of marauding tribes from the mountains to the west, such as the Cherokees, who would suddenly descend on frontiersmen and their families living in the Carolinas. Young children, like Andrew, learned early on about the danger the Indian represented and the need to protect themselves. No doubt Andrew picked up his hostile attitudes about Native Americans from his brothers, his uncles, and most probably his schoolmates and playmates. It was reported that he learned to make bows and arrows, just like the Indians, and became something of a marksman "in shooting snipes, partridges and wild turkeys" with his handmade weapons. Susan Alexander remembered him as a "lank, leaning-forward fellow," tall of his age with "a large forehead and big eyes." All in all, she said, he "was an independent boy in his manner . . . [and] could not well be idle."[3]

As he entered his teenage years, Andrew gained a reputation as an unruly, wild, and headstrong ruffian. He never forgot an affront or insult, and he never suffered them without responding in kind. He was a mischievous troublemaker, stubborn and quick to anger. Perhaps his undisciplined behavior could be chalked up to his youth or his lack of an appropriate role model. An early biographer described him as "a wild, frolicksome, willful, mischievous, daring, reckless boy." At the same time he demonstrated unswerving loyalty to his friends and could be "singularly tender" toward them.[4]

The fighting streak in Andrew soon had a worthy target when the colonial leaders in Philadelphia signed a Declaration of Independence from Great Britain in July 1776 and took up arms to defend their newly declared freedom. In time, the British brought the war to South Carolina and Georgia by capturing Charleston and Savannah. Then, in the spring of 1780, approximately 300 mounted British soldiers, under the command of Lieutenant Colonel Banastre Tarleton, rode into the Waxhaws in a surprise attack and killed 113 locals and wounded another 150. Their assault was so savage that the raid was rightly called a massacre. They pillaged and burned homes and virtually destroyed the community.

The meetinghouse was converted into a hospital, and Elizabeth Jackson and two of her three young sons tended the wounded. The eldest, Hugh, had joined the regiment of William Richardson Davie and later died of "the fatigues of the day" at the battle of Stono Ferry.[5] At the time, Andrew was 13.

Elizabeth encouraged Robert and Andrew to attend the drills and general muster of the local militia. The two boys quickly learned the commands and exercises of military service. Andrew, in particular, understood the value of the militia and how important it was to keep the men well trained. Discipline was essential, something he never forgot. But he also recognized the political and social values that accompanied membership in this military organization. Holding rank in the militia provided a high position—perhaps the highest—in American frontier society.

Following the Tarleton raid, the Waxhaws community kept pleading for protection, and it finally arrived in the person of Colonel Davie and a small fighting force intent on avenging the massacre. Andrew and Robert joined Davie's force and may have served as messengers or errand boys. As part of this fighting group, Andrew had the opportunity of observing the actions, attitude, and operation of the commanding officer.

An early biographer said that if General Andrew Jackson had any model for soldiering, that model was William Richardson Davie. The colonel cared for his men, looked after their needs, and regularly showed attention to their well-being. He hardly rested. He was constantly on the move, constantly vigilant and concerned and involved in every aspect of his command. In addition, he was bold in planning his military operations but extremely cautious in exercising them. Many of these same characteristics can be seen in Jackson's later struggles with the Indians, the British, and the Spanish.[6]

The following winter, 1781, the enemy returned to the Waxhaws, and fierce fighting broke out again. It turned into a vicious civil war between those loyal to the crown and those supporting independence. "Men hunted each other like beasts of prey," wrote one biographer, "and the savages [Indians] were outdone in cruelties to the living and indignities to the dead." Andrew and his brother participated in many of the skirmishes between the two factions, and they were both taken prisoner when a Tory neighbor notified British dragoons that they were hiding in their uncle's home. The troops surrounded the house, then burst in and captured the two boys.

One of the British officers ordered Andrew to clean his boots and when the boy refused, the officer drew his sword and aimed it directly at the lad's head. Andrew threw up his left arm to ward off the blow and received a deep gash on his forehead and fingers, a lifetime reminder of British brutality.

Robert and Andrew, along with 20 other captives, were taken to a concentration camp in Camden, South Carolina, where they were "inhumanly" and "harshly" treated, reported one early biographer. Never would Andrew forget the experience. Thrown in with 250 other prisoners, the boys were robbed and abused. Lacking proper food, medicine, and beds, they soon contracted smallpox. Fortunately, Elizabeth arrived at the exact time that an exchange of prisoners was being arranged by Lord Rawdon and Captain Walker of the American militia. Faced with the desperation of an imploring mother, the officers agreed to include her children in the exchange. They were surrendered, along with several other Waxhaws neighbors, in return for a number of British soldiers.[7]

Elizabeth could not believe what she saw: her two sons wasted by malnutrition and disease. She procured two horses and placed the dying Robert on one and rode the other herself. Andrew walked the 45 miles to their home, barefoot and without a jacket. Two days later, Robert died and Andrew was delirious. Fortunately, the attention and care of his mother, the help of a local doctor, and his own strong constitution brought Andrew through the crisis. He remained weak for months but finally recovered.

Once her son was out of danger, Elizabeth decided to go to Charleston to help nurse American prisoners of war held on prison ships in the harbor. Lord Cornwallis and his army had moved out of South Carolina and had arrived in Virginia, where he fortified Yorktown. So it seemed safe for her to travel the 160 miles to Charleston. Along with other nurses she reached her destination safely, but she later contracted cholera and died.

Alone at the age of 15, Andrew was an orphan and a veteran of the Revolutionary War. He had endured intense personal suffering, having lost his entire immediate family and having survived a bout with a deadly disease. For the next few years, he showed signs of developing into an angry, resentful, and depressed young man—and one still weak from his past illness. He lived for a time in the home of his Uncle Thomas Crawford. Another boarder in the house, one Captain Galbraith, took offense on one occasion to something Andrew said or did and raised his hand to strike him. At that, Andrew lost control and showered the captain with angry curses. He swore that if the hand touched him, Galbraith was a dead man. And he never forgot the incident. "I had arrived at an age to know my rights," he said, "and although weak and feeble from disease, I had courage to defend them, and if he attempted anything of that kind I would have most certainly Sent him to the other world."[8]

Andrew spent the next few years carousing in Charleston with several other rowdies, drinking, gambling, cockfighting, and mischief making in a wild, carefree spree that bordered on the manic. It is remarkable that he did not get into serious trouble. But the record shows no collision with the law. Finally, when he had frittered away what little money he had from an inheritance, his buddies deserted him and he returned to the Waxhaws. Having given his anger, grief, and resentment unbridled indulgence in Charleston, he finally came to his senses back home.

It was there that he realized he had no future in South Carolina and decided to move north to Salisbury in Rowan County, North Carolina, where he knew he could find employment in a lawyer's office and begin the study of the law. He was now 17 years of age. It was 1784, and he figured that the law would allow him to get ahead in the new nation that had achieved its independence and established a republican government. He packed up his belongings and left the Waxhaws. He never looked back.

He found employment in the law office of Spruce McCay, an eminent attorney, and for the next two years he ran errands, copied documents, cleaned the office, read law books, and attended legal proceedings of one kind or another. After a few years of this course of study he could presumably be admitted to the North Carolina bar. He found living quarters in town with a number of other law students, and without any plan or intention he became their leader. It was natural. Unfortunately, some of his activities offended other townspeople. One of them remembered him as "the most roaring, rollicking, gamecocking, horse-racing, card-playing mischievous fellow that ever lived in Salisbury."[9] But this wildness was unlike his manic behavior in Charleston. He was no longer assuaging his anger and resentment. He was simply having fun and letting off steam after a long day of tedious work in the law office.

Andrew was not much of a student of the law, but rather preferred the stables and horses. And apparently he was well liked by those who knew him best. There was something attractive about his manner and presence. He was charismatic. People were drawn to him. It was later reported that if Andrew Jackson joined a party of travelers and they were attacked by Indians, he would instinctively take command of the party and conduct the defensive actions. Even at the early age of 18, he possessed qualities of command that would later achieve great success on the battlefield.[10]

An obvious reason for his commanding presence was his appearance. He stood six feet one inch tall and was extremely slender, never weighing more than 140 pounds. He carried himself with an air of self-confidence and strength. He had a shock of sandy-colored, bushy hair that stood as straight as he did, and it gave him another inch or two of height. He had very sharp features with a jutting jaw and a long straight nose. Most important of all, he had deep-blue eyes that instantly conveyed his pleasure or displeasure at what was going on around him and added strength to his appearance.

Andrew finally ended his apprenticeship at McCay's in 1786 and completed his study of law in the office of Colonel John Stokes, considered the best lawyer in North Carolina. He had apparently learned enough law to appear on September 26, 1787 before two judges of the Superior Court of Law and Equity of North Carolina and win the right to practice as an attorney in the several courts of pleas and quarter sessions within the state.

For the next six months he wandered around the state looking for a place to practice but had little luck. Then he heard that John McNairy, a fellow student at McCay's, had been elected by the North Carolina legislature to serve as the superior court judge for the western district of the state, the area that later became Tennessee, and given the authority to appoint the district's public prosecutor. McNairy offered the position to Jackson who readily accepted. He and Bennett Searcy, another McCay student who had been appointed clerk of the court, and three or four others agreed to form a party, rendezvous in Morgantown, and then head west for Tennessee. Two western settlements had already been formed in Tennessee, one around Knoxville and the other around the Cumberland River Valley centered in Nashville.

These frontier communities were dangerous places, regularly attacked by marauding Indians, especially Cherokees. Their assaults were so numerous that settlers frequently had to flee their homes and take refuge in Kentucky. Militias from several communities would then band together and drive the Indians back to their tribal lands. The settlers would return to find burned-out houses and devastated fields. With determination they rebuilt as quickly as possible.

Jackson knew the dangers involved in heading into Tennessee, but they did not deter him. Still, for added safety, he, McNairy, and the others decided to join a party of 60 families, numbering about 100 persons, which had a sizable escort. On November 28, 1788, they all set off to the west, heading for Nashville, a distance of 183 miles.[11] When they arrived at what was considered the most dangerous segment of their journey, they kept moving, never stopping to rest or make camp. For some 36 hours (or a night and two days), they did not halt for more than an hour. They knew that once they reached a particular place, they would be relatively safe from attack. Only then did they feel comfortable about resting and making camp.

Luckily they reached this point of safety without incident and they immediately lit fires and set up tents for the women and children to sleep. The men, except for those on guard duty, wrapped themselves in blankets and lay down on the ground. Soon complete silence enveloped the camp. All slept—all except Andrew Jackson, who sat on the ground with his back against a tree, smoking a corncob pipe. But soon even he began to doze off. As he did so, he heard the hooting of owls in the forest around him. Strange, owls in this country. The hooting became louder and closer. Then it suddenly hit him: These were no owls. He bolted awake and jumped to his feet, grabbed his gun, and shook the sleeping Bennett Searcy.

"Searcy," Jackson whispered, "raise your head and make no noise."

"What's the matter?" mumbled the dazed and semiconscious Searcy.

"The owls—listen," hissed Jackson. "There—there again. Isn't that a little too natural?"

"Do you think so?" asked the now fully awakened Searcy.

"I know it," said Jackson. "There are Indians all around us. I have heard them in every direction. They mean to attack before daybreak."[12]

Most probably Jackson learned the ways in which the Indians signaled one another during his early years in the Waxhaws. White children were taught to beware of strange or unusual sounds emanating from the forest.

Jackson and Searcy awoke the other members of the camp. Some older members of the party confirmed Jackson's suspicions. So, quickly but noiselessly, the settlers were roused, the camp was broken up, and the entire company moved out. During their evacuation, they neither saw nor heard Indians, but an hour later a group of hunters came upon the abandoned camp and decided to take advantage of the still-smoldering fires and get some rest. Just before dawn the Indians attacked and all but one of the hunters were killed.[13]

Around the end of October 1788, Jackson, McNairy, and the others arrived in Nashville, a frontier community in central Tennessee. Jackson found lodgings at the home of the widow Donelson, whose husband, John, was one of the original settlers but who had been killed by Indians. Jackson also met the widow's youngest daughter, Rachel, who was married to Lewis Robards of Kentucky. Jackson and Rachel immediately fell in love, and when Robards returned to Kentucky he began divorce proceedings. After a long delay and misunderstandings, the divorce was finally granted, and Andrew and Rachel were married in 1793 by a justice of the peace.

In Nashville, Jackson gained an enviable reputation as a prosecutor and established his own private law practice. Together with John Overton and Samuel Donelson, one of Rachel's many brothers, he formed a partnership to buy and sell land and operate a store on the Cumberland River.

But the situation with the Cherokees did not improve. Indeed, no settler dared to live more than five miles from the central stockade in Nashville. Several stations, or primitive forts, along the Cumberland River had been set up for protection against the Indians, and they guarded a white population of approximately 5,000 men, women, and children who had come to this remote frontier, starting in 1779. On average, the Cherokees killed a settler every 10 days. And the constant arrival of white men seeking land only exacerbated the situation.

Naturally, upon settling in Nashville, Jackson participated in the protection and defense of the community. He "aided alike in garrisoning the forts, and in pursuing and chastising the enemy," according to one early report.[14] As a matter of fact, virtually upon his arrival in Nashville, he was conscripted into an expedition to punish the Cherokees, who had made a daring attack on the Robertson Station in broad daylight when the men were out plowing the fields. The force consisted of 60 or 70 men, commanded by Captain Sampson Williams. They tracked the hostiles and caught up with about 30 Cherokees encamped on the south side of the Cumberland River. At daybreak, they made a surprise attack. Several Indians were killed, but the rest of them splashed across the river to the north side and disappeared into the forest. The Indians left behind 16 guns, 19 shot pouches, and all their luggage, consisting of blankets, leggings, moccasins, skins, and other articles.[15] This was Jackson's "first Indian campaign and Indian fight" in Tennessee, said an early historian. He had the rank of private in this operation, but, according to Williams, he was "bold, dashing, fearless, and *mad upon his enemies.*" The two men became close friends and "had great ambition for encounters with the savages."[16]

As it developed, Jackson had any number of opportunities to achieve his "great ambition." In the pursuit of his legal business, he was obliged to travel regularly from Nashville to Jonesborough. During the first seven years of his residence in Tennessee, he made this trip a total of 22 times—this when the Indian menace was at its height. He usually traveled in the company of other men. They had any number of encounters with the "savages," and in the process he learned a great deal about Indian habits and practices and soon gained a reputation as one of Tennessee's best Indian fighters. Moreover, his leadership ability became immediately apparent, and he was soon taking charge of some of these expeditions.[17]

To Jackson and virtually all the men in Nashville, killing Indians and driving them farther south and west was a vital necessity. It was the only way they knew to protect themselves and safeguard the Tennessee frontier. One way or another, they believed, the "savages" had to be disposed of.

The Indian problem worsened because of the presence of the Spanish in Florida and Louisiana who regularly supplied the Cherokees, Creeks, Choctaws, and Chickasaws with guns and ammunition, a situation that convinced most frontiersmen that Spain, like England, had to be expelled from the continent. Worse, the Spanish controlled the mouth of the Mississippi River. If settlers wished to sell their produce in Natchez or New Orleans or even ship it to the east via the Gulf of Mexico, they had to have Spanish approval, which cost 15 percent of the produce. Relief from this tax and an end to the devastating effects of Indian assaults prompted some Tennesseans to consider separating from the United States. This Spanish Conspiracy, as it was called, influenced many frontiersmen, including Andrew Jackson. "I think it the only immediate way," Jackson wrote to Brigadier General Daniel Smith, "to obtain a peace with the savage."[18]

Tennesseans turned to their government for help but received little support. A new Congress was formed in 1789 under the Constitution, and George Washington became President of the United States. A year later Congress established the Territory of the United States South of the Ohio River out of the vast country between Kentucky and the territories of Alabama and Mississippi. William Blount of North Carolina was appointed governor and General Smith secretary.

To improve the situation, the new American government attempted to hold peace talks with the Indians, something Jackson sneered at. Peace talks are nothing but "Delusions" to put white men off their guard, he wrote to his friend John McKee. Why hold them when experience "teaches us that Treaties answer No other Purpose than opening an Easy door for the Indians to pass through and Butcher our Citizens"? Jackson ended his letter with a clear reference to the Spanish Conspiracy. Unless the United States government can provide adequate protection, "this Country will have at length to break or seek a protection from some other Source than the present."[19]

Governor Blount became acquainted with Jackson and his rising reputation as an Indian fighter, a prosecutor, and a political presence in Nashville. In fact, Blount began a correspondence with the young man, and at one point asked him to serve as his agent in the purchase of land. Then, on September 10, 1792, he appointed Jackson as judge advocate for the Davidson County cavalry regiment commanded by Lieutenant Colonel Robert Hays. The appointment was a recognition not only of Jackson's legal ability but also of his long service as a volunteer in the armed militia fighting Indians on the frontier.

Now Jackson, at 25, had an official position in the militia. A month later Blount tried to promote him. "Can't you contrive for Hays to resign," he asked General Robertson, "and I will promote John Donelson and appoint Jackson second Major." Robertson warned the governor against such a politically unwise move, and Blount backed off. But it was another sign of Jackson's growing recognition as an important presence in Tennessee.

For the next several months Jackson put in a great deal of military time as the Cherokees continued "to prowl around and infest the settlements" and kill white inhabitants. They planned their raids from the five "Lower Towns" near Chattanooga along the Cumberland River, frequently with the aid of Creeks and Chickasaws. On September 6, 1794, said one early historian, an expedition of 550 mounted infantry descended on the Cherokee town of Nickajack and killed "a considerable number of warriors." They also destroyed the Indian town of Running Water, the largest and "among the most hostile towns of the Cherokees." Reportedly Jackson not only helped plan the attack on Nickajack but demonstrated "good conduct generally in the campaign." Among the war trophies captured by the Tennesseans were guns and ammunition recently delivered by the Spanish government.[20] The Nickajack campaign effectively ended the war with the Cherokees, and the western region around Nashville became more pacified. The frontier moved farther west.

Blount and his friends decided in 1794 that the only way to settle the Indian problem was for Tennessee to become a state and manage its own affairs without any direction from the central government. So he guided the territorial legislature into arranging a plebiscite on the question and a census to make sure the population was large enough to apply for statehood. The calling of a constitutional convention was also scheduled. As it turned out, the census showed that 77,000 white males, females, free blacks, and slaves inhabited the territory, of whom 6,504 favored statehood and 2,562 did not. An election of delegates to the constitutional convention followed, held on December 18 and 19, 1795, and among the five men elected from Davidson County was Andrew Jackson. His election was a further sign of his growing reputation as a leader in the western district and his popularity among his neighbors.[21]

The delegates wrote a constitution for the territory, Congress approved it, and President Washington signed the legislation making Tennessee a state on June 1, 1796. Blount was elected U.S. Senator along with William Cocke. And, as their single representative in the U.S. House of Representatives, the people of Tennessee elected Andrew Jackson. He had no opposition in the western districts of the state and only token opposition in Washington County to the east. He received 1,113 votes, while his opponent, James Rody, won 12.[22]

Before taking his seat in Congress, Jackson made a bold attempt to win election as major general of the state's militia. In those days, selection of commanding officers in the militia was done by election. The state was divided into three districts, each having a brigade with a cavalry attached to it, and a regiment. Members of the militia elected regimental and company officers; field officers elected the brigadier generals. And the major general, who commanded the militia of the entire state, was elected by the field officers of all three districts plus the brigadier generals.

This bold move by the 29-year-old Jackson says a great deal about his character. He was intensely ambitious and probably had been planning to run for the office of major general for some time. He had a strong sense of his own worth, and because he had fought Indians for the past several years and demonstrated his leadership skills, he figured he was more than qualified to command the state's fighting force. But John Sevier, the Revolutionary War general and presently the governor of Tennessee, had other ideas. He preferred George Conway for the post and through political manipulation defeated Jackson's bid to head the militia.

Jackson learned several lessons from this experience. If he expected to be elected major general of the Tennessee militia, he would need to work at preparing the ground by attracting a personal following within the corps and also show a deep interest in the affairs of the organization. Most especially he needed to participate actively in all future elections, whether it involved regimental and company officers, field officers or brigadier generals.

Conway's election took place in November 1796, and Jackson took his seat in the House of Representatives a month later. During the second session of the Fourth Congress meeting in Philadelphia, the capital of the government until it moved to Washington, D.C., in 1800, the young representative hardly said a word. But when a petition was received from Hugh Lawson White, a fellow Tennessean, requesting compensation for his services in a campaign against several Cherokee towns led by General Sevier in 1793, Jackson sprang to attention and became not only vocal but very active. President Washington had refused the claim on the advice of Secretary of War Henry Knox, who declared that the expedition was not justified. The attack was offensive, not defensive, declared Knox, and a violation of the specific orders from the War Department.

Jackson bolted to his feet on the House floor. He roared his rage. He insisted that the raids were "just and necessary. When it was seen that war was waged upon the State, that the knife and the tomahawk were held over the heads of women and children, that peaceable citizens were murdered" by the "savages," it necessitated a swift and forceful response. He ended his outburst by offering a resolution:

"Resolved, That General Sevier's expedition into the Cherokee Nation, in the year 1793 was a just and necessary measure, and that provision ought to be made by law for paying the expenses involved."[23]

The vote was put off until the next day. Meanwhile, Jackson solicited help from his colleagues, speaking privately with them. He also gave several more speeches on the floor about the expedition and even demanded that the entire expeditionary force, not just White, be compensated for their service. If the cause was just for one man, he said, it was just for all the others. A long debate followed in which Jackson presented supporting documents along with a summary that he himself wrote listing all the "depredations" that had been submitted to the secretary of the territory back in 1793.

A select committee was formed with Jackson as chairman to bring a recommendation to the House. A month later the committee submitted its report, written by Jackson, and, not surprisingly, it recommended full compensation for the entire militia. The bill passed and the militia received $22,816.[24]

This outstanding success in obtaining compensation for the militia raised Jackson to new heights of popularity among the people of the West, and especially the members of the militia. "The payment of Seviers expedition," wrote William C. C. Claiborne, the future governor of Louisiana, to Jackson, "has heighten[ed] the esteem of the people for the General Government and secured to yourself a permanent interest."[25]

The congressman followed up this success by demanding payment to those who participated in the Nickajack expedition. This was a bit self-serving, but Jackson probably did not realize or consider that fact. He simply felt that those involved in making the frontier safer should be compensated. When the names of all those who participated in the attack could not be found, Jackson asked the expedition's commanding officer to help obtain them. "I wish you to publish this letter for the information of those citizens, who served under your command on the expedition." The information was obtained, again adding to Jackson's reputation as an outstanding representative, and a payment of $12,000 was authorized for the members of the expedition.[26]

Although Jackson's views about Indians who wantonly killed or attacked settlers were harsh, he also condemned whites who deliberately murdered Indians, stole their land, and acted without authority from any legitimate government. He told Governor Sevier he hoped that those white men guilty of such crimes would be apprehended and brought to trial.

When Jackson's term in the House ended, he did not seek reelection. Instead he stood for election in the U.S. Senate, after Blount had been expelled from that body for inviting the British to subsidize filibusters in Florida and Louisiana. On September 26, 1797, the Tennessee legislature elected Jackson to the Senate by a vote of 20 to 13.

He should never have done it. The Senate was no place for a man like Jackson, and he soon discovered his mistake. He was completely out of his depth. His record in the upper house is virtually a blank. Bored, frustrated, and weary, he finally resigned his office on April 16, 1798, without apology or explanation. He simply walked away from a job he could not perform.

It is very possible that he made the decision to resign because the possibility of a judgeship opened up that proved very attractive, one that would advance his political and military ambitions by taking him to all the districts of the state. The position would seat him on the bench as a state superior court judge and require him to attend court in various localities. Shortly after his return to Nashville, the Tennessee legislature approved his appointment, and Governor Sevier signed his commission on December 22, 1798 at a salary of $600 per annum. Jackson, then 31, served on the bench for the next six years.

Although his knowledge of the law was a little shaky, several commentators claim that he performed his duties quite well. "Tradition reports," said an early biographer, "that he maintained the dignity and authority of the bench, while he was on the bench; and that his decisions were short, untechnical, unlearned, sometimes ungrammatical, and generally right." Respect for the law was something he insisted on in his courtroom. And no one who faced him ever forgot it.[27]

The best example of Jackson's character in this regard involved one Russell Bean, a "great hulking fellow" who was hauled into court for cutting off the ears of his child in a "drunken frolic." He marched into the room, cursed the judge, jury, and spectators, and then brazenly walked out the door.

"Sheriff," roared Justice Jackson, "arrest that man for contempt of court and confine him."

The sheriff obeyed but in a short while he reported back that he could not apprehend Bean.

"Summon a posse, then," Jackson ordered, "and bring him before me."

Once again the sheriff, with the posse, could not get near the man. Bean threatened to shoot the "first skunk that came within ten feet of him," so not a single member of the posse tried to apprehend him.

"Mr. Sheriff," the judge raged, "since you can not obey my orders, summon me, yes, sir, summon me."

"Well, judge if you say so, though I don't like to do it; but if you will try, why I suppose I must summon you."

Jackson adjourned the court as he headed out the door. He found Bean a short distance away, at the center of a crowd, cursing and flourishing his pistols and threatening death to anyone who might try to take him into custody.

Jackson walked straight toward the man, eyes blazing, a pistol in each hand. "Now," he roared as he looked straight at Bean, "surrender, you infernal villain, this very instant, or I'll blow you through."

Bean stared at Jackson and in an instant a complete change came over him. "There judge," he meekly answered, "it's no use. I give in." He dropped his weapons and was carted off to jail.

What had happened to bring about this miraculous transformation? In his jail cell he was asked why he had surrendered to the judge after defying the sheriff and an entire posse. Why, responded Bean, "when he came up, I looked him in the eye, and I saw shoot, and there wasn't shoot in nary another eye in the crowd; and so I says to myself, says I, hoss, it's about time to sing small, and so I did."

It was Jackson's bright, blue, blazing eyes. They instantly registered whatever passion or emotion surged within him. There was no mistaking their meaning. And when they started to blaze, they sent a signal to the object of his wrath to get out of harm's way. Indians came to appreciate the meaning of the signal. They said he merely had to look at them that way and they fell lifeless to the ground. Later the soldiers he commanded would also learn the signal.

For the next several years Jackson attended his judicial duties, regularly touring the state, visiting with various officials in the several counties. He was especially attentive to the officers of the militia, listening to their complaints, cultivating their friendship, commiserating with their problems, and demonstrating his concern with the affairs of their command. It was a deliberate and well-planned pattern of behavior to win their friendship and support. There is no doubt that Jackson was determined to be elected major general of the militia, and this was the only way he knew to make it happen. So intense was his desire that it had become an obsession. And in 1802 it looked as though he would achieve his goal.

Unfortunately, John Sevier had run out his string of three successive terms as governor allowed by the state's constitution and was replaced by Archibald Roane, one of Jackson's close friends. So Sevier decided that at the next election for major general, he would run for the office, not expecting any opposition in view of his reputation as the hero of the Battle of King's Mountain during the Revolution and as a recognized leader in the ongoing wars with the Cherokees and Creeks. Needless to say, he was aghast when he learned that Jackson also intended to run for major general. He was appalled that a *"poor, pitiful petty fogging Lawyer,"* as he once called Jackson, had the temerity to stand against a veteran of the wars with Great Britain and Native Americans.[28]

His displeasure turned to cold fury when the results of the election held on February 2, 1802, were announced. Jackson and Sevier tied! Both had 17 votes, while Brigadier General James Winchester had 3. It was a remarkable showing for Jackson and demonstrated how far he had come in cultivating the friendship and loyalty of the other members of the militia since the previous election. Unquestionably, he would have won, had he not run against a man as formidable and distinguished as Sevier.

To break the tie, the election went to the new governor, who did not hesitate to choose his friend Andrew Jackson. Thus, in 1802, at the age of 35, Mr. Justice Jackson became Major General Jackson of the Tennessee militia, a position he held until May 1814, when he became a major general of the United States Army.

But that did not end the matter. On November 5, 1803, Sevier's friends shepherded a bill through the legislature, dividing the military command and creating two militia districts, one in the east and one in the west. Jackson was to retain command over the western district, while command of the eastern district went to Sevier.

The rivalry between Sevier and Jackson intensified over the next several months and finally resulted in a duel held in the Indian territory of South West Point. Fortunately, neither sustained any injury and their seconds managed to convince them to end their quarrel and return peacefully to Knoxville.

Jackson then began to take up his duties as a major general, and he performed them with such skill and intelligence that all the criticism about his age and arrogance in taking on Sevier soon disappeared. There was an immediate demonstration of leadership that surprised many and won the admiration and affection of his officers and men. For one thing, he showed genuine concern for their care and comfort. He went out of his way to make it clear that his first priority was their well-being. And he played the part of a major general to the hilt. He knew how to do it. He conducted himself with an intelligence that revealed his innate understanding of the meaning of leadership, and he quickly emerged as a figure of commanding presence and dignity that won the respect of his men. No one questioned his authority, and no one dared to disobey him. He brought a higher level of discipline to the militia, which made it a more effective fighting machine.

It is not possible to document how he learned the various skills that made him such a distinguished general. Whether he observed the actions and behavior of other generals and tried to emulate them cannot be verified. But leadership was native to him, and he knew how to put it to good use. Although he might not have known much about the rules of military strategy, he was quick to size up a situation and then instinctively do what would bring about military victory.

One of his first actions as major general came in May 1802, when Governor Roane informed him that an Indian had been murdered in a place close to the Cherokee boundary and that Major William Russell, a commissioned officer in the South County militia, had raised a party intent on taking the law into their own hands by searching a number of Indian camp sites and "breaking them up." On receiving this information, Jackson immediately contacted Colonel Henry McKinney of Jackson County (named for Jackson in 1801 in tribute to his many political successes) and instructed him to arrest Russell if he had indeed taken the law into his own hands. If not, McKinney was to order him to cease and desist his searching operation. If Russell refused to obey the order "I command you immediately to arrest him, and to furnish Brigadier [General James] Winchester [of the Mero District militia] with the charges against him so that a court martial may be called and a Speedy enquiry had into his conduct."[29]

This is the earliest known action taken by Jackson as major general, and it clearly demonstrated a degree of fairness and justice that characterized his reactions and behavior when dealing with Indians and the men of the militia. As he explained to McKinney, "the militia are considered to be the bulwark of our national peace prosperity and happiness, and for an officer thus to violate the law and hazard the peace of our country, is Such an example to those of a lower grade, that it ought and must meet, with speedy corrective."[30]

In addition to fairness, this letter is an obvious example of his racism, an attitude shared by many frontiersmen. He regarded Indians and slaves as "those of a lower order." Much as he might admire the courage of Indians and treat them with respect when they obeyed his orders, he looked down on them as inferiors who were prone to violence and barbarism.

Jackson also contacted Winchester and explained what he had ordered McKinney to do. He wanted Winchester to investigate and "if the facts are true" to "pursue the Legal steps to have a Speedy . . . court martial."[31]

This incident was typical of the sorts of activity that regularly required his attention. It did not take long for the militiamen to know that their commanding general would not tolerate violations of the law or of Indian treaties approved by the U.S. government. The troops learned, said Jackson, that they were expected to behave as "guardians of our national peace liberty and happiness."[32]

Throughout the early years of the young republic, white settlers continued to gain access to Indian lands. Sometimes the lands were acquired by treaty; sometimes, by war. From 1791 to 1819, the Cherokees signed 25 treaties with the federal government, usually because of debts they had incurred and the need to settle them by giving up their land. In fact, President Thomas Jefferson urged shopkeepers and factors to keep the Indians in debt so that they were obliged to agree to land cessions. The chiefs of the various tribes were usually bribed with goods and annuities to get them to approve the treaties that were negotiated by American agents. And once the land had been lawfully ceded, there was Major General Jackson to see to it that there was compliance by both white settlers and Indian tribes. And he brooked no violators.

For the next several years, Jackson diligently attended to his responsibilities as major general. He held regular drills of the militiamen, conducted meetings of the officers and staff, and, when necessary, he "chastised" those whites and Indians who violated the law. Of course, he also continued to act as judge, lawyer, land speculator, and businessman. Moreover, he kept an eye on the Spanish in Florida and Louisiana and did what he could to prevent Spanish interference with Indians living within the United States. Things got more worrisome when Napoleon, in the hopes of rebuilding France's North American empire, cajoled the Spanish into returning Louisiana to France in the secret Treaty of San Ildefonso in 1800. When rumor of this treaty became rampant, President Jefferson immediately recognized the danger and what it meant if Napoleon, the colossus of Europe, should take control of New Orleans and the entire Mississippi Valley. But the danger dissolved with the disastrous defeat of Napoleon's army in Santo Domingo. To rebuild a French empire in the New World necessitated a strong presence in the Caribbean and the disaster in Santo Domingo made that impossible. So Napoleon agreed to sell Louisiana to the United States—in violation of the San Ildefonso treaty—in 1803 for $15 million.

Once Louisiana became part of the United States, Jackson seriously considered seeking appointment as governor of the territory, using what political influence he could muster to bring it about. But President Jefferson, who had seen Jackson in action in Congress and declared him contemptuous of laws and constitutions, waved him aside. Instead, he appointed William C. C. Claiborne to the post. Worse, he chose James Wilkinson as general of the U.S. forces in New Orleans. Wilkinson was a double agent who acted and was paid to spy for the Spanish still present in the Floridas.

Despite this disappointment, Jackson continued to bolster his reputation as an energetic and skillful commander of the Tennessee militia who acted promptly whenever unlawful activity broke out among the tribes or the whites living on the frontier. He frequently ran into trouble with U.S. agents sent to particular tribes not only to protect the Indians from white exploitation but to distribute annuities to their chiefs. Silas Dinsmore, agent to the Choctaw Nation, Benjamin Hawkins, agent to the Creeks, and James Robertson, agent to the Chickasaws, all defended their charges against the intrusion of white settlers. A particular problem, for example, involved the fact that the treaties with the Indians called for them to hand over any tribe member guilty of murdering American citizens. They would be tried under the laws of the United States and punished. Yet, wrote Jackson to his friend George Campbell, *"the Creek law says the Creeks will punish them themselves."* Justice is demanded, he insisted. "We want and do expect the murderers delivered up agreeable to treaty."[33]

And Jackson's insistence was well taken. The first U.S. treaties with the southern tribes began with the Treaty of Hopewell. In it, the Cherokees in 1785, and then the Chickasaws and Choctaws in 1786, agreed to Article 5, which said that if American citizens violated the boundary established between the tribes and the United States, they forfeited the protection of the government and could be punished by the tribes as they thought best. Article 6 specifically stated that if an Indian committed a capital crime against an American, the tribe must turn over the culprit to U.S. authorities to be punished according to U.S. law. The Treaty of New York with the Creeks in 1790 contained similar provisions.[34] So Jackson was right.

The problem of Indian-white relations became so bothersome, even when violence was not involved, that Jackson began to consider Indian removal as a solution. In 1809 he discussed the matter with Willie Blount, the brother of William, and now the head of the Blount faction in Tennessee. Willie Blount had just been elected the new governor of the state, and he wrote to the major general about his concern. The time is "fast approaching," he wrote, when the federal government would have to propose to the Creeks and Cherokees "an exchange of territory" by which the tribes would leave their present location and move to the "vacant lands west of the Mississippi," that is, the land purchased from France in 1803. The Indians living along the Gulf Coast are a "direct threat to our national security," he continued. Any European power, be it England, France, Spain, whatever, with designs on American independence or American territory, would certainly ally itself with the southern tribes and incite them into declaring war against the United States. The tribes would be supplied with guns and ammunition in a probable invasion by the European power from the Gulf. "For our benefit," Blount readily admitted, "I wish them led away from us." At present "they are surrounded by States thickly populated by people who have different interests." If they go west they will find other Indians "whose manners and customs are more assimilated to their's [sic] than those of the people where they now live." Every Tennessean should advocate this "exchange of territory," and "I am convinced," he told Jackson, "yours will not be withheld."[35]

Indeed not. Exchange of territory. That was the answer. Unfortunately, Jackson's reply to this letter has not survived. But the two men did begin a long correspondence, for the major general became an early convert to the removal doctrine first put forward by Thomas Jefferson. The argument about national security resonated deeply inside Jackson's mind. It was incontestable. It made sense. Furthermore, it was in the interest of the Indian to move. With all the killing that had been going on for decades, with white settlers moving ever westward, it seemed inevitable that the annihilation of Native Americans would result if they did not move. They would end up like Yamasees and Delawares and Mohigans—all dead, all gone.

Then an incident occurred that drove Jackson to take military action. A party of Creeks returning from a visit to the Shawnees on the northern lakes "massacred" several white families living near Duck River on May 12, 1812. The massacre "aroused strong feelings against the Creeks among the people of Tennessee," most especially Major General Jackson. "My heart bleeds within me," he raged in a letter to Willie Blount, "on the receipt of the news of the horrid cruelty and murders committed by a party of Creeks, on our innocent wifes [sic] and little babes. . . . *They must be punished*—and our frontier protected—and as I have no doubt that they are urged on by british [sic] agents and tools, the sooner they can be attacked, the less will be their resistence, and the fewer will be the nations or tribes that we will have to war with." He urged Blount to give him the "provisions and munitions of war" and "by your orders" he said he would lead 2,500 volunteers to "quell the Creeks, and bring them to terms without presents or annuities." He would show the Creeks the meaning of retributive justice.[36]

Jackson also wrote to George Colbert, the mixed-blood Chickasaw chief, having learned that the Creek "murderers" had passed through "your nation carrying along with them stolen horses, scalps, and a white woman prisoner." He had also learned that the Chickasaws relieved the Creeks of two of the horses. "Brother," the general ranted, "could you not also have taken the woman?" The "creeks have killed our women and children, we have sent to demand the murderers, if they are not given up, the whole creek nation will be covered with blood, fire shall consume their Towns and villages: and their lands shall be divided among the whites." You know, Chief Colbert, "that I am your friend, and the friend of your nation," but if the Chickasaws persist in permitting Creeks to have access through your Nation, my friendship and the friendship of the United States "will stop." Jackson urged the chief to remember how the Creek Nation came to destroy Chickasaw towns and how "a few hundred chickasaws aided by a few whites chased them back to their nation, killing the best of their warriors, and covering the rest with shame?" Do you remember? Brother, we will do the same "if the Creeks dare to touch you for your friendship to us." But "mark what I say." If the chief allowed any more scalps or stolen horses to pass through his Nation by the Creeks, "your Father the President" will know that the Chickasaws had violated the treaty with the Americans and had taken the enemy "by the hand." I want the names of the murderers and the towns where they live. Brother, you say you are a friend of whites—"now prove it to me."[37]

This letter is also very instructive about Jackson's manner and tone when dealing directly with Native Americans. He always addressed them as if they were children, irrespective of their age, education, or intellectual maturity. The President was their "Father," and he their "Brother and Friend." Of course, Jackson's friendship was based on how well they obeyed his instructions and performed as he directed. And the Indians played along. They always referred to the President as "Father" and themselves as his "red children."

On the other hand, Jackson felt that "little confidence . . . ought to be placed in the aid or friendship of Indians." They were not to be trusted. He also believed that sound policy and strategy dictated "the propriety of inlisting one nation against another." Here he was attempting to "inlist" the Chickasaws against the Creeks. He was also anxious to "inlist" Cherokee chiefs, such as Lowry, Walker, and Major Ridge, against the Creeks—or so he told Governor Blount. If the Cherokees can be "inlisted," said Jackson, they "will be obliged to be friendly with us to preserve themselfs [sic]—I believe self interest and self preservation the most predominant passion—fear is better than love with the indian."[38]

Fear is better than love. That says a great deal about how Jackson behaved toward Indians, how he felt and operated as major general. And now he was prepared to spread that fear throughout the Creek Nation. He informed the governor that he expected to begin his military operation no later than July 25 with whatever arms and supplies he could muster and "penetrate the creeks Towns, until the [woman] captive, with her captors are delivered up, and think myself Justified in laying waste their villages, burning their homes, killing their warriors, and leading into Captivity their wives and Children." Clearly, Andrew Jackson could be as cold-blooded and ruthless as the Indians. But he always felt "Justified."[39]

Jackson conveyed his thirst for revenge to the people of Tennessee when he published an article in the *Democratic Clarion* on July 8, 1812, in which he said that "no vengeance has yet been taken, no atonement has yet been made" against the perpetrators of this "cruel outrage" at Duck River. We cannot allow the assassinations "of women and children to escape with impunity and with triumph." If we do not exact "atonement," there will be further "depredations." Be assured that the "zeal" of your major general "has not been stopped. Just as the Nickajack expedition brought an end to the Cherokee War," so too there must be another expedition to put down what is obviously a new war by the Creeks. "Citizens," he cried, "hold yourself in readiness: it may be but a short time before the question is put to you: *Are you ready to follow your major general to the heart of the Creek nation*[?]"

Revenge of sorts was achieved when those who participated in the Duck River massacre were sought out and killed by a Creek war party. The white woman held captive was released. She was "very feeble," her mind seemed "impaired by suffering," and "her limbs and feet" still "wounded" on account of the hardships she had endured. She was taken to George Gaines's home, and after a week's nursing by Gaines's wife, her "mind appeared to be restored."[40]

But before the major general could administer adequate revenge, he was abruptly notified by Governor Blount in June 1812 that the United States had declared war against Great Britain as a consequence of such outrages as the seizure of ships, the impressment of seamen, territorial incursions, and assisting Indians in their attacks on American settlers. Most important of all, perhaps, was the widespread feeling among Americans that the United States needed to prove to itself and to Europe that this nation had won its independence and could defend itself, even against the greatest military power in the world.

The War of 1812 was a colossal mistake because shortly after war was declared, Britain rescinded some of its worst policies that affected the United States. But it was too late. War had been declared, and several American military disasters, such as the surrender of Detroit by General William Hull to a combined force of British soldiers and Indians, occurred before it ended. To prosecute the war, the administration of President James Madison sent Governor Blount 70 blank commissions for volunteers to take part in an expedition to New Orleans, and Blount gave one to Jackson, ordering him to proceed directly to the city. The major general of the Tennessee militia was now Major General of United States Volunteers.

Without wasting a moment's time, Jackson assembled his army at Nashville, and despite the inclement weather and a countryside covered with snow, the expedition took off for New Orleans on January 7, 1813. Troops came from every corner of the state and were expected to bring their own weapons, especially rifles, although the government promised to provide guns to those who did not have them. Blount ordered the infantry and riflemen to be transported by boat to New Orleans while the cavalry and mounted infantry were to proceed by land. The governor also congratulated Jackson on his skill and efficiency in raising and organizing the volunteers. But the general replied that he was only doing his duty. Once his army began to move, Jackson notified the secretary of war that he was under way with 2,071 volunteers. The boats carrying this army floated down the Cumberland, the Ohio, and Mississippi rivers to Natchez, where they halted temporarily.[41]

It was there in Natchez that Jackson received a blow from the new secretary of war, John Armstrong, that convulsed him and left him shaking with rage. He was ordered to dismiss his army and turn over "all articles of public property" to General James Wilkinson, who was stationed in New Orleans.

Dismissed! He could scarcely believe it. Here he was with over 2,000 troops, 500 miles from his home base, in a wilderness alive with Indians, and he was told to dismiss them and return home. Jackson had 150 men on sick report, 56 of whom could not raise themselves from their pallets. The order struck the general as absolutely insane, the sort of thing politicians decree in Washington when they have no idea of the circumstances facing the military on the ground. It was a situation that occurred repeatedly in future military operations. More than likely his troops would attempt to link up with General Wilkinson rather than brave the terrors of a return trip to Nashville. Thus, the imbeciles in Washington would deprive Jackson of his command and humiliate him by forcing him to return home alone.

Actually, the authorities in Washington had decided to abandon a planned attack on Spanish Florida and for this reason had decreed the dismissal of Jackson's army. Initially, the possibility of seizing East Florida was tempting, but on more mature thought it was abandoned because the United States did not need or want war with Spain. Furthermore, Spain was allied with Russia, and the czar was attempting to mediate the conflict between the United States and Great Britain. However, Congress did later authorize the seizure of what remained of West Florida, claiming it was part of the Louisiana Purchase, and in

1813 American forces captured Mobile and forced the Spanish garrison to withdraw to Pensacola.

Jackson knew none of this. All he did know was that his military operation had been halted and he had been ordered to dismiss his army. Well, he would not do it. He would disobey the secretary's order. He would not disband his army; rather he would lead his men back to Tennessee—at his own expense if necessary. Jackson discussed his plan with his aides and found them all adamant about keeping the troops together. In a letter to Secretary Armstrong, toned down from his original draft by the wise recommendations of his staff, Jackson said that "these brave men . . . deserve a better fate and return from their government." At the call of their country they "voluntarily rallied around its insulted standard. They followed me to the field; I shall carefully march them back to their homes."[42]

The secretary of war "must have been drunk when he wrote" the order, said Jackson to his congressman, Felix Grundy, "or so proud of his appointment as to have lost all feelings of humanity & duty." To his friend and neighbor William B. Lewis, the general's tone and voice were sharper and louder: "Is this the reward of a virtuous administration, to its patriotic sons, or is it done by a wicked *monster,* to satiate the vengeance, of a combination of hypocritical Political Villains, who would sacrifice the best blood of our Country, to satiate the spleen of a villain [Wilkinson] who their connection with in acts of wickedness they are afraid to offend[?]"[43]

So he headed home with his army intact. Ironically, the journey back to Tennessee proved to be a personal triumph for the commanding general. Everything the volunteers admired about Jackson was amplified in their presence: his courage, his outstanding leadership skills, his determination, his deep and personal concern for the welfare of his troops, and his patience and understanding. Moreover, something quite extraordinary emerged in Jackson during that homeward march, a quality that helps explain the reason for his many military successes. That quality was his indomitable willpower. It was truly demonic. It was a total, concentrated, and absolute determination to succeed. So if he decided to march his men back to Nashville, he would do it even at the risk of death.

What distinguished Jackson as a general was his will to succeed—no matter the cost. As a result, he was capable of extraordinary feats of bravery, of daring maneuvers and perseverance, even against impossible odds. He took risks. Caution in a military operation was foreign to him. Only victory satisfied him. Defeat was unacceptable.

This titanic force of will, buttressed by outstanding self-confidence and genuine leadership ability, shaped the many military successes he achieved over the Indians, the British, and the Spanish during the next few years. But make no mistake. He was not a great general in the traditional sense. Although he was better than most of the military leaders in the War of 1812, that is not saying much. He was not a tactician. He had little real training in military matters and did not know or understand the art of warfare. And he made a number of colossal military blunders. Fortunately, as he said many times, pure luck prevented him from suffering the consequences of his mistakes.

Yet Jackson was indeed a great general because, despite his lack of military training and despite mistakes, he won colossal victories over his country's enemies, and he won them because he was a outstanding leader who inspired in his troops the loyalty and devotion that made them heroic warriors who destroyed the enemy.

And from the moment he began his march back to Nashville from Natchez, a more mature General Jackson emerged to handle the problems he now faced. His first problem was the size of his sick list. He had only 11 wagons to carry them. He therefore ordered his officers to turn their horses over to the sick. He himself surrendered his own three horses for this duty.

As the army began to move, Jackson instinctively knew how to behave in this situation. "It is . . . my duty," he explained to his wife, Rachel, "to act as a father to the sick and to the well and stay with them until I march them into Nashville."[44]

And he planned the operation very carefully. All things considered, Jackson's army of volunteers moved quite rapidly once it got started, averaging 18 miles a day. As gently as possible, he regularly urged his men to keep moving. When a delirious invalid lifted himself up and peered over the wagon and asked where he was, Jackson brightly responded, "On your way *home*," with a strong emphasis on the word "home." Whereupon all the volunteers who heard him let out a loud cheer.[45]

Jackson seemed to be everywhere as the army moved north, walking back and forth and up and down the columns, supervising the distribution of rations, calling to his men to be brave and of good heart, and always on the lookout for any sign of trouble. He was indomitable. His men could think of no other word to describe him than "tough." Tough as hickory, which was about as hard as anyone could imagine. So they began referring to him as "Hickory," and because they admired and revered him, they called him "Old Hickory," his nickname for the rest of his life.

Within a month, the army arrived back in Nashville, and soon word of Jackson's monumental leadership spread through the town. The *Nashville Whig* broadcast it far and wide. "Long will their General live in the memory of his volunteers of West Tennessee," it reported, "for his benevolence, humane and fatherly treatment to his soldiers; if gratitude and love can reward him, General Jackson has them. It affords us pleasure to say, that we believe there is not a man belonging to the detachment but what loves him." Yes, love. The soldiers love him, said the newspaper, and are not ashamed to admit it.[46]

Thus, at the age of 46, General Andrew Jackson became a father figure, a protector of his troops as well as a strong force guarding the people of the frontier. He was "the most beloved and esteemed of private citizens in western Tennessee."[47]

Jackson being Jackson, he managed to tarnish that reputation immediately by becoming involved in a dispute between William Carroll, his brigade inspector, and Jesse Benton, the brother of Thomas Hart Benton, his aide-de-camp. He foolishly agreed to stand as Carroll's second in the resulting duel. In the duel, Jesse receiving a grazing wound across both cheeks of his buttocks. The humiliation outraged both brothers, and they especially faulted Jackson for participating in the duel. As general of the militia, as father figure, as an older man, Jackson should never have allowed himself to become involved, the brothers protested. The incident festered over the next several months and finally resulted in the Benton boys ambushing Old Hickory in a hotel bar and shooting Jackson in the arm and shoulder. The general collapsed and was rushed to a doctor, who managed to staunch the flow of blood. But the bullet remained embedded against the bone in the upper part of his left arm. It remained there until 1832 when a Philadelphia surgeon, operating in the White House without anesthesia, removed it. Jackson and Thomas Hart Benton later reconciled, and Benton became one of Old Hickory's strongest supporters in the U.S. Senate. But Jesse never forgave the general nor his brother for the humiliation he had suffered in the duel.

This was the second time Jackson was shot. Earlier, on May 30, 1806, he was shot in the chest by Charles Dickinson in a dispute over a horse race. Jackson killed Dickinson but the bullet he sustained in the duel remained lodged in his chest for the rest of his life.

Jackson lost a great deal of blood as the result of the barroom shooting and for weeks lay prostrate in bed. It took nearly a month for him to recover sufficiently to resume normal activities. But his arm remained in a sling for support for a considerable length of time.

While the general was recovering, Creek Indians attacked Fort Mims in Alabama (then part of the Mississippi Territory) on August 30, 1813, under the leadership of William Weatherford, the mixed-blood son of a Scot trader and Creek mother and known as Chief Red Eagle. They massacred more than 300 American settlers. Red Eagle commanded the most militant Creeks, called Red Sticks, because they painted their war clubs a bright red. They lived in the upper Creek region around central Alabama along the Coosa and Tallapoosa rivers. Their goal was to join a Shawnee chieftain, Tecumseh, in his plan to organize the northern and southern tribes into a great confederation and with it drive the white settlers back into the ocean from whence they had come. Opposed to the Red Sticks were those Creeks of the lower region east of Alabama and west of Georgia around the Chattahoochee River who wished to assimilate with whites and learn the skills of modern farming and industry.

Following the massacre at Fort Mims, Governor Blunt ordered the state's major general to call out the militia and punish the Creeks. Now at last Jackson could wreak "vengeance and atonement" on the Creek Nation for the 1812 massacre of several families and the kidnapping of a woman at Duck River. The Indians responsible for the Duck River killings had already been executed by their own people, responding to the demands of the Chickasaws who feared they too would be held responsible for the murders. But the executions split the Creek Nation into two factions, and a bloody civil war broke out between the Creeks of the upper and the lower regions.

On September 24, 1813, Major General Jackson issued a general order to his militia to rendezvous at Fayetteville for immediate duty against the Creeks. They would avenge not only the Duck River murders but the massacre at Fort Mims. "The late attack of the Creek Indians . . . call a loud for retaliatory vengeance. Those distressed citizens of that frontier . . . implored the brave Tennesseans for aid. They must not ask in vain. . . . They are our brethren in distress and we must not await the slow and tardy orders of the General Government. Every noble feeling heart beats sympathy for their sufferings and danger, and every high minded generous soldier will fly to their protection." Since virtually everyone in Tennessee knew he had been gunned down in Nashville by the Benton brothers, he felt obliged to mention his physical condition. "The health of your general is restored," he assured them; "he will command in person."[48]

It is important to point out that Jackson regularly addressed his troops in person and spoke to them about his plans and what he expected of them. He realized that this method of communication strengthened the ties between himself and his soldiers. Henceforth, he rarely missed an opportunity to speak directly to his men through public addresses and use them to bolster their determination to defeat the enemy.

The Tennessee legislature had authorized Governor Blount to raise 5,000 men, including another 1,500 regulars enrolled in the U.S. Army, for a three-month tour of duty. Jackson was told to march with 2,500; another force of 2,500 from eastern Tennessee, commanded by Major General John Cocke, was also ordered against the Creeks. To destroy the Creek menace a basic strategy was devised in which four armies would invade the Creek Nation and converge where the Tallapoosa and Coosa rivers joined to form the Alabama River. The two forces under Jackson and Cocke were instructed to join in northern Alabama. Commanded by Jackson, these two armies would proceed to the juncture of the Tallapoosa and Coosa rivers, where they would be met by two additional armies, one from Georgia under General John Floyd and the other consisting of the Third Regiment of U.S. Army regulars and the forces of the Mississippi Territory commanded by Brigadier General Ferdinand L. Claiborne.

A problem of command immediately arose because the Creek Nation straddled the Sixth Military District, headed by Major General Thomas Pinckney with headquarters in Charleston, South Carolina, and the Seventh Military District, commanded by Brigadier General Thomas Flournoy with headquarters in New Orleans. The incompetent secretary of war tried to resolve the problem by placing the entire Creek War under General Pinckney while reserving Flournoy's authority within his own district except in matters dealing with the Creeks. But this decision only increased the friction between the two generals, and eventually Flournoy resigned.

It was a situation inviting disaster. Still the overall strategy remained in place, although it was slightly modified from time to time during the course of the war. All four armies were expected to destroy the Red Sticks, burn their villages, destroy their crops, and run them off U.S. land. The armies were further ordered to build forts about one day's march from one another in order the divide the Creeks from north to south and east to west. It was anticipated that this line of blockhouses would permanently break up the Creek Nation. The entire operation was expected to take no longer than two or three months.

All things considered, it did not look like a recipe for success. Fortunately, Major General Jackson had been commanded to march against the Creeks, and he would tolerate nothing but total and complete victory over these murderous Indians.

CHAPTER 2

The Creek War

ON OCTOBER 7, 1813, MAJOR GENERAL ANDREW JACKSON, looking pale and feeble, with his left arm in a sling, assumed command of his West Tennessee army at Fayetteville. Three days later he broke camp and headed south to link up with his cavalry, commanded by his good friend and business partner, John Coffee. Moving along at the astounding speed of 36 miles a day, the army joined the cavalry and then proceeded into Creek territory and reached the southernmost tip of the Tennessee River, where Jackson built Fort Deposit, a depot for supplies and arms that had been ordered but had not yet arrived.

The general waited impatiently. Then he decided to move on. "I am determined to push forward, if I have to live upon acorns," he growled.[1] Since he lacked adequate supplies, prudence might dictate that he remain at Fort Deposit until they arrived. Not Jackson. He could not, he would not wait. To his soldiers he said that he would "face the danger of the enemy, and with them he will participate in the glory of a conquest."[2]

So he continued driving southward to the Coosa River, where he established a base at Fort Strother. He hardly had a week's rations on hand, but he expected momentarily to link up with General Cocke and his East Tennessee army. He was about 13 miles west of the hostile village of Tallushatchee and its 200 fighting warriors. Jackson ordered Coffee to destroy the town, and on the morning of November 3, 1813, a force of 1,000 soldiers surrounded the village and systematically slaughtered virtually all inhabitants. "We shot them like dogs," boasted Davy Crockett.[3] "We have retaliated for the destruction of Fort Mims," Jackson reported to Blount, and he expected to cap that victory with the destruction of other Creek villages farther south. But it all depends, he said, on the speedy arrival of rations. "If we had a sufficient supply of provisions, we should in a very short time, accomplish the object of the expedition."[4]

Upon inspecting the bloody battlefield a dead Indian woman was found still clutching her living ten-month-old child. The infant was brought to Jackson's camp, along with other captives, whereupon the general asked that the women of the village care for the infant. But they refused. "No," they said, "all his relations are dead, kill him too."

Something inside Jackson resonated at the words "all his relations are dead," reminding him of his own past. He dismissed the women and sent the boy back to his home at the Hermitage in Tennessee. "I want him well taken care of," the general instructed his wife, Rachel. "[H]e may have been given to me for some valuable purpose—in fact when I reflect that he as to his relations is so much like myself I feel an unusual sympathy for him."[5]

The child, named Lyncoya, grew up as a pampered son of southern planter. Jackson treated him as a son and called him his son. He intended to send the boy to West Point for an education, but the young man died at the age of 16 of a "pulmonary complaint." He caught a bad cold and after "very severe sufferings," reported the

United States Telegraph, Lyncoya "expired under the roof of the hero who conquered his nation but who followed his remains to a decent grave, and shed a tear as the earth closed over him forever."[6] Surely Jackson did not hate Indians as such, having virtually adopted one as his son. Yet here was the man who as President initiated the removal of the southern tribes beyond the Mississippi River, resulting in the terrible "Trail of Tears."

Following the Tallushatchee massacre, a number of Creek villages wisely decided to avoid a similar catastrophe and proclaimed their allegiance to Jackson. One of these was the small town of Talladega, about 30 miles south of Fort Strother across the Coosa River. Incensed by this act of treachery, Red Eagle decided to make an example of the village and raze it to the ground. First off, he surrounded it with 1,000 warriors, and then he planned to kill all 154 people living within it.

When Jackson was informed by his spies of what was happening, he realized he had a chance of destroying a large hostile force. He had hoped by now to have met up with General Cocke's army coming from East Tennessee. But there was no sign of Cocke or his army.

Jackson faced a dilemma. If he did nothing, the destruction of Talladega would surely follow, inflicting a blow on American prestige among friendly Indians. But if he marched to Talladega's relief without reinforcements, that meant he must leave behind his sick and disabled, who would be prey to roving Indian raiders.

It took only a moment to decide. He chose to move. At midnight his army, consisting of 1,200 infantry and 800 cavalry, began to march. As always, the general advanced his army in three columns. He had double the size of Red Eagle's warriors. As a commander, Jackson believed in outnumbering the enemy.

At dawn on November 9, the army arrived at Talladega and deployed for action. They were within half a mile of Red Eagle's warriors. First, the infantry advanced in two columns, militia on the left and volunteers on the right. The cavalry formed two separate wings on the flanks and were ordered to advance in a crescent-shaped curve, the points directed toward the town and the rear of the cavalry connected to the advance units of infantry. A mounted reserve was placed behind the main line.

Jackson's strategy was simple enough: he ordered an advance guard to move forward, engage the enemy, and then fall back and join the main force, drawing the pursuing Indians into the curved arms of his army.[7] And the strategy worked beautifully—at least in the beginning. The vanguard moved forward, and as they did so the Red Sticks came "screaming and yelling" from behind trees and bushes. The guard fired four or five rounds of shot and then fell back. The Indians, numbering nearly 1,000, raced after them and entered the trap. The two curving arms of the troops closed in and shut tight around them. The circle of Tennesseans then fired at the Red Sticks at point-blank range. The killing would have been completed, except that suddenly one portion of the infantry on the right—perhaps in a moment of confusion over orders—retreated instead of advancing.

The line broke. A hole opened up, and the Indians dashed through it by the hundreds as they attempted to escape the withering fire. The reserves quickly dismounted and rushed to fill the hole. Once in place, those Red Sticks still in the trap were shot to death. Those who escaped were pursued by Coffee's cavalry for three or four miles, shooting as many of them as possible. But around 700 of the hostiles made good their escape and prepared to renew the war at a later time. Even so, over 300 Indians lay dead on the battleground. Jackson's losses included 15 dead and 85 wounded.[8]

The first thing Jackson did was bury his dead and have litters made for the wounded. Then he swung his army back to Fort Strother, where he expected to find the supplies he had requested weeks ago. When he got to the fort, he was dumbfounded to learn that no supplies had arrived from Nashville. All the food they had was a few dozen biscuits and a small amount of meat, hardly enough to feed his army. So the remaining cattle were slaughtered, and the meat distributed to the troops. Jackson and his officers made do with the offal.[9] The newspapers later printed a story about a starving soldier who asked Jackson for something to eat. "I will cheerfully divide with you what I have," responded "Old Hickory." He thrust his hand in his pocket and drew out a few acorns. "This is the best and only fare I have," he said.[10]

Day followed day, and still no supplies. The troops grew angry as their hunger mounted. They bordered on mutiny. Finally the field officers came to Jackson with a petition requesting that the army be allowed to return home. The petition was respectful and rational. It made sense. The soldiers needed to be fed; winter was approaching and they required proper clothing; the frontier was relatively safe.[11]

Leave before the Creek Nation was completely crushed? Not Jackson. He rejected the petition with haughty disdain, reminding the men that they were soldiers and expected to act accordingly. Then things began to fall apart. The militia broke camp and headed for home. But they did not get far. When the general heard what was happening, he drew up the volunteers in front of them and forced them to return. The next day the situation was reversed. The volunteers headed homeward and the militia forced them back.[12]

Jackson appealed to his men. "I have no wish to starve you," he protested, "none to deceive you." Then, having heard that supplies had already reached Fort Deposit, he made his officers and men a promise. "Stay contentedly," he pleaded, "and if supplies do not arrive in two days, we will all march back together, and throw the blame of our failure where it should properly lie." The love his men had for him and the sincerity of his appeal produced the desired effect. The troops agreed to stay two more days.[13]

Two days passed. Still no supplies. So the army insisted that their general keep his promise and allow them to return home. Overwhelmed by the thought of the humiliation of returning to Nashville before the Creeks had been completely vanquished, Jackson threw up his hands and cried out in desperation, "If only two men will remain with me, I will never abandon this post."[14]

Suddenly there was movement in the ranks, and a Captain Gordon stepped forward. "You have one, general, let us look if we can't find another." And to the amazement of many, 100 soldiers volunteered to stay with their general. Overwhelmed with gratitude, Jackson reformulated his plans and asked these volunteers to remain at Fort Strother while he and the remainder of the army set off for Fort Deposit. He felt certain that they would meet the supply train along the way and that the troops would return to Fort Strother and renew the campaign against the Creeks.[15]

So, on November 17, the weary, hungry, angry army broke camp and headed north. Most of them hoped they would not meet a supply train and could continue their march until they arrived back in Nashville. Then, to their surprise and disappointment, they came upon 150 "beeves" of cattle and 9 wagons of flour not 12 miles from the camp. They feasted, and when their hunger had been appeased, they were ordered to head back to camp.

Loud grumbles responded to the order. Some of the soldiers had no intention of returning to camp. One company formed and then started marching toward Nashville. Jackson reacted swiftly: He mounted his horse and raced ahead of the mutinous soldiers. About half a mile ahead of these troops, Jackson met Coffee with a few cavalrymen. The general positioned these men across the road and directed them to shoot any deserter who refused to go back. Then he took a position in front of them.

When the mutineers arrived at the spot, Jackson started berating them. Sitting high in the saddle, his eyes blazing, he threatened to kill any man who defied him. Turn back, he thundered, turn back. After a moment or two, the mutineers turned around and headed back to the camp.

But that did not end the rebellion. When Jackson reached the camp where he had left the bulk of his army, he found an entire brigade in the act of deserting. This was mass disobedience and a supreme challenge to his leadership.

Again Jackson responded quickly. He snatched a musket and rested it on the neck of his horse, since his left arm was still useless. He rode in front of the brigade and aimed the gun directly at the deserting troops. They looked into his eyes and saw "shoot," just like Russell

Bean, and they knew he would kill the first man who took another step toward Tennessee.

General Coffee and Jackson's aide, John Reid, galloped forward and took positions alongside Old Hickory. A volley of threats poured down on the soldiers but no one moved. No one had the temerity to tempt the "shoot" in Jackson's eyes. Minutes passed. Still no movement. Then several loyal companies formed behind Jackson to block the road. And that broke the stalemate. A few mutineers headed back to their posts. Others followed. Soon the remainder of the brigade recognized the hopelessness of their situation and backed away.

These incidents only added to Jackson's reputation as a great commander. Soldiers later recounted what had happened and emphasized the fact that almost single-handedly he had faced down the rebellion of an entire brigade. Actually the musket he aimed at the troops was so ancient it could not be fired. Had the brigade risked his threats, they might have gotten away with it.[16]

The worst seemed to be over. The troops marched back to Fort Strother, more supplies arrived, and Jackson expected to link up with General Cocke momentarily. But the volunteers had other ideas. Their one-year enlistment would expire on December 10, 1813, and they fully intended to break camp and go home. Of course, as part of their one year enlistment, they counted the days they spent at home waiting to respond to Jackson's summons to duty; but the general insisted that a year's enlistment meant 365 days of actual service in the field. The men kept arguing their legal right to leave, and Jackson threatened them if they did. "You can have no idea of the clamours of the men," wrote one officer, "all disorder here and daily desertions etc. etc."[17]

Jackson was just as determined that they remain and perform their duty. "The disquietude of the volunteers has grew to a hight [sic]," he wrote to Coffee, "that it is impossible to tell in what it may end. I have been on yesterday threatened with disagreeable events on the 10th, unless they are discharged. . . . What may be attempted tomorrow I cannot tell, but should they attempt to march off in mass, I shall do my duty, should the mutineers be too strong, and you should meet any officers or men, returning without my written authority, you will arrest and bring them back in strings, and if they attempt to disobey your order you will immediately fire on them and continue the fire until they are subdued, you are to compel them to return."[18]

On the evening of December 9, one of Jackson's aides informed him that the entire brigade of volunteers planned to slip away during the night. Jackson jumped to his feet and issued an order commanding the brigade to parade on the west side of the fort. At the same time he ordered the artillery company to take a position in front and behind the rebellious troops, their two small fieldpieces aimed at the mutineers. The militia was strung along an adjacent "eminence" commanding the road to Tennessee. Then Jackson mounted his horse and rode along the line of the volunteers, speaking gently at first, praising them for their excellent service and reminding them of the humiliation they and their families would suffer if they were publicly condemned as mutineers and deserters.

No one spoke. "It was a scene," Jackson later told Rachel, "that created feelings better to be judged of than expressed ... a whole Brigade whose patriotism was once the boast of their Genl and their country ... turning their backs on an enemy fifty miles in advance."[19]

Jackson demanded an answer from the mutineers. He received none. Thereupon he ordered the artillery gunners to light their matches. He himself remained motionless before the brigade and in the line of fire. The volunteers had seen enough of Jackson to know that he would not hesitate to order the artillery to fire. Having an artillery piece explode in their faces had little attraction, and a general movement within the ranks indicated they were ready to surrender. Several officers stepped forward and pledged that they and their men would remain at the fort until reinforcements arrived—at which time they expected to be released from service. Jackson agreed. The volunteers nodded their consent and were dismissed to their quarters.

Jackson wrote to Rachel about what had happened. The volunteers had sunk from the "highest elevation of patriots—to mere, wining, complaining, sedioners and mutineers—to keep whom from open acts of mutiny I have been compelled to point my cannon against, with a lighted match to destroy them—This was a grating moment of my life—I felt the pangs of an affectionate parent, compelled from duty, to chastise his child—to prevent him from destruction & disgrace and it being his duty he shrunk not from it—even when he knew death might ensue."[20]

He was hard on his men, but they loved him nonetheless. They loved him because they knew he cared about them, about their welfare, safety, and comfort—and their honor and reputation in Tennessee. Said one: "Never did a man labour more incessantly in the cause of his country & of those who have abandoned him. Day & night his whole soul has been devoted to the honor & the welfare of both. Yet this man has been traduced by those who have abandoned the campaign. He is represented as a tyrant & a despot. Never was there a milder man, when mildness could possibly succeed—never a more energetic one, when energy was necessary, but at all times never did a general love his army so much or labour so much to promote their interest."[21]

Finally, on December 12, General Cocke and his army of 1,500 men arrived at Fort Strother. Their arrival forced Jackson to keep his promise and release his volunteers. But, as it turned out, the enlistment of Cocke's troops was also due to expire within a few days, and they did not have adequate clothing for the coming winter. Disappointed, Jackson ordered Cocke to march his troops back to Tennessee and discharge them. On top of that disappointment, he received a letter from Coffee, who had been sent to Tennessee to procure horses and winter clothing, telling him that his cavalry had deserted. Coffee was ill at the time but he mounted his horse and rode after the deserters. He caught up with them and tried to persuade them to return to their duty. His men listened to him and then turned away. "I am really ashamed to say anything about the men of my Brigade," he wrote to Jackson. "They are now lying encamped with that holy body of Infantry that deserted you and their country in the hour and moment of danger."[22]

The enlistment of Jackson's second brigade would also expire on January 4, 1814, and they informed him that they were prepared to leave on that day. His army dissolving around him, the general took several more body blows when his ally and friend Governor Blount suggested that he abandon Fort Strother and retreat to Tennessee. In addition, he agreed with the militia about their interpretation of their terms of enlistment. And the secretary of war had approved it.

One disappointment after another. But Jackson was one of those extraordinary individuals who gains strength from adversity. The more he faced disaster, the more he was determined to overcome it. He gritted his teeth and swore he would hang on and destroy the Creek Nation. Retreat? Never. Still, he told his troops that Governor Blount had agreed with them about their enlistment, and he gave them the choice of staying and completing the campaign or returning home. To his dismay, they chose to go home. As they left the fort, Jackson wished them each "a smoke tail in their teeth, with a Peticoat as a coat of mail to hand down to their offspring."[23] It was his way of calling them all a bunch of cowards.

As bad as Jackson's situation appeared to be, it was no better in other parts of the Creek country. General John Floyd and the Georgia militia destroyed the Creek village of Auttose on the left bank of the Tallapoosa River in November 1813. In turn, the Red Sticks struck Floyd's camp in a surprise move and killed or wounded more than 200 soldiers before they were finally driven off. Shaken by what happened, Floyd abandoned any further offensive action, and his command was discharged. Georgia simply withdrew from the war.

At approximately the same time, an expedition of volunteers from the Mississippi Territory, led by General Ferdinand L. Claiborne, penetrated into southern Alabama and won a victory at Enotachopco, but because of mass desertions when enlistments terminated, Claiborne was forced to withdraw. The expedition proved to be a total failure.

The Creek War was now left to General Jackson and the handful of troops he still had at Fort Strother. Still, there were at least two bright spots. By the end of 1813, a great number of Red Sticks had been killed and much of their food supply destroyed. Unfortunately the Americans did not follow through with a decisive military victory. A large part of the American force withdrew. They abandoned the war.

Not Jackson. He remained, waiting for reinforcements so he could resume his assault on the Creek Nation and destroy it. According to his report to General Pinckney, commander of the regular army for the Department of the South, Old Hickory had no more than 130 men under his command at Fort Strother.[24] Then, to Jackson's complete surprise, 800 raw recruits marched into the fort and reported for duty. He could scarcely believe it. They appeared without prior notice, and knowing how quickly they could be disillusioned by life in the wilderness under his command, Jackson marched them forthwith into Creek territory to fight.

What a mistake! These raw recruits lacked experience or discipline. This action by the general bordered on the insane. It was certainly rash and inexcusable. He should have known better, and he almost paid a terrible price for it.

Worse, he decided to head for the heavily fortified Creek encampment at Tohopeka, or the Horseshoe Bend, a 100-acre peninsula formed by the looping action of the Tallapoosa River. Jackson was inviting a massacre of his troops. Fortunately, he never got there at this time. On January 21 he camped at Emuckfaw Creek, three miles from the fortification, and sent out his spies to locate any hostiles in the area. At midnight the spies returned with information that they had located the Indians who, by their dancing and whooping, probably knew of Jackson's presence and planned to attack in the morning.

Sure enough, at dawn they struck. But Jackson was ready for them. An hour-long struggle ensued with the heaviest fighting on the left wing. There was a pause. Then the Creeks attacked again, this time on the right wing. It was only with difficulty that the Indians were repulsed. The raw recruits proved brave, but they lacked the experience and discipline to be successful.

Then came the main attack, again on the left side. Jackson expected it and had prepared for it. The Red Sticks showered the army with "quick irregular firing, from behind logs, trees, shrubbery, and whatever could afford concealment."[25] The general ordered Brigade Inspector William Carroll to lead a charge against a group of Indians hiding behind logs. The Creeks would rise, fire, and then duck down to reload. Carroll and his men "broke in on them, threw them into confusion" and subsequently drove them from their position.[26]

All in all, the Indians had devised an excellent plan of attack, namely, to hit three different sections of the American line at once. But something happened that nullified the proper execution of the plan. For some unknown reason, possibly jealousy among the chiefs, one contingent designated to hit Jackson's front line decided to retire to their village.[27] Had they cooperated in the general assault, they might very easily have cut Jackson's army to pieces. Here is one instance where pure luck saved Old Hickory from catastrophe.

Jackson realized how fortunate he had been, and decided not to subject his raw recruits to any further engagement with the Creeks. He also realized that with 900 or so soldiers he could never overcome the Red Sticks at Horseshoe Bend. That would invite mass slaughter. So he wisely ordered a return to Fort Strother.

But the Creeks he had attacked at Emuckfaw were not through with Jackson yet. They stealthfully followed him, and when he reached Enotachopco Creek and started across it, they jumped him, attacking just as the artillery entered the water behind the front guard and the flank column. Moving rapidly, Jackson ordered the rear guard to engage the Indians and instructed the left and right columns to wheel around, recross the creek above and below the Creeks, and surround them—in imitation of his strategy at Talladega. "But to my astonishment and mortification," he reported to Pinckney, " . . . the rear guard precipitately gave way. This shameful action was disastrous in the extreme."[28]

The raw recruits scrambled to escape the punishing firepower of the Indians. Fortunately, Jackson managed to reform his columns and after a great deal of intense fighting, the troops drove off the Creeks. John Reid, his aide and an early and friendly biographer, described this action and claimed that Jackson was a "rallying point," even for the brave. "Firm and energetic, and at the same time perfectly self-possessed, his example and his authority alike contributed to arrest the flying, and give confidence to those who maintained their ground. . . . In the midst of a shower of balls, of which he seemed unmindful, he was seen . . . rallying the alarmed, halting them in their flight, forming his columns, and inspiring them by his example."[29]

Twenty Americans were killed in the struggle and 75 wounded, many of whom later died. Approximately 200 dead Indians were counted as they lay on the ground or were fished out of the creek. No doubt Jackson's masterful skill in handling his men in a desperate situation saved them from annihilation. But he should never have attempted this expedition. Again, he was lucky that his army survived and returned safely to Fort Strother.

Although the Emuckfaw and Enotachopco engagements in no way constituted a military victory over the Creeks, they nonetheless were vitally important. First, the Red Sticks had suffered a great many casualties and as a result they abandoned their aggressive policy and withdrew to their stronghold at Horseshoe Bend. Second, these engagements, when reported in Tennessee, sounded like genuine victories and encouraged many Tennesseans, who wanted to share the honor of destroying the Indian menace, to enlist in large numbers. Governor Blount ordered a new levy of 2,500 troops and was surprised to find not only popular support for his action but approval by the War Department. A number of the officers of the disbanded companies who had served under Jackson now began to raise new companies, and General Pinckney offered Jackson the use of the Thirty-ninth Regiment. When Jackson returned to Fort Strother, he was amazed and delighted to find several thousand troops ready and eager to do battle with the Creeks. Third, Jackson's exploits had opened up a road into the heart of the Red Stick territory that further weakened the Creek Nation. Finally, Emuckfaw and Enotachopco increased enormously Jackson's reputation as a general. He was seen as an inspiring leader who had the skill to rally his army in the face of possible devastating defeat. His superior, General Pinckney, wrote to the secretary of war and enumerated Jackson's many talents as a military commander. "Without the personal firmness, popularity and exertions of that officer," Pinckney explained, "the Indian war, on the part of Tennessee, would have been abandoned at least for a time. . . . If government think it advisable to elevate to the rank of general other persons than those now in the army, I have heard of none whose military operations so well entitle him to that distinction."[30]

In early February, Jackson received information that 2,000 east Tennesseans would join him, and on February 6, the Thirty-ninth Regiment of the U.S. Infantry, commanded by Colonel John Williams, arrived. Not much later, General Coffee's reconstituted cavalry brigade and a troop of dragoons appeared at Fort Strother. By March 1814, Old Hickory had over 5,000 troops under his command, more than enough to "exterminate" the Creeks at Horseshoe Bend.

And he had learned from his previous mistake. These raw recruits needed to acquire military discipline if they were ever to function as a professional army. Now he had regular army troops to serve as models and aid in the process. Jackson let it be known that any infringement of the regulations would meet with severe punishment. No more pleading with the men to act like soldiers, said Jackson, no more cajoling or arguing. They would obey orders promptly and without argument or they would suffer court-martial and possibly the supreme penalty. So the general set about training his troops in an effort to create a professional army.[31] Such a disciplined machine, powered by his iron will, would at last bring about the extermination of the Red Sticks. "There never was so thorough going a man, not one who so well knew how to inspire his men with ardor & enthusiasm as our officer," wrote his aide, John Reid. "Had he been appointed to the command of the armies in the North I am well assured the war had long ago been at an end. He will not be delayed or trifled with by the contractors. He *makes* them do their duty. Indeed every officer & every soldier—every man . . . connected with the army, is here, compelled to the strictest observance of what appertains to his duty." In the field the army was required to rise at 3:30 A.M., the staff at 3:00 A.M. Jackson insisted on this schedule because experience had taught that the Red Sticks usually struck early in the morning.[32]

When Jackson heard that General Cocke and General Isaac Roberts, out of jealousy, were engaged in subverting his program of discipline, he sent them home under arrest. Roberts tried to compel Jackson to agree to allow his men to return home after serving three months. When Old Hickory refused and the men assembled to begin their homeward march, he arrested Roberts and declared the men deserters. Later he relented and promised pardons if the deserters returned to duty. Eventually most of them did.

To make the movement of men and supplies easier and quicker, Jackson put his men to work improving the road between Forts Deposit and Strother. At this stage of his generalship, Jackson was trying to think ahead and prepare the logistics necessary to ensure success against the enemy.

He was so focused on victory and so determined to form a disciplined army that he sometimes went too far. One such incident occurred when John Woods, an 18-year-old who had enlisted in the militia, was given permission by one officer to leave his post. He went to his tent and ate breakfast. Another officer appeared and ordered Woods to return to his post. The young man refused, saying he had permission to go to his tent. An argument ensued whereupon the officer ordered Woods's arrest. At that the young man lost control of himself, grabbed his gun, and threatened to shoot anyone who attempted to take him into custody.

Someone rushed to Jackson's tent and informed him that a "mutiny" was under way. When he heard the word "mutiny," the general bolted from his tent. "Which is the ___ rascal?" he shouted. "Shoot him! Shoot him! Blow ten balls through the ___ villain's body!"[33]

Most soldiers believed nothing would come of this incident except that Woods would be dismissed without pay or drummed out of the camp. After all, it had happened many times and the incidents were easily disposed of. Besides, Woods was young and had temporarily gone berserk. He was a militiaman, and militiamen enjoyed special rights, such as being exempt from capital punishment for mutinous actions.

But Jackson had every intention of making an example of Woods, and he ordered a court-martial. The young man pleaded not guilty to mutiny, but the court found him guilty and ordered his execution.[34] Several efforts were made to win clemency for the young man, but the stiff-backed Jackson refused to listen. On March 14, two days after the trial, John Woods was shot to death by a firing squad in the presence of the entire army.

This incident severely damaged Jackson's reputation, on both a military and a political level. When he ran for the presidency, he was depicted by his enemies as a pitiless, ruthless killer, a man who could snuff out the life of anyone who displeased him. But John Reid insisted the execution had a "most salutary effect" on the other soldiers. "That mutinous spirit," he wrote, "which had so frequently broken into the camp, and for a while suspended all active operations" had to be crushed once and for all, and subordination observed. As "painful" as the execution was to Jackson, "he viewed it as . . . essential to the preservation of good order." It produced the "happiest effects," said Reid. "That opinion, so long indulged, that a militia-man was for no offence to suffer death, was, from that moment, abandoned, and a strict obedience afterwards characterized the army."[35]

A stern, demanding general was forged by the incident. His determination intensified. He became an insistent, driving, indomitable force committed absolutely to the destruction of the Red Sticks. And nothing would stop him.

The same day Woods was executed, Jackson recommended the campaign to bring the Creek War to a successful conclusion. On March 14, 1814, leaving 450 men to guard Fort Strother, he headed south toward Horseshoe Bend. He planned to travel along the banks of the Coosa River, then head east toward Emuckfaw, which was near Horseshoe Bend. After destroying the Indian fortification at the Bend, he would march to the Hickory or Holy Ground, which was approximately at the center of the Creek country at the junction of the Coosa and Tallapoosa rivers. Indians believed this place was protected by the deities and that no white man could violate it and live. Jackson had every intention of disproving their superstition.[36]

First, he sent Colonel John Williams and the Thirty-ninth Regiment ahead of the army. They floated down the Coosa on flatboats and were instructed to build an advance post about 30 miles south of Fort Strother in order to provide lines of communication and protect provisions. This post was named Fort Williams by a topographical engineer to honor the commander of the regiment.

Jackson was very cautious, moving very slowly at first. Then, when he heard from General Pinckney that reinforcement and supplies would be sent from Mobile to meet him at the Holy Ground, Old Hickory picked up speed. Once he reached Fort Williams, he immediately headed east toward the Bend, some 60 miles away. He now commanded a force of about 4,000 men, including a number of Cherokees and Creek allies. His spies informed him that Indians from the Oakfusky, Newyorka, Hillabees, Fish Ponds, and Eufaula towns had gathered at the Bend in expectation of Jackson's attack. Approximately 1,000 Indian warriors and 300 women and children were already holed up inside the fortress.

Horseshoe Bend was a 100-acre heavily wooded peninsula almost completely surrounded by water with a breastwork running across its 350-yard neck. The breastwork was constructed of "large timbers and trunks of trees" laid "horizontally on each other, leaving but a single place of entrance." It was five to eight feet high and had a double row of portholes "artfully arranged" to give the defenders "complete direction of their fire."[37] Because of the breastwork's curvature, no hostile force could approach without being subjected to a withering crossfire. Few believed that Indians were capable of such an engineering feat. It was a place, said Jackson, "well formed by Nature for defence & rendered more secure by Art."[38]

After leaving a strong contingent of soldiers at Fort Williams to protect his rear, Old Hickory headed eastward on March 24 with an army numbering between 2,000 and 3,000. He had a two-to-one advantage over the Creeks in terms of manpower, something he always tried to maintain before launching into battle. This time he took every precaution in protecting his army. Each move was carefully planned. Nothing rash or impulsive was allowed. He had too much to lose. Obviously, he had matured as a commander.

At ten o'clock in the morning of March 27, he and the army arrived at the Bend. He was amazed by what he saw. "It is impossible to conceive a situation more eligible for defence than the one they have chosen," he informed Pinckney, "and the skill with which they manifested in their breast work, was really astonishing."[39]

The first thing Jackson did was dispatch Coffee and his cavalry and a company of spies along with the entire force of friendly Cherokees to the opposite side of the Tallapoosa River, just opposite the Bend, to prevent any Creeks from escaping. His plan was to bottle up the hostiles inside the Bend and systematically destroy them. In addition, he told Coffee to make some feinting motion to distract the Indians from the main point of attack, which would take place in front of the breastwork.

Next the general planted his artillery on a small eminence about 80 yards from the closest and 250 yards from the farthest points of the breastwork. His artillery consisted of one six-pounder and one three-pounder. At 10:30 A.M. he opened fire, and it continued for two hours. But the cannonballs thudded harmlessly against the thick logs or whistled through the works without shaking the wall. Whenever the Indians showed their faces by peering over the breastwork the soldiers raked them with musket and rifle fire. The failure of this initial attack started the Indians whooping with derision, and several medicine men, their heads and shoulders decorated with the plumage of birds and other animals, danced and called upon the deities to bring death to the invaders.[40]

Meanwhile Coffee sent a number of swimmers to cut loose the Creek canoes that provided a means of escape, if that became necessary, and bring the canoes to the other side of the river so they could be used to ferry soldiers in their attack on the rear position of the fortification. Once the canoes were obtained, a small party of soldiers, commanded by Captain Gideon Morgan, crossed the river and set fire to the huts standing at the turn of the Bend, killing any Indian who attempted to stop them. This force was much too small to inflict any serious damage on the encampment, but it did provide the diversion that Jackson ordered. Once the general saw the smoke from the burning huts, he immediately ordered his troops to storm the breastwork in force.

Shouting their response to the order, the soldiers charged forward. The Thirty-ninth Regiment moved rapidly under a withering blast of bullets and arrows from the Indians. When they reached the breastwork, they thrust their rifles through the portholes and fired. It was point-blank shooting, muzzle to muzzle, "in which many of the enemy's balls were welded to the bayonets of our musquets."[41]

Major Lemuel P. Montgomery of the Thirty-ninth Regiment was the first man to reach the breastwork. He leapt over the wall, called to his men to follow, took a bullet to the head, and fell lifeless to the ground.[42] Thereupon Ensign Sam Houston mounted the wall and repeated Montgomery's order. An arrow pierced his thigh just as he jumped into the compound. A large contingent of regulars followed him, swarming over the wall, shooting every Indian within sight.

They breached the breastwork. The soldiers poured into the compound in force.

Stunned and incredulous, the Indians backed away from the wall and tried to hide in the thick brush that covered the ground. The soldiers went after them with a vengeance. The Indians continued to fight, despite the fact that they were hopelessly outnumbered. The killing then became savage. The troops kept up the relentless pursuit, and the retreating Indians suffered a devastating round of fire. "The *carnage was dreadful*," Jackson told Rachel.[43] The Indians who dove into the river to escape ran into Coffee's soldiers. Others tried to conceal themselves in the bushes or behind fallen trees, but the troops flushed them out and shot them at close range. The compound became one enormous killing field. Hour after hour throughout the afternoon the killing continued. In total disarray, the Indians bolted from place to place and the Americans systematically slaughtered them.

Still, the brave Creeks would not surrender. Jackson sent a flag with an interpreter to those positioned in their last stronghold on the bluffs of the river and asked for their surrender. The Indians responded with a blast of gunfire that killed one member of the peace party. At that, Jackson turned his artillery on them, riddling the cliffs with cannonballs. The Indians still would not surrender. So Jackson ordered lighted torches to be thrown down the cliffs which set the brush and fallen trees ablaze and creating an inferno. As the Indians raced to escape the flames, the soldiers shot them one by one. The killing continued into the night and only came to a halt when the light faded in the evening and soldiers could no longer see their targets. A few Indians managed to cross the river and escape under cover of darkness. But they were very few.

The following day Jackson ordered a count of the slain Indians lying within and without the compound. To keep the count accurate, the soldiers cut off the tip of each Indian's nose. They found 557 slain hostiles on the ground, and Coffee estimated that approximately 300 Creeks lay dead in the river. Later a few dozen more bodies were found in the woods, making a total of approximately 900 Indians killed in the engagement. Besides cutting off the tip of each Indian's nose, the soldiers also sliced away long strips of skin to make bridle reins.[44] It was gruesome.

As the count progressed, a wounded 18-year-old Creek was brought before Jackson. A surgeon was summoned to dress his severely wounded leg. While the surgeon attended to the wound, the proud Indian looked at Jackson and asked, "*Cure 'in, kill 'm?*" Jackson shook his head and told the lad that he would not be killed. Jackson was so impressed with the youth's "manly behavior" that he sent him to the

Hermitage as a ward and, after the war, bound him out to a trade in Nashville. Later the Indian married a "colored woman" and established himself in business.[45]

In looking over the dead, the soldiers came upon three Indian prophets, one of whom was the notorious Monahoee, "shot in the mouth by a grape shot," reported the general, "as if Heaven designed to chastise his impostures by an appropriate punishment."[46] Three hundred captives were taken, all of them woman and children, except for four. Jackson regretted to learn that about two or three women and children were also killed during the battle. He never made "war on females," he said; only the base and the cowardly do that. His own casualties amounted to 47 dead and 159 wounded as well as 23 friendly Creeks and Cherokees killed and 47 wounded.[47]

As he looked over the battlefield, Jackson knew that the power of the Red Sticks had been broken. But he was not satisfied. Chief Red Eagle—William Weatherford—who had led the assault on Fort Mims, was not among the dead or the captives. Unfortunately the chief was away from Horseshoe Bent at the time. In any event, Jackson expected the surviving Creeks to sue for peace. "Should they not," he explained to Rachel, " . . . I will give them, with the permission of heaven the final stroke at the hickory ground." He also told her how proud he was of his men. "Every officer and man did his duty—the 39th distinguished themselves and so did the militia, who stormed the works with them. There never was more heroism or roman courage displayed."[48]

Unquestionably, the Battle of Horseshoe Bend is one of the most important battles in the War of 1812. Not only did it end the Creek War and remove over 3,000 warriors from further involvement in the war, but it came at a time when the British were about to land an invading army in the South and supply Indians with guns and ammunition to fight and defeat the Americans. Had not the Creeks been crushed so decisively, they would have become a powerful force to aid the British in their coming invasion. The entire southern half of the United States would have been in jeopardy.

Jackson buried his dead in the river to prevent their being scalped. He knew that Indians frequently dug up dead soldiers and stripped and mutilated them. In fact, any number of Red Sticks at Horseshoe Bend were found wearing the clothing of those soldiers who had died and been buried at Emuckfaw.

Once his dead had been properly buried, Jackson and his army marched back to Fort Williams to obtain fresh supplies. As he traveled he burned and obliterated every Indian village he came across. He showed no mercy. "At my approach," he informed Rachel, "the Indians fled in all directions. . . . I have burnt the Verse Town this day that has been the hot bed of the war, and has regained all the Scalps, taken from Fort Mims."[49] He systematically destroyed the Creek food supply so that both friendly and hostile Indians verged on starvation. Facing famine, the few remaining Red Sticks either surrendered or fled into Spanish Florida.

At Fort Williams, Old Hickory had the army stand at parade to hear an address from their commander. It was Jackson's regular habit to write these addresses in order to inspire the army, commend their heroism, and advance its professionalism. They had utterly destroyed, he told them, the "fiends of the Tallapoosa." Never again would they "murder our women and children." Never again "would their midnight flambeaux" light their council house "or shine upon the victims of their infernal orgies. . . . By their yells, they had hoped to frighten us, and with their wooden fortifications to oppose us. Stupid mortals! their yells but designated their situation the more certainly; whilst their walls became a snare for their own destruction. So will it ever be, when presumption and ignorance contend against bravery and prudence."[50]

After allowing his men a few days of rest following their long campaign, Jackson moved out on April 5, 1814, and headed for the Hickory Ground at the junction of the Coosa and Tallapoosa rivers. Again he destroyed Indian villages and towns in his path. It was ruthless, scorched-earth campaigning. He was determined to snuff out whatever remained of Creek resistance. As a result, the Upper Creek country was reduced to a scarred and devastated ruin.

Jackson also wished to meet the Georgia and North Carolina militia that General Pinckney was sending him to strengthen his army. Actually, for all intents and purposes, the war was over. In recognition of this, chiefs of hostile groups came to Jackson's camp under a flag of truce professing their friendship and saying they wished to end the war and live in peace. The stiff-necked Jackson, whom many Indians now called "Sharp Knife" or "Pointed Arrow," rudely informed them that peace could come only if they moved north of Fort Williams so that they would not have any contact with the Red Sticks who had fled to Florida or with the Spanish or British. When they had relocated themselves and their people, they would learn his final terms of surrender. Then they would have peace.

The Indians had no choice but to accept his ruling and they stoically nodded their consent.

On April 17, 1814, Jackson reached the Hickory Ground and raised the American flag over the ruins of the old Toulouse French fort, which was rebuilt and renamed Fort Jackson. More chiefs appeared and professed friendship and asked for peace. Again Jackson directed them to remove to the northern territory above Fort Williams. And he asked each chief if they knew where William Weatherford was hiding. None knew. They suggested he might have fled to Pensacola in Spanish Florida with many other Red Sticks, such as Peter McQueen, Josiah Francis, and the other "instigators of the war." Actually a few of them did know Red Eagle's whereabouts, and they prevailed upon him to give himself up so that the war could end and peace be reestablished. They assured him that unless he surrendered, Sharp Knife would never bring an end to the suffering which women and children were enduring. William Weatherford, a brave man, realized his duty and agreed to turn himself over to Jackson, even though it probably meant that he would forfeit his life.

Without being recognized, Chief Red Eagle entered the American camp. He made no sound as he searched out and found Jackson's tent. Sitting at the entrance of the tent was Big Warrior, "a man of gigantic size" and the principal Chief of the Upper Creeks, who had refused to join Tecumseh in his plan to unite Indian tribes and drive the white man out of their country. He opposed the Red Sticks from the beginning, and now the great leader of those warriors stood defiantly before him.

"Ah! Bill Weatherford," cried Big Warrior, "have we got you at last?"

"You—traitor," stormed Red Eagle, "if you give me any insolence I will blow a ball through your cowardly heart."

The ruckus brought Jackson out of his tent. He stared at Weatherford for a moment and finally recognized him. Then came the explosion. "How dare you, sir, to ride up to my tent after having murdered the women and children at Fort Mims?"

The proud Indian stood very straight and looked into the flashing eyes of Sharp Knife. "General Jackson," he replied, "I am not afraid of you. I fear no man, for I am a Creek Warrior." But he understood his situation and submitted to it. "I am in your power," he said. "Do with me what you please. I am a soldier still."

Jackson stared at him in disbelief—and a discernible degree of admiration.

"I have done the white people all the harm I could," continued Red Eagle. "I have fought them, and fought them bravely. If I had an army, I would fight them still. But I have none! My people are no more! Nothing is left me but to weep over the misfortune of my country."

"Kill him! Kill him! Kill him!" shouted several soldiers who had heard the noise coming from the tent and surrounded it.

"Silence!" commanded Jackson. "Any man who would kill as brave a man as this would rob the dead." Then he turned to Red Eagle and said, "I had directed that you should be brought to me confined; had you appeared in this way, I should have known how to have treated you." Red Eagle finally declared that he desired peace and an end to the suffering of his people. Continuing the war was impossible. "Once I could animate my warriors to battle; but I cannot animate the dead. My warriors can no longer hear my voice, their bones are at Tal-ladega, Tallushatchee, Emuckfaw, and Tohopeka."

Then, with an audacity that shocked the soldiers, he demanded of Jackson the same terms that he had extended to other chiefs. You are a courageous man, he told the general, and "I rely upon your generosity." The Creek people must go north as you directed. If they refuse to listen to the terms of your peace "you will find me amongst the sternest enforcers of obedience." He ended with a simple statement. "This is a good talk, and my nation ought to listen to it. They shall listen to it."[51]

Jackson could not help but admire the bravery if not the arrogance of this proud warrior. He also recognized how important this chief's appeal to his people would be in ending the war. Instead of shooting or imprisoning Red Eagle, Jackson agreed to let him go to meet with his people and convince the remaining Red Sticks in Alabama to lay down their arms. Red Eagle agreed to search the forests for his followers and get them to surrender. Before he left, Weatherford heard Jackson deliver a stern warning. "If you choose to try the fate of arms once more, and I take you prisoner, your life shall pay the forfeit of your crimes. But if you really wish for peace, stay where you are and I will protect you." And on that note the meeting ended, and Red Eagle departed from the camp.[52]

Naturally, Jackson did not rely on Red Eagle to round up the holdouts. He set up a schedule in which detachments of troops scoured the river basins of the Coosa and Tallapoosa river valleys and the countryside "to scatter and destroy any who might be found concerting offensive operations."[53] Finally he spread the word through his spies and emissaries that any Indian found below Fort Williams would be treated as an enemy. "Every hour brings in more" Creeks, he reported, "all thankful to be received upon unconditional submission." A number of black slaves captured at Fort Mims were recovered in one town, along with a white woman, Polly Jones, and her three children. "They will be properly taken care of," the general promised. Jackson also found 150 scalps, "the greater part of which were females supposed to be taken at Fort Mimms [*sic*]."[54]

Although the Creek War appeared to be over on the American side of the U.S.–Florida border, the Red Sticks who fled to Pensacola, such as Peter McQueen and Josiah Francis and their followers, merged their forces into the larger conflict between the United States and Great Britain. At the same time, John Armstrong, the secretary of war, appointed General Pinckney and Benjamin Hawkins, the United States commissioner to the Creek Nation, to work out a peace treaty with the surrendering chiefs of that tribe. They were instructed to obtain an indemnity in land equivalent to the cost of the war. Moreover, they were told to include in the treaty a statement that all trade and communication with the Spanish in Florida must cease. In addition, the right of the United States to build roads, trading posts, and military forts in Creek territory must be acknowledged. On the whole these were very generous terms and Hawkins informed the friendly chiefs that for their loyalty during the war their land claims would be respected. For those who had distinguished themselves in battle, they would be repaid in the form of additional land.

Because Hawkins was generally known to be exceedingly friendly toward the Indians and prone to protect them, a great many westerners were infuriated by his appointment. They were convinced that neither negotiator, Pinckney nor Hawkins, would punish the Indians to the extent they deserved. And they took their complaints straight to Washington. Unless a huge cession of land was demanded from the Creeks, they contended, the government could expect additional trouble in the future. Jackson agreed. He believed that the Creeks, both friend and foe, should be stripped of their land east of the Coosa and north of the Alabama rivers in order to insure complete separation of the Creeks from the Spanish in Florida. Then, said Jackson, the government should "adopt every means to populate speedily this section of the Union." Preference should be given to "those who have conquered it." Surely such a "hardy race" settled in this area would defend it against all invaders. He also wanted the government to extinguish all

Cherokee and Chickasaw claims to land within the state of Tennessee. "Our national security require it and their [the Indians'] security require it: the happiness and security of the whole require this salutary arrangement." Here in essence was his policy for removing Native Americans beyond the Mississippi River. Shortly thereafter Armstrong directed that the treaty should involve a military capitulation and therefore only Pinckney would undertake the negotiations, not Hawkins.[55]

In the meantime, Jackson continued accepting the surrender of Indians and rebuilding and strengthening several forts in Alabama. He succeeded in establishing a string of posts down the length of Alabama through the heart of the Creek territory, forming a line of protection from Tennessee and Georgia to Alabama and Mississippi. Then, on April 20, General Pinckney arrived at Fort Jackson to assume command and begin his negotiations with the defeated Creeks. He was unstinting in his praise of what the Tennessee troops and their commander had accomplished. And he was sincere. There was no jealousy. Finally he directed Jackson to march his men back to Tennessee and discharge them.

Three days later Jackson led his army back to Fort Williams, a distance of 60 miles. Once there he took the occasion to issue another address to his men, one in which he expressed his pride in their bravery and their skill, loyalty, and stamina. Because of these addresses, the troops knew that he not only appreciated the suffering and hardship they had endured but would proclaim it to their countrymen.

"Your vengeance has been glutted," he told them. Whenever these infuriated allies of our archenemy assembled for battle, you pursued and dispersed them. "The rapidity of your movements and the brilliance of your achievements . . . will long be cherished in the memory of your general." Then he notified Pinckney that he and his troops were on their way to Fayetteville, "where I shall discharge them: after which, I shall no longer consider myself accountable for the manner in which the posts may be defended, or the line of communication kept open."[56]

The arrival back home of this victorious army and their general touched off elaborate celebrations throughout the state, considering how few victories Americans enjoyed at this point in the War of 1812. When Jackson arrived home in Nashville, he was given a hero's welcome by a frenzied mob of friends and neighbors, something he relished unstintingly. As a matter of fact, Jackson's pride in his military accomplishments was such that he could not nor would not accept any criticism of it, however justified. He wanted his military accomplishments in fighting for his country properly acknowledged by both the people and the government.

And Washington did indeed acknowledge his victory over the Creeks. When General Wade Hampton resigned after failing in his invasion of Canada, the administration offered the rank of brigadier general in the United States Army to Jackson with the brevet of major general and the command of the Seventh Military District, which included Louisiana, Tennessee, the Mississippi Territory, and the Creek Nation.

So proud was Old Hickory of his victory at Horseshoe Bend that he was outraged by the offer from Washington. He expected to be named a major general, the same rank he held in the militia. Sheepishly, Armstrong admitted that it was the best the government could do. No major general's rank was available, so on June 8 the disgruntled hero accepted what had been offered. But the problem was resolved when Major General William Henry Harrison, after a long dispute with the administration, resigned his commission, whereupon Armstrong immediately offered it to Jackson. The offer went out on May 28 and Jackson accepted it on June 18.[57] In addition, he received a base salary of $2,500 a year; but with allowances for servants, rations, transportation, and miscellaneous expenses, his total salary came to $6,500, a handsome amount at that time.

Clearly, Jackson deserved this honor, for he had demonstrated his ability to command an army, maintain it in the field despite adverse conditions, and deploy it effectively to pacify the frontier. When necessary, he could move his army quickly, and he understood the importance of gaining accurate information about enemy movements. He used his spies effectively, and they brought him very useful information of what he might expect from marauding Indians. Most important of all was his demonic will to succeed, his extreme determination to destroy the enemy and achieve total victory.

That indomitable will was amply demonstrated by his ability to keep functioning despite the infirmities of ill health. In the relatively short space of eight months, his constitution was shattered by diarrhea and dysentery brought about by the wild conditions, lack of adequate food and medicine, and his own indifference to his physical suffering. When he began his campaign, he was recovering from his gunfight with the Benton brothers. His left arm was tied up in a sling and he could hardly move it. Then pieces of bone "came out of my arm," and he sent them to Rachel as a souvenir. And his arm got better as a result. "I hope all the loose pieces of bone are out," he told his wife, "and I shall not be longer pained with it."[58] As for the dysentery, he could not get rid of it. When the attacks occurred in the field and were particularly severe, Jackson would bend over the branch of a tree and in that way find a measure of relief; in camp he pressed his chest against the back of a chair, which apparently helped him get over the worst of the spasms. When eating became impossible, he sipped weak gin and water. The pain at times was excruciating but he forced himself to keep going. He would not indulge his body. It too must obey the sovereign demands of his titanic will. By the end of the war his health was so shattered that he never fully recovered. He lived with pain for the rest of his life.

Extremely proud of his new position as Major General of the U.S. Army, Jackson outfitted himself with a new and rather spectacular uniform. He wanted everyone to know they were in the presence of a distinguished member of the armed forces. He also informed Rachel that he wanted her carriage "well repaired or exchanged for a new one . . . you must recollect that you are now a Major Generals lady—in the service of the U.S. and as such you must appear, elegant and plain, not extravagant—but in such stile as strangers expect to see you."[59]

And this elegant gentleman finally took command of the Seventh Military District from General Pinckney on June 15. At the same time Old Hickory was notified of his appointment to the regular army, Armstrong also informed him that President Madison wished him to proceed immediately to Fort Jackson and take over the peace negotiations with the Creeks. He was to be guided by the instructions sent to Pinckney and Hawkins, and the treaty was to take the form of a military "capitulation."[60] As Jackson soon learned, Pinckney had offered the Indians the easiest terms imaginable. Old Hickory himself believed the long-term effects of leniency could be disastrous to the interests of the United States. The Spanish were close enough to cause trouble, and now the general learned from his spies that the British were also nearby. In a letter he informed Armstrong that "300 British had landed and are fortifying at the mouth of the Apalachacola [in Florida], and are arming and exciting the Indians to acts of hostility toward the United States." These may be rumors but "we ought at least to be prepared for the worst." Then he added a question that promptly brought a response: "*Query—If the hostile Creeks have taken refuge in East Florida, fed and armed there by the Spanards and British; the latter having landed troops within it and fortifying, with a large supply of munitions of war and provisions, and exciting the Indians to hostility*—Will the government say to me . . . proceed to _____ and reduce it—If so I promise the war in the south has a speedy termination and British influence forever cut off from the Indians in that quarter."[61]

On receiving Jackson's letter, Armstrong consulted with President Madison. Then, on July 18, he wrote a response. "I am so directed by the President to say, that there is a disposition on the part of the Spanish Government not to break with the U.S. nor to encourage any conduct on the part of her subordinate Agents, having a tendency to such rupture. We must therefore in this case be careful to ascertain facts & even to distinguish between what, on the part of the Spanish authorities, may be the effect of menace & compulsion, or of choice & policy. The result of this enquiry must govern. If they admit, feed, arm and cooperate with the British and hostile Indians, we must strike on the broad principle of self-preservation. Under other & different circumstances, we must forbear."[62]

But the letter was not sent—at least not at this time. It was not until January 17, 1815—nearly 10 days after the Battle of New Orleans—that Jackson received this response to his query. Had he gotten it in July, he most probably would have taken immediate action, for it said "we must strike" if the Spanish were cooperating with the British and Indians. Jackson knew such cooperation was taking place. Most likely Old Hickory and his army would have crossed the border and slammed into Florida without a moment's delay.

Why did Madison wish the letter to be delayed? Armstrong does not explain. Most probably the President wanted to keep his options open in case he really did want Jackson to invade. To send the letter in July and trigger an invasion would have violated Spain's sovereignty in Florida, and Madison was not prepared to do that just yet.[63]

When the general arrived at Fort Jackson on July 10, 1814, he notified the Indian commissioner, Benjamin Hawkins, that he was calling a general meeting of Creek chiefs, both friendly and unfriendly, to meet with him at the fort on August 1. He wanted Hawkins to use his considerable influence with the Indians to get them to attend the meeting wherein the final terms of a peace treaty would be dictated. And he meant business. "Destruction will attend a failure to comply with those orders." For some reason he seemed to think a large number of the Indians would disregard his orders. In a letter to Coffee he declared, "If they do not come in and submit, against the day appointed which is the first of next month, a sudden and well directed stroke may be made, that will at once reduce them to unconditional submission."[64]

It is clear that Jackson meant to strip the Creeks, both friendly and unfriendly, of much of their landholdings. He believed, as did most westerners, that the Indians were warlike because they occupied too much land, which resulted in "wandering habits of life" that brought them into collision with white settlers. By substantially reducing the amount of land they held, their roaming habits would subside "until at last, necessity would prompt them to industry and agriculture, and the only certain and lasting means of support."[65] Thus, Jackson reasoned, for the Indians' own sake and for that of the country at large, it was necessary to reduce their property and restrict their movement.

A prescription for outright theft! But one honestly believed by most Americans at the time. For national security and the preservation of Indian life and culture, the tribes needed to be confined and restricted—and eventually removed to a place where they could do no harm.

The Creek chiefs knew better than to defy Sharp Knife, and so on August 1 they assembled at the fort to hear his "talk." Most of them, as it turned out, were his allies, the friendly Creeks. But, they asked themselves, why the threatening tone of his orders? Why the talk about destruction for absentees? They soon found out.

"Friends and Brothers," Jackson began when the general meeting convened, we wish to save our friends and destroy our enemies. "*We will destroy our enemies* because *we love our friends & ourselves.*" To accomplish this we have drawn up a treaty for you to examine. "Our friends will sign the treaty . . . our enemies must depart." Your signature will prove your friendship "Consult—and this evening let me see & know who will sign it and who will not. I do not wish to force any of you—act as you think proper."

The treaty was read aloud. As the terms were spelled out, the chiefs' shock and disbelief was visible on their faces. Jackson demanded some 23 million acres of land, about half of the entire Creek territory. It was roughly three-fifths of the present state of Alabama and one-fifth of Georgia, much of it from the property of the friendly Creeks, those allied to him and fought with him. In addition, Sharp Knife called for 4 million acres of Cherokee land and a strip along the Florida border stretching from the Perdido River to the Pearl River. Virtually every southern tribe suffered a loss of their land.[66]

This callous dismissal of what Pinckney and Hawkins had promised, this outright theft of Indian land, this terrible punishment of his friends, stupefied the chiefs. Both the Upper and Lower Creeks must surrender land so that the United States would be better protected against its enemies.

The Speaker for the Creek Nation, Big Warrior, tried to reason with Jackson. "The president, our father," he said, "advises us to honesty and fairness, and promises that justice will be done. I hope and trust it will be." Then he pointed to the Indian agent, Benjamin Hawkins. "There sits the agent he sent among us. Never has he broken the treaty. He has lived with us a long time. . . . By his direction, cloth was wove, and clothes were made, and spread through our country, but the red sticks came, and destroyed all—we have none now. Hard is our situation, and you ought to consider it."

"The United States," Sharp Knife responded, "would have been justified by the Great Spirit, had they taken all the lands of the nation." Why? Because they did not inform their Great Father, the President, that Tecumseh had tried to talk them into killing Americans. The entire Nation was therefore guilty of maintaining silence and breaking treaties. They must therefore pay for their treachery.

Big Warrior protested. We did not listen to Tecumseh. The Nation had done what was right.

No, you did not, growled Jackson. You should have seized Tecumseh, bound him, and sent him as a prisoner to your Great Father. Or, he snarled, "cut his throat."

The words, once again, sent shock waves into the crowd of assembled chiefs.

Shelocta, another friendly Creek, spoke next. He had fought alongside the Americans against the Red Sticks and had won Jackson's confidence. He spoke eloquently of his strong feelings for his white brothers and how he had tried to maintain peaceful relations with them. He agreed that the land to the south along the Alabama–Florida border should be turned over to the white man as a way of preventing an invasion by the British or Spanish. But to demand the land lying west of the Coosa would cause havoc among the friendly Creeks. They could not survive without it.

Shelocta looked directly into Jackson's eyes and "appealed to his feelings," to the dangers they had faced together, and to his "faithfulness." But Sharp Knife was unmoved. "You know," he said in reply, "that the part you desire to retain is that through which the intruders and mischief makers from the lakes reached you, and urged your nation to . . . acts of violence. . . . That path must be stopped. Until this is done, your nation cannot expect happiness, nor mine security. . . . This evening must determine whether or not you are disposed to become friendly." Those who refuse to sign can go to the British for protection. But "then I would persue and drive them and the British into the sea."

For a moment Jackson paused so that his words could sink in. "Your rejecting the treaty will show you to be the enemies of the United States—enemies even to yourselves."[67]

Still the Indians persisted. What about the promises of indemnity to the friendly Creeks for the losses they had sustained in fighting the Red Sticks? Pinckney had written to Hawkins and said, "You may likewise inform them that the United States will not forget their fidelity, but, in the arrangements which may be made of the lands to be retained as indemnity, their claims will be respected; and such of their chiefs as have distinguished themselves, by their exertion and valor in the common cause, will also receive a remuneration in the ceded lands, and in such manner as the Government may direct."[68]

So, General Jackson, what about the indemnity? Actually, he knew nothing about it. Nothing in his instructions mentioned an indemnity. He was embarrassed by this disclosure and to get rid of it, he promised to refer it to Washington, where a response would take months.

Meanwhile Jackson demanded that they act now. Consult with one another and let me know, he said, who are our friends and who are not.

The chiefs withdrew. They could scarcely believe the harsh terms being imposed on them. And they had done nothing against the

United States. They were the friendly Creeks, not the Red Sticks. Still, they had little choice. Sharp Knife's overwhelming strength and their total weakness dictated that they give their consent to his treaty. "He threatened us," said Big Warrior, "and made us comply with his talk. . . . I found the General had great power to destroy us." Even Hawkins recognized the hopelessness of their situation. Jackson "marked his line, and demanded their acquiescence," he explained to General Pinckney. Hawkins then advised the Creeks to capitulate—and his influence was powerful, which Jackson was the first to acknowledge.[69]

The situation among the Creeks was really appalling. As Jackson told the secretary of war, "The whole creek nation is in a most wretched State, and I must repeat, that they must be *fed* and *clothed* or necessity will compell them to embrace the proffered friendship of the British."[70]

At 2:00 P.M. on August 9, 1814, the Creeks surrendered themselves to Jackson's vengeance. The treaty was placed before them, and 35 chiefs signed it under protest. Only one of those who signed it was a Red Stick. The others were Jackson's allies, his comrades in arms. He had actually signed a peace treaty with his friends and in the process deprived them of their means of survival.

The chiefs then withdrew to carry the word of their disgrace and ruin to the other members of the Nation.

"I have just finished the business with the creeks," Jackson told Rachel the following day, "the convention was signed yesterday at 2 oclock P.M. and tomorrow at 12 I embark for Mobile. . . . Could you only see the misery and wretchedness of those creatures perishing from want of food and Picking up the grains of corn scattered from the mouths of horses and troden in the earth—I know your humanity would feel for them, notwithstanding all the causes you have to feel hatred and revenge against."[71]

The Creeks had ceded more land than any other southeastern tribe had ever surrendered to the United States. Jackson hurried the signed document to Washington and sent copies to his friends and officials in Tennessee. He enthusiastically informed John Overton, his partner in land speculation, that he had acquired for the United States over 20 million acres "of the cream of the Creek Country, opening a communication from Georgia to Mobile."[72] Now it was necessary to bring American settlers into this rich land so that the frontier could be better protected, an opinion he repeated again and again to many of his correspondents. Congress should pass the necessary legislation, he said, to provide "to each able bodied man who will settle upon this land a section at two dollars per acre, payable in two years with interest—this measure would insure the security of this frontier, and make citizens of the soldiers who effected its conquest." He told Rachel that he could foresee the time when "the banks of the allabama will present a beautiful view of elegant mansions, and extensive rich & productive farms and will add greatly to the wealth as well as the security of our Southern frontier."[73]

For the moment the immediate Indian menace had been settled. But the greater war with Great Britain still raged, and the American coast was about to be invaded through the Gulf of Mexico with help from the Spanish and the Red Sticks and other Indians in East Florida. It was now up to Jackson to attend to this danger, and he recognized it at once. "I owe to Britain a debt of retaliatory vengeance," he told Rachel, no doubt thinking of his own experiences during the American Revolution; "should our forces meet I trust I shall pay the debt— she is in conjunction with Spain arming the hostile Indians to butcher our women & children."[74]

But it was one thing to attack the British, since a state of war existed between that country and the United States, and quite another to invade Spanish Florida, since war had not been declared against Spain. Of course Jackson would not hesitate to attack the Spanish, operating on the broad principle, later approved by the administration, that if Spain aided and abetted the British and the hostile Indians in any way, then he had the right to intervene and put a stop to it. And his spies assured him that this was exactly what was happening. Consequently, he wrote a letter to the Spanish governor of Pensacola, Don Matteo González Manrique, and informed him of the terror he could expect if he did not attend to Jackson's complaints. Those complaints he specified as follows: There were "refugee banditti from the creek nation" escaping into Florida and "drawing rations from your government and under the drill of a British officer." They should be arrested, tried, and punished for their crimes. "Such should be your Excellencys conduct toward [such Red Sticks as] Francis, McQueen Peter and others forming that matricidical band for whom your christian bowels seem to sympathize and bleed so freely." The United States would no longer tolerate such a situation. So, your "Excellency," be warned of my creed: "An Eye for an Eye, Toothe for Toothe and Scalp for Scalp."[75]

A cruel, ruthless, and determined warrior had been spawned by the Creek War—and a superb commander intent on victory. General Andrew Jackson now sought "retaliatory vengeance" against the remaining enemies of the United States.

CHAPTER 3

The Battle of New Orleans

AS OLD HICKORY PREPARED TO HEAD SOUTH FROM FORT Jackson to "instruct" the Spanish in East Florida about their responsibilities regarding the United States and its wars with the Indians and Great Britain, the Madison administration faced a series of devastating defeats. In Europe, Napoleon had been captured, and the British were now free to concentrate their forces against the United States and deliver the knockout blow that would end the American war. Already the effects of this new situation had been realized. A British force under the command of Sir George Cockburn had invaded the Chesapeake Bay area, marched on Washington, burned the Capitol, the White House, and most government buildings, and then bombarded Baltimore. Another army swept into New York State from Quebec but failed to secure Lake Champlain and did not dare to risk a further penetration until its rear could be protected. And a third force, commanded by Vice Admiral Sir Alexander Cochrane, prepared to invade the United States from the Gulf of Mexico. It was assumed that it would take only a few thousand professional British soldiers, together with Indian and Spanish friends and allies, to sweep the coast and drive the Americans out of West Florida and up the Mississippi Valley.[1] In this way, they could control the valley, link up with forces from Canada, and reduce the United States to an island surrounded by Great Britain in the north, west, and south.

In documenting his case for such an invasion to his superiors in the Admiralty in London, Cochrane included a report he had received from Captain Hugh Pigot, who had landed his ship *Orpheus* at the mouth of the Apalachicola River on May 10, 1814, consulted with a large number of Indians, and found that 2,800 Creek refugees from the north were prepared to assist the British in their invasion. As a follow-up, Cochrane dispatched Major Edward Nicholls of the Royal Marines with over 100 men to Pensacola in order to arm the Indians and enlist African runaway slaves to recapture Mobile. This action in and of itself violated Spanish neutrality. Once Mobile was retaken, it would be a simple task to invade and cut across to the Mississippi River somewhere north of Natchez, thereby isolating New Orleans and rendering its capture a simple landing operation.[2] Once New Orleans had been secured, it would be an easy march northward to Canada.

When Cochrane transmitted a letter from a number of Creek chiefs stating their readiness to assist in the invasion, the Admiralty approved of the invasion plan and directed that the army in the Chesapeake be moved to Cochrane's command. In addition, 2,000 troops from Europe would join the force and could be expected to arrive in Jamaica around the middle of November 1814.

Meanwhile Jackson had hurried south and arrived in Mobile on August 22, a distance of 400 miles which he accomplished in eleven days. The first thing he did upon arrival was dispatch Major William Lawrence and 160 men to repair and strengthen Fort Bowyer, which stood at the end of a long sand spit commanding the entrance to Mobile Bay, a distance of 30 miles from Mobile itself. Lawrence completed the repair and equipped the fort with 20 guns, mostly of the 9 and 12 pound variety, along with two heavier guns. Jackson's rapid rush to Mobile and his strengthening of Fort Bowyer were strategically splendid, actions that immediately thwarted British intentions and dictated a different invasion plan. Once Cochrane learned that Jackson had entered the town with a large army and fortified the entrance to the Bay, Mobile was no longer an easy route to the Mississippi Valley. For him to try and take Mobile and then link up with the Spanish and Creeks before pushing on to the Mississippi presented serious problems, although it was still worth a try. Since New Orleans was totally unprotected, Cochrane eventually decided, especially when an expedition into Mobile Bay failed, to bypass Mobile and head directly for the Crescent City.

Jackson, as always, sent out his spies to learn more about the movement of the British within Spanish Florida. Since Spain was supposedly neutral and its ports open to trade, the general dispatched Captain John Jones to Pensacola to study its defenses, no doubt with the object of using the information in a subsequent invasion. Clearly, Jackson was itching to drive into Florida. In a letter to Secretary Armstrong, he complained about not hearing a response to his request for permission to undertake the invasion. "I can but regret that permission has not been given by the government to have seized on Pensacola, had this been done the american [sic] Eagle would now have soared above the fangs of the British Lyon," he wrote.[3]

As for New Orleans, Jackson gave it little heed. He inquired about its defenses and was told that Fort St. Charles and Fort St. John were badly in need of repair. Fort St. Philip, which was 60 miles below the city and on the Mississippi River, had 28 guns in relatively good condition, but the barracks were old and falling apart and could be easily set on fire by shells from warships sailing up the river.

Still Jackson stayed in Mobile, knowing that it was the best route for the British to invade the United States and make contact with Indian allies. So he appealed to various governors of nearby states for their militia, warning of the imminent invasion and likelihood that the British would have a force of 25,000 of the Duke of Wellington's best soldiers.

Because of Jackson's dire threats, the Spanish governor in Florida, Manrique, finally invited the British to land in Pensacola and help him protect his town. Acting on his own, he was convinced that the "Napoleon of the Woods," as the Spanish often called Jackson, would attack his village and destroy it.[4] So when Major Nicholls arrived in Pensacola on August 14, he assumed complete control of the area and, since he was unaware of any change in the invasion plans, prepared to retake Mobile. Together with 130 Indians, Nicholls and his marines sailed for Mobile and reached it on September 12 aboard a fleet of ships, the *Hermes,* the *Carron,* the *Sophie,* and the *Childers,* all commanded by Admiral Sir William Percy. They were put ashore six miles east of Fort Bowyer. Then, in a joint land and sea operation, they attacked the fort.

At four o'clock in the afternoon of September 15, the *Hermes* and *Sophie* sailed within range of the guns at Fort Bowyer. But because of the dying wind and the shallowness of the channel, the other two ships could not get into position. If they had, there would have been a total of 78 guns firing at the fort. That was triple the firepower that the American could bring to bear on the attackers. As it was, the *Hermes* and *Sophie* spat out one broadside after another. The battle raged for an hour. Then a lucky shot from the fort severed the anchor cable on the *Hermes* and the ship drifted to shore, directly under the American guns. Finally the ship blew up with a deafening roar, heard by Jackson himself at a distance of 30 miles.

And that ended the British attempt to take Fort Bowyer. The ships withdrew and sailed away, and Nicholls and his men returned to Pensacola. The *Hermes* suffered 22 killed and 20 wounded, the *Sophie* 9 killed and 13 wounded, and the *Carron* 1 killed and 4 wounded. The Americans lost only 4 killed and 5 wounded.[5]

This was an important victory for Jackson because it nullified Nicolls's attempt to contact Indian allies through the Mobile corridor and prepare the way for the principal invasion. Cochrane was obliged to alter his plans and forget about capturing Mobile and the surrounding countryside. Most probably, if the British had attacked Fort Bowyer with adequate forces, they might have captured it and with it Mobile. This was a lesson Jackson never had to learn, namely any military operation must be executed with overpowering might. Halfway measures invariably end in disaster, a mistake that the United States would make again and again over the next two centuries.

Unfortunately, the action also convinced Jackson that the British were indeed planning to invade through Mobile, so he sat and waited for it to happen. Weeks went by without anything taking place. He did nothing to right the weaknesses in and around New Orleans. Then, on October 10, the new secretary of war, James Monroe (who also continued as secretary of state), notified Jackson that he had received important intelligence from the American commissioner in Ghent (in what is now Belgium) who were negotiating a treaty with their British counterparts to end the war. The information concerned a British expedition that had left Ireland in September and was headed for New Orleans to assist in the invasion of the American continent. The invasion must be repelled, said Monroe, and therefore he had ordered the governors of Tennessee, Kentucky, and Georgia to make 12,500 men available to Jackson so that he could defend the city.[6]

Still Jackson did not move. He knew from his spies that the British intelligence operation was centered in Florida. He was much more anxious to lead his troops into Spanish Florida than head them toward Louisiana. Such an invasion at Pensacola would wipe out the enemy's spy system and also punish the Spanish for violating their neutrality. Finally Jackson decided he could wait no longer. Operating on the general principle of "self-preservation," he quit Mobile on October 25 and headed for Pensacola with an army of 4,000 men, including 1,000 regulars and a few Indian allies. He informed Monroe of the reasons for his action at the same time that the secretary sent him a letter explaining that the administration did not want him to do anything that would jeopardize the current "peaceful" relations be-tween the United States and Spain.[7]

On the afternoon of November 6, 1814, Jackson reached the outer defenses of Pensacola. This village was protected by two small forts, St. Rose and St. Michael. More imposing was Fort Barrancas, which guarded the entrance to the bay. Under a flag of truce he sent his demands to Governor Manrique. "I have come not as an enemy of Spain," said Jackson, "but I come with a force sufficient to prevent the repetition of those acts so injurious to the U.S. and so inconsistent with the neutral character of Spain." Then he spelled out his demand: the possession of Fort Barrancas with its munitions "until Spain can preserve unimpaired her neutral character." If this demand is not met, he warned, "I will not hold myself responsible for the conduct of my enraged soldiers and the Indian warriors."[8]

But the flag of truce was fired on, probably by the British, and the letter was not delivered at that time. "Turn out the troops," com-manded Jackson in response, and before daybreak four columns of troops, fully armed, assembled, three of them American, one Choctaw.[9] The Spaniards were taken completely by surprise as one column of 500 mounted men created a diversion with a noisy attack on the west side of town while Jackson led the main force on the east side. After a sharp exchange of fire in which two British-made and manned cannons took part in the defense, the Americans poured into the town and drove the Spanish soldiers from their hiding places. Jack-son expected the British ships in the harbor to open fire, "but they re-mained silent from the dread of our Artillery."[10] Indeed, the British ships had no time to get into position to deliver their salvos because the assault was so swift that resistance collapsed within minutes. Jack-son was very pleased with what happened. Not only did his troops act bravely but "we have given the British such an alarm at Pensacola, that they will dread an approach on this quarter."[11]

So rapid was the destruction of Spanish authority in Pensacola that Governor Manrique came forward under a white flag and surren-dered the town and its fortifications to Jackson. The next day "a tremendous explosion" rocked the village, and a column of smoke rose over Fort Barrancas. Nicholls and his men blew up the fort and then retreated to their ships and sailed away, leaving the wreckage to the American commander. At least, said Jackson, "I had the Satisfaction to see the whole British force leave the fort and their friends to our Mercy." American casualties included 7 dead and 11 wounded; the Spanish suffered 14 dead and 6 wounded. There is no documentation of British and Indian casualties, but it may be assumed that they were also light.[12]

His goal accomplished, Old Hickory proposed to return the town to Spanish authority. If nothing else, he had convinced the officials in Pensacola that the United States would not tolerate violations of neutrality by the Spanish that jeopardized American safety. Besides, the Florida adventure had been strategically wise in that it sealed off potential avenues of invasion by the British, avenues that were militarily far better than a frontal assault up the Mississippi River from New Orleans. The Crescent City area, with its bayous, lakes, streams, creeks, and soggy ground, would play havoc with the movement of heavy landing equipment and large numbers of troops involved in an invasion. Moreover, Jackson's capture of Pensacola meant that the British could no longer count on the Spanish or Indians for help. Both groups gained respect for the American ability to wage war. Henceforth Cochrane operated without Indian or Spanish support.

While in Pensacola, Jackson learned from his intelligence—which had picked up a leak in Jamaica—that the British were about to launch a full-scale invasion of New Orleans. Even so, he remained certain the assault would come through the Mobile area. In any event, he knew he had to leave Florida, so with a ceremonial flourish he returned his conquest to Manrique. The "enemy having disappeared and the hostile creeks fled to the Forest," he said, "I retire from your Town, and leave you again at liberty to occupy your Fort."[13] The governor responded graciously by "asking God to preserve your life many years."[14] And with that, Jackson and his army marched out of Pensacola and headed for Mobile.

Once back in Mobile, Jackson strengthened Fort Bowyer and increased the number of men defending it. Then he sent General Coffee and 2,000 of his brigade to cover New Orleans by riding to Baton Rouge and meet the newly mustered militia coming from Tennessee and Kentucky. From there, Coffee could be easily summoned, depending on whether the British invaded through Mobile or New Orleans. At the same time, he directed Colonel Arthur P. Hayne, his inspector general, to go to the mouth of the Mississippi River and search for sites on which batteries could be mounted that would command the river and prevent the British from crossing the bar. He also summoned Rachel to come to New Orleans and bring beds, tables, carriages, servants, his adopted son Andrew Jr. (one of Rachel's nephews), but not Lyncoya, and a nurse. He said he was close to a physical collapse and needed her. Before leaving Pensacola, he told Rachel, "I was taken verry ill, the Doctor gave me a dose of Jallap & calemel, which salavated me, and there was Eight days on the march that I never broke bread. My health is restored but I am still verry weak."[15]

Finally, on November 22, 1814, General Jackson set out for New Orleans with 2,000 soldiers. He turned Mobile over to General James Winchester, admonishing him to keep the town secure. Should the British land in Pensacola, he said, Winchester must cut their lines of supply and communication. He gave him this wide discretion so that he could post troops "in the best positions to give security to the country committed to your care."[16]

That done, debilitated but determined to throw back the invasion, General Jackson struggled to his horse and headed for the Crescent City, New Orleans. The city acquired that name because it sat on a looping curve of the Mississippi River, approximately 100 miles from the mouth of the river. It was a swampy area, filled with bayous, many parts of which lay below sea level. The river itself was protected by Fort St. Philip, a military post 65 miles south of New Orleans and was garrisoned by regular troops manning twenty-eight 24-pounders. North of this fort and about 25 miles below the Crescent City was Fort St. Leon. It was situated at a point where the river makes a wide looping bend and is known as the English Turn. All sailing ships had to stop there to wait the shift in the wind before they could navigate the bend. Hostile ships fell easy prey to the guns of the fort as they waited for a wind shift.

So any invasion upriver would be extremely difficult, although not impossible. There were two other approaches, both from the east. The most obvious was the one through Mobile. This route made military sense, and it was the one Jackson was sure the British would attempt. The other was a water route from the Gulf of Mexico into Lake Borgne and then into Lake Pontchartrain. These two lakes were connected by a narrow, shallow strait called the Rigolets, situated only a few miles to the north and east of New Orleans. Bayou St. John flows out of Pontchartrain and comes within two miles of the city limits. Fort St. John, a small brick fortification badly in need of repair, guarded the entrance to the bayou. The terrain around the lakes and between the lakes and the city was very swampy and virtually roadless. However, there was a narrow ridge of dry land that swept northeastward from the city, called the Plaines of Gentilly. And on the plains was a road called Chef Menteur, which connected the Rigolets with New Orleans.

Many citizens of New Orleans figured that an invasion would come from the lakes to Chef Menteur or from any one of a number of bayous that fingered their way between Lake Borgne and the Mississippi.

General Andrew Jackson rode into New Orleans early in the morning of December 1, looking gaunt and emaciated. His complexion was sallow but he carried himself with military stiffness. He was 47 years of age but looked much older because of his recent illness. His hair was iron gray, his face drawn, but he radiated confidence, determination, and enormous energy. One observer described him at the time as "erect, composed, perfectly self-possessed, with martial bearing. . . . One whom nature had stamped a gentleman."[17]

Riding alongside Jackson as he made his way into town were Robert Butler, his adjutant general; John Reid, his aide; and Major

Howell Tatum, his topographical engineer. Waiting to greet them were the governor of Louisiana, W. C. C. Claiborne; Commodore Daniel T. Patterson, the commandant of the naval district; Nicholas Girod, the mayor; and Edward Livingston, who had served in Congress with Jackson back in 1796 and who soon became a confidential adviser, translator, secretary, and aide de camp.

After a short welcoming address by Claiborne before a large crowd, General Jackson gave a spirited speech in which he said he had come to save the city and its inhabitants, and would drive the invaders into the sea or die in the attempt. He called on the citizens of New Orleans to join him in the effort, to put aside their differences and bring honor to their city. The differences were definitely present. They involved race, class, and ethnic background.

Livingston translated into French what Jackson had said. In no time the crowd caught the fervor of his remarks and showed their appreciation with loud and prolonged applause. They felt new confidence that this man would indeed do as he said and save their city from the ravages of an invasion.

When the welcoming ceremony concluded, Jackson got into a carriage, a cavalcade formed, and he rode to 106 Royal Street, where, in one of the few brick buildings in the city, he established his headquarters.[18]

Not much later, Jackson received a frantic letter from Secretary Monroe, telling him that the administration had learned that a large invading force under Admiral Cochrane was headed toward New Orleans. Monroe hoped that Jackson had already taken up a suitable position of defense there. "Mobile is comparatively a trifling object with the British government," he explained. "Your presence at such a point, on the river, with the main body of your troops will be of vital importance." It is essential that you save the city. "All the boasted preparation which the British government has been making thro' the year, with veteran troops from France and Spain, after having been gloriously foiled, in attacks on other parts of our Union, is about to terminate in a final blow against New Orleans. It will, I hope, close there its inglorious career, in such a repulse as will reflect new honor on the American arms."[19]

Monroe spoke correctly in more ways than one. On November 27–28 an armada of 60 British ships, consisting of frigates, sloops, gunboats, and various other transports, carrying 14,000 men put out to sea from Jamaica commanded by Admiral Cochrane aboard his flagship *Tonnant*. With Cochrane was Major General John Keane, who would soon be replaced by Lieutenant General Sir Edward Michael Pakenham, the nephew of the Duke of Wellington, who was on his way from Europe to take command of the invading army. The armada was a grand display of British military and naval might. It carried every imaginable tool and weapon needed for the invasion, including a printing press for the publication of a newspaper. Cochrane still had the option of landing at Mobile, but he chose New Orleans because of its apparent weakness and the money to be found in this glorious city. "Beauty and booty" was the cry of these invaders as they thought about what lay ahead.

Almost immediately Jackson began preparations for the defense of the city. The greatest problem he faced was the fact that there were so many possible invasion routes into New Orleans, given all the bayous, creeks, a long, twisting river and other existing waterways. Like others, he soon came to accept the fact that the Chef Menteur route was the most likely entrance for an invading army. But he took no chances. He ordered Major A. Lacarrière Latour, the chief engineer for the New Orleans district, to close all water routes leading to the city, an assignment that Latour turned over to the chief of the militia, General Jacques Villeré. Next, Jackson ordered that a guard be posted at the mouth of every bayou to give warning if the enemy approached. Unfortunately, Jackson did not personally undertake the task of making sure that his order was properly executed, nor did he assign a responsible person to do the job for him. He learned of his mistakes soon enough. He also directed that additional batteries be installed at Fort St. Philip. He personally inspected the fort and examined the existing diagrams provided by Latour, after which he suggested specific alterations to increase its ability to defend the river. In addition, at Commodore Patterson's direction, a fleet of five gunboats consisting of 23 guns and 182 men under the command of Lieutenant Thomas Ap Catesby Jones was stationed on Lake Borgne. Jones was ordered to retire if attacked and try to lead the British ships into the Rigolets, where they could be pounded by the guns at Fort Petites Coquilles. As for the defensive force within the city itself, on paper it numbered 700 men, many of whom, as it turned out, were absent from duty.

Among the many problems facing Jackson in repelling an invading enemy was the presence of pirates who operated out of Barataria Bay, a large body of water some 70 miles southwest of New Orleans that provided numerous water routes to the west side of the Mississippi at a point opposite the city. Heading this band of freebooters was Jean Lafitte, who, with his brothers Pierre and Dominique, lived on the island of Grand Terre in the Bay and had built houses, erected crude fortifications with heavy guns, and regularly engaged in an unlawful but lucrative practice of privateering and smuggling, much of it in the waters near Spanish Florida and Mexico. They frequented New Orleans regularly, and with the help of merchants and prominent citizens who traded in the stolen merchandise, Lafitte and his band grew rich and exercised considerable influence in the area. Even Edward Livingston became legal adviser to the Lafittes. Indeed, the brothers were frequently seen walking "arm in arm with Livingston's brother-in-law, Davezac" along the streets of New Orleans.[20] The situation became so scandalous that the Spanish governor in Florida reproached Jackson for allowing the operation to continue. "Turn your eyes to the Isle of Barataria," he wrote, "and you will perceive that within the very Territory of the United States, Pirates are sheltered and protected with the manifest design of committing hostilities by sea, upon the Merchant vessels of Spain, and with such scandalous notoriety that the cargoes of our vessels taken by these Pirates, have been sold in Louisiana."[21] What was happening in New Orleans, he said, violated the neutrality obligation of the United States with regard to foreign nations not currently engaged in combat. What hypocrisy for Jackson to lecture Spain about the Indians while consorting with pirates!

The charge nettled Jackson because it was true. And he chided Governor Claiborne about the matter. "Permit me to express my extreme regret and astonishment," he wrote, "that these wretches, the refugees from Barataria and its dependencies, should find an asylum in your city, that they should even be permitted to remain in it, without being strictly scrutinized under your existing vagrant laws."[22]

Early in September 1814, prior to Jackson's arrival in New Orleans, the British sloop *Sophie,* captained by Nicholas Lockyer, sailed into Barataria Bay bearing letters of introduction from Colonel Nicholls that invited the pirates to join the British in carrying out their intended invasion. In return for the use of their ships and supplies, the pirates were offered land and a guarantee that their persons and property would be protected. In addition, the pirates had to promise not to prey on Spanish or British shipping. Jean Lafitte himself was offered the rank of captain in the British navy.

The pirate asked for two weeks to think it over. Actually, he had no intention of joining the British. He much preferred the Americans since he had so many friends in the city and so many of his men were born in the United States. However, he did recognize that the letters could be used to negotiate an agreement with his allies in New Orleans. So he sent the letters to Governor Claiborne and offered to help defend Louisiana in return for a general amnesty for himself and his followers.[23]

The letters arrived in the governor's office just as he was about to launch an attack on the pirates' lair in Barataria Bay. He already had Pierre Lafitte in jail and hoped to imprison the rest of the pirates. Thus, Claiborne's advisers saw Lafitte's offer as nothing but a ploy to prevent the attack on his stronghold and a way of getting Pierre out of jail. So the planned attack went forward. As a precaution, Claiborne sent copies of the letters to Jackson.

An American expedition, headed by Commodore Patterson, sailed for Barataria Bay on September 13, reaching Grand Terre three days later. Patterson captured nine ships, a hoard of valuable merchandise worth $500,000, and 80 pirates. But Lafitte, brother Dominique, and most of his men managed to escape aboard his best vessels. Patterson then destroyed the stronghold. Despite this action, Lafitte still preferred to fight with the Americans, provided he could work out a deal.

When Jackson arrived in New Orleans in December, he found a considerable amount of sentiment in favor of enlisting the pirates in the defense of the city. Edward Livingston, naturally, gave the plan his support, and a legislative committee headed by Bernard Marigny urged acceptance. Then the Louisiana legislature passed a series of resolutions asking Jackson to use his influence to win amnesty for the pirates if they would lend their aid in defeating the British.[24] Furthermore, a group of prominent citizens reminded Jackson of the pirates' talents as gunners and marksmen. They also went to Judge Dominick A. Hall of the United States District Court and got him to agree to release those pirates already in jail if they promised to fight to save the city. Hall obliged, and, in addition, he granted a safe conduct to Lafitte so he could come to New Orleans and plead his case personally with General Jackson. Since the crimes committed by the pirates violated federal law more so than any other, Hall's safe conduct decree carried great weight.

Jackson bristled at this attempt to persuade him. He regularly called the pirates "hellish banditti."[25] Still, he knew the worth of the pirates as gunners, and this fact alone proved very persuasive. With the protective safe conduct order issued by Judge Hall, and with the boldness and bravery he was known to possess, Jean Lafitte returned to the city, found Jackson, and told him there were none more ready than he and his followers "to defend the country and combat its enemies."[26] He asked for the privilege of joining Jackson's army to repel the approaching invasion. Knowing that the pirates could provide powder, shot, flints, 1,000 men, and incomparable marksmanship, General Jackson readily accepted. He then ordered Lafitte to assist in the defenses between Barataria and the city. The pirates manned two batteries during the Battle of New Orleans and served with one company of marines. For their contribution to the defense effort, they were later exonerated of all charges against them. Meanwhile, the British Captain Lockyer kept his appointment with Lafitte, returning two weeks later as requested. But he found Grand Terre in ruins and deserted so he sent back a report that his mission had failed.[27]

Besides the pirates, Jackson also accepted the aid of the free blacks in the city. The request was first advanced by Governor Claiborne to whom Old Hickory sent this reply: "Our country has been invaded and threatened with destruction. She wants Soldiers to fight her battles. The free man of color in your city are inured to the Southern climate and would make excellent Soldiers. They will not remain quiet spectators of the interesting contest. They must be for, or against us—distrust them, and you make them your enemies, place confidence in them, and you engage them by every dear and honorable tie to the interest of the country who extends to them equal rights and privileges with white men."[28] Jackson directed that white officers command these troops and that they be treated the same as all other volunteers. He also permitted blacks to serve as noncommissioned officers. Pierre Lacoste was given command of this battalion, and later when a second battalion of refugee Santo Domingo blacks was formed, Jackson assigned Major Jean Daquin to lead it. Old Hickory issued a proclamation to these soldiers that promised each the regular bounty of 100 acres of land and $124 if they served, along with the regular pay, rations, and equipment furnished all American soldiers.[29]

Of course there were those rednecks in Louisiana who resented Jackson's decision to accept "coloured" men and place firearms in their hands. They predicted a bloody revolt would result. And when the assistant district paymaster challenged the general's authority to enlist blacks into service and put them on the payroll, he received a blast he did not forget. "You will in future," Jackson angrily told him, "be pleased to keep to yourself your Opinions upon the policy of makeing payments to particular Corps—It is enough for you to receive my order for the payment of the troops with the necessary muster rolls without inquiring whether the troops are white, Black, or red."[30]

To demonstrate to the people of New Orleans his regard for these troops, Jackson held a review of the black battalions. He also reviewed the city militia, a group of young men from the best families in New Orleans. They were commanded by Major Jean Plauché. He could not review his Tennessee militia because they were in Baton Rouge with Coffee, and he soon learned that General William Carroll was on his way down the Mississippi with an additional 2,000 soldiers from West Tennessee. Jackson wrote to Coffee and urged him to keep his brigade in "compleat readiness to march at a moments warning. We may or may not have a fandago . . . in the christmas holiday. If so you and your Brave followers must participate, in the frolic. I hope the west Tennessee militia and the Kentuckians will reach here in due time to participate."[31]

Jackson had been in New Orleans a little less than two weeks when he wrote this letter to Coffee. Two days later, on December 13, 1814, the British armada was sighted off Cat Island at the entrance of Lake Borgne. A small force of American gunboats commanded by Captain Jones hovered ahead of them, trying to coax them toward the Rigolets, as he had been instructed. Admiral Cochrane immediately ordered 45 barges carrying 42 cannons and a crew of 1,000 sailors and marines to pursue the American vessels. The gunboats beat a hasty retreat when they saw the size of the expedition coming toward them, but they were suddenly becalmed and the strong current at the western end of the lake nudged them toward Malheureux Island, where several of them grounded. Then the British barges lined up and prepared to blow the gunboats out of the water. Within minutes, the British captured the flagship, turned her guns against the other American ships, and peppered them with shot and shell. By noon, all the gunboats surrendered. Both Lockyer and Jones were severely wounded. The American lost 6 killed, 35 wounded, and 86 captured. The British suffered 19 killed and 75 wounded.[32] Lake Borgne was now free of any American military presence.

It was a disaster for the United States. It extinguished Jackson's watch on the lakes and prepared the way for the invasion of the mainland. But it had one salutary effect. The American prisoners all swore that Jackson had an army four or five times larger than he really did have, and that gave the British pause. Actually, no one knew the precise number of American troops in New Orleans, including Jackson. The best estimate is that he had about 3,500 to 4,000 soldiers at the time of the British appearance on the lake. But he soon had many more when witnesses of the battle between the barges and the gunboats rushed to the city to inform the general of what had happened. Jackson had just returned to the city from an inspection of Chef Menteur. Once he learned of the British presence, he summoned all available troops to New Orleans immediately. "I need not say to you, to reach me by forced marches," he wrote to Coffee, "it is enough to say that [Co]chrane is on our coast with about [eighty sa]il great & small, and report says has t[ake]n all our gun Boats in the lake—I have still a hope it is not true." He also instructed Coffee to send an express to the commanders of the Tennessee and Kentucky militias to "proceed night and day untill the[y] arrive." And notify the commander of the 44th Regiment at Baton Rouge to rush to New Orleans "without delay."[33]

Because of the reported size of Jackson's army and the fact that the shallow waters of the lake made it impossible for his large war vessels to sail into Lake Pontchartrain, Cochrane decided to disembark all the troops on the ships and take them to Pea Island, just to the east of the Rigolets, at the mouth of the Pearl River as it flows into Lake Borgne. So began a gigantic ferrying operation. Day after day the barges rowed back and forth from the anchorage to the island, carrying as many troops was safety allowed. It was backbreaking. To make matters worse, the weather grew cold, and it rained every afternoon. At night the temperature dropped below freezing, and the soldiers' wet clothing turned to ice. The operation began on December 17 and continued through December 22, giving Jackson plenty of time to prepare for the invasion by bringing more troops to New Orleans.

Coffee and his brigade arrived on December 20, and the following day they were joined by General Carroll and 3,000 Tennessee recruits, along with a regiment of Mississippi Dragoons commanded by Colonel Thomas Hinds.

Pea Island proved to be an insect- and reptile-ridden sand spit, a bleak, inhospitable stretch of desolation. And that was only the beginning. The troops still had to be ferried to the mainland. In questioning fishermen and Spaniards who were former residents of New Orleans, Cochrane learned that approximately 30 miles due west of Pea Island was a bayou that stretched from Lake Borgne to within a dozen miles of the Crescent City itself. This was the Bayou Bienvenu. The admiral immediately sent Captain Robert Spencer and Lieutenant John Peddie to explore the bayou and report back. With the help of Spaniards and Portuguese who lived in Fisherman's Village, a quarter of a mile from the entrance of the bayou, they discovered that the route was indeed a practical one, that it was navigable for large barges, and that it was virtually unattended—despite Jackson's order that all bayous leading to the city were to be closed.

Although New Orleans now teemed with soldiers prepared to defend it against the enemy, the citizens of the city panicked when they heard that the British had arrived. Under the circumstances, Jackson decided he must take control of all aspects of civilian life, so on December 16 he proclaimed martial law, making all citizens potential soldiers and directing that every person entering New Orleans must report to the adjutant general's office. No one could leave the city without written permission signed by Jackson or one of his staff. Ships must have passports to clear the port, and a nine o'clock curfew was imposed. Anyone found on the streets after that hour would be arrested as a spy.[34] This was the first time martial law had been imposed in the United States.

To bolster the spirit of the frightened citizens and reassure them that the enemy would be defeated, Jackson held a review of the militia on Sunday, December 18. He tried to make it as colorful and lively as possible. The square before the cathedral was jammed with people as they heard Jackson exhort his troops to show the world that they were worthy sons of those who had fought and won their freedom during the American Revolution. "The enemy is near," he cried, "his 'sails cover the lakes,' but the brave are united, and if he finds us contending among ourselves, it will be for the prize of valour and the rewards of fame."[35]

Two days after this pageant, the British completed their landing on Pea Island. Then at 9 A.M. on December 22, Cochrane sent an advance army of 1,800 men under Colonel William Thornton, who had led the successful assault on Bladensburg when the British first invaded the Chesapeake area, aboard shallow-bottomed boats, to head straight for Bayou Bienvenu. Major General John Keane, who was temporarily in charge of the invasion and would make all the wrong decisions for the expedition, accompanied the advance.

The flotilla glided with perfect order into a wide, flat expanse of swamp that was covered with reeds. The progress was slow but by dawn of the next morning they reached the mouth of the bayou without attracting any notice. The pickets at Fisherman's Village, who were expected to sound an alarm if the invasion came within eyesight, were easily captured. One did escape, but he spent the next three days wandering in the swamp before finally reaching an American camp.[36] The British spent the remainder of the day paddling up the bayou, which was 100 to 150 yards wide and 6 to 9 feet deep. When they found a strip of solid land along the bank, they debarked and formed a single line as they moved inland. The ground became firmer and the path more distinct. Gradually the swamp melted away and cypress trees came into view. Then it changed again to canebrakes until it finally opened up to the cultivated fields that formed the plantation of General Jacques Villeré of the Louisiana militia.

Thornton quickly formed his lines and headed for the plantation houses, which were no more than a 1,000 yards from the Mississippi River. Major Gabriel Villeré, son of the general, sat on the porch of the main house smoking a cigar and talking with his brother, Celestin. He had been charged with guarding the Bienvenu approach. Suddenly he saw red-coated soldiers dashing through the orange grove and heading toward the river. Realizing the invasion was before him, he tried to make his escape through a back door but ran headlong into several armed men, including Thornton. Captured, he was taken under guard to another room to await the arrival of General Keene. Conscious of his responsibility to spread the alarm of the invasion, he sprang from his captors and jumped out the window. He raced across the yard, hurdled a picket fence, and plunged into the cypress forest.

"Catch or kill him," shouted Thornton to his men.[37] But Villeré outran them and reached a neighbor, Colonel de la Ronde, who helped him get to the river, where they boarded a boat. Together they rowed to the opposite shore. There they found Dussau de la Croix, a member of the New Orleans Committee of Public Safety. The three men saddled horses and rode as quickly as they could to the city.

Meanwhile, the invaders congregated alongside the Mississippi. Keane joined them and ordered the troops into battalion formation. Then they marched forward, wheeling right at the levee road that paralleled the river, passing Villeré's house and halting at the edge of the plantation between the Mississippi and the cypress swamp. Thornton urged Keane to continue the march and capture the obviously defenseless city. The number of troops at hand were large enough to accomplish their goal, he insisted.

And he was probably correct. Jackson had no knowledge of the British presence, nor did he have adequate defenses against a surprise attack. He would have been reduced to street fighting, guerrilla fashion, and the city would have been torched.

But Keane was cautious. The pickets they captured at Fisherman's Village confirmed what the prisoners of the gunboats had told them, that Jackson had a huge army, maybe close to 20,000 men under arms. Another consideration was Keane's unwillingness to stretch his lines of communication and supply with the main fleet too far. So he decided to wait until the main body of his command caught up with the advance column. Then he would head north along the river to New Orleans.

Keane established his camp approximately 10 miles south of the city. At the same time, Jackson was in the parlor of Royal Street headquarters, reading reports and dispatching orders. At about half past one on the afternoon of December 23, the sentry notified him that three men wished to see him. They had important information. The men were instantly ushered in.

"What news do you bring, gentlemen?" Jackson asked.

"Important! Highly Important!" de la Croix gasped. "The British have arrived at Villeré's plantation nine miles below the city and are there encamped. Here is Major Villeré, who was captured by them, has escaped, and will now relate his story."[38]

Villeré blurted out his account in French with de la Croix translating as he spoke. When he finished, Jackson rose from his seat, his face contorted with anger because of the "treason" that had allowed the British to get from the lake to the river undetected. "With an emphatic blow upon the table with his clenched fist," Old Hickory cried out, "By the eternal, they shall not sleep on our soil!" Then he summoned his aides and secretary. When they appeared, he said to them, "Gentlemen, the British are below, we must fight them to-night."[39]

Bold, aggressive, and determined, he was spoiling for a fight. "I will smash them," he allegedly thundered, "so help me God!"[40]

Orders were hurriedly given to assemble the regulars, the battalions of city guards, the Mississippi Dragoons, the free black battalions, and Coffee's cavalry. They were to move down the river quickly and engage the enemy. Carroll's Tennessee troops and the Louisiana militia were left behind in case the column below the city was a feint while the main force proceeded along Chef Menteur, as Jackson originally supposed. Then he ordered Commodore Patterson to direct his warship, the *Carolina,* to sail down the river to a point opposite the British camp and open fire at 7:30 P.M. That would be the signal for the start of a general attack. Jackson planned to employ his usual tactic of setting up a pincher situation, so he told Coffee to move his troops along the cypress swamp on the left and strike the British on their flank, while the main force would attack along the river. Orders were also sent down to General David Morgan, commanding the Louisiana militia at the English Turn, to create a diversion from the rear. Old Hickory himself expected to arrive well beforehand to direct the entire operation. All told, he put into play about 2,000 troops, only a few hundred more than Keane's force.

By seven o'clock it was dark. The *Carolina* reached its position in the river, about 300 yards from the British camp. A half an hour later the ship opened fire with a broadside that roared over the delta and took the British completely by surprise. For 10 minutes the redcoats stumbled about in confusion, searching for their weapons, extinguishing their campfires, and running for protection next to the levee. Then, as the *Carolina* slackened its fire, Jackson ordered a frontal assault. For several hours the fighting was a confused tangle of men frequently fighting hand to hand. And then a thick fog rose from the river and, said Jackson, "occassioned some confusion among the different [American] Corps."[41]

It was now 9:30 P.M., the fog got thicker and the moonlight completely disappeared. "Fear of the consequences, under this circumstance, of the further prosecution of a night attack with troops then acting together for the first time," Jackson reported to Secretary Monroe, he disengaged.[42] He pulled his troops several hundred yards away from the enemy, straddled the road leading to New Orleans, and waited for daylight.

It was a wise move. Shortly after eight o'clock Keane began receiving reinforcements from Bayou Bienvenu. Soon he outnumbered the American force. Had the engagement continued, the British troops would have severely mauled the American army.

By their own count, Jackson's army suffered 24 killed, 115 wounded, and 74 missing or captured in the encounter. The British admitted to 46 killed, 167 wounded, and 64 missing.[43] Both sides lost a high percentage of their troops—around 10 percent—which they could hardly afford. At best, Jackson got away with a draw. The British could and did claim victory. After all, the Americans failed to destroy the advance guard and had withdrawn from the battlefield. Even so,

Jackson had initiated an offensive, returning a surprise invasion with a surprise counterattack, and so alarmed the British that they halted their advance. Had he not attacked, Keane would surely have renewed his march toward the city when the reinforcements arrived. And undoubtedly he would have captured it.[44]

The following morning, December 24, 1814, Christmas Eve, American commissioners in Ghent signed a treaty of peace with their British counterparts, thereby ending the war once the treaty had been ratified by both countries. That same day, Jackson decided to withdraw his army another mile to the north and set up his defense behind an old millrace called Rodriguez Canal, a ditch 10 feet wide and 4 feet deep that ran from the eastern bank of the Mississippi River to a cypress swamp, a distance of about three quarters of a mile. The trench provided a natural means of defense and would add strength to his position. Rather than attempt another attack on well-disciplined and professional British soldiers, Jackson recognized the wisdom of crouching behind a well-fortified wall and waiting for the enemy to attack him. He himself set up his headquarters at the Macarte house, 200 yards behind the ditch.

Pickaxes and shovels were immediately ordered from the city, and the soldiers began the work of digging, widening and strengthening the canal. Earthen ramparts were raised along the northern rim of the ditch, the rim closest to the city, and artillery pieces were strategically installed at regular intervals. Jackson ordered his engineer, Latour, to cut the levee and flood the ground immediately in front of the line. Unfortunately, the river would not cooperate. The temporary swell of the Mississippi subsided. It seemed as though the river wanted no part of the contest that was about to take place.[45]

To keep the British pinned down, Jackson ordered a second warship, the *Louisiana,* to join the *Carolina* in the river and lob cannonballs into the enemy's camp on a regular basis. Night and day the two ships pumped shot and shell into the British camp, and while they caused little physical damage, they played havoc with the morale of the invading soldiers.

At the same time the British completed the backbreaking task of bringing all their troops from the transports to the camp alongside the river. John Reid, Jackson's aide, estimated that the enemy now had 7,000 troops "against our 3,000."[46] Then, on Christmas Day, the British camp broke out with shouts of welcome with the arrival in the camp of its new commander. The troops set off a salvo that captured Jackson's attention two miles away. It was not the Duke of Wellington, as many Americans feared, but his wife's brother, Lieutenant General Sir Edward Michael Pakenham. He had finally caught up with his command. Originally General Robert Ross had been designated to lead the invasion, but his death during the action in Chesapeake Bay necessitated a new appointment.

It was an admirable choice. Pakenham was a splendid officer who had risen rapidly through the ranks. During the Peninsular War against Napoleon, he won military distinction by breaking the French line with a daring but costly attack. He was 37 years of age at the time he arrived in Louisiana and was generally regarded as one of the best officers in the British army.

On his arrival, Pakenham took one look at the impossible position his troops occupied, cramped as they were in a narrow strip of land between a river and a swamp. In front of him were entrenched Americans, crouched behind a fortified wall; in addition, two armed river vessels guarded the enemy's right flank and subjected his own left flank to a deadly crossfire any time he attempted to move his army forward.[47] Pakenham immediately decided that the first thing he needed to do was silence the *Louisiana* and *Carolina* or at the very least drive them away. So he called up nine fieldpieces to the riverbank to do the job: two 9-pounders firing hot shot, four 6-pounders firing shrapnel, two 5.5-inch howitzers, and a 5.5-inch mortar—along with furnaces to heat the shot.[48] Once in place, the expert British gunners opened up on the *Carolina* in a devastating display of accurate firepower. On the second round of hot shot the ship caught fire, which soon raged out of control. The ship's crew dove into the water. And not a moment too soon. Suddenly the *Carolina* blew up with a tremendous roar, shaking the ground for miles and spewing burning fragments in every direction.

From his headquarters at the Macarte house, Jackson ordered the heavier and better-armed *Louisiana* to get out of range of the British gunners, and it took several small boats to tow it to safety a half mile away. The ship now occupied a position across the river, which enabled it to rake lengthwise any column of troops that advanced toward the mud rampart. As for the *Carolina,* its crew escaped, except for one killed and six wounded, and joined the American line at the ditch and helped with the artillery.

Jackson regularly sent out an advance corps to observe the enemy and make reports to his headquarters. Then, on December 28, Pakenham ordered a general advance. They formed two columns and easily drove away the observation corps as they smartly marched toward the rampart. British officers and men had the mistaken notion that one whiff of their firepower and the Americans would flee in panic—as they had done so often during the American Revolution. They would soon learn otherwise.

One column moved along the river, the second near the cypress swamp. The "red coats," as Jackson regularly called them, were about to show the "dirty shirts," as the British called the Americans, what havoc and destruction professional soldiers could inflict. Most of these "dirty shirts" had never witnessed professional soldiers in action. What they now saw "was certainly a formidable display of military power and discipline."[49]

Letting loose with a shower of Congreve rockets, a new and frightening pyrotechnic, and with the constant firing of their artillery, the British column near the river crossed the open plain in front of Jackson's rampart. When they got to within 600 yards of the ditch, the Americans opened fire in a stupendous roar of cannonading; and, with help from the *Louisiana,* they caught the British in a deadly crossfire. So devastating was the response to the attack that the British soldiers were forced to dive into nearby ditches to escape. Some had to wait until dark to withdraw; others who were farther away retreated as best they could. Those next to the swamp on the right who were out of range of the *Louisiana* and the American artillery might have defeated Coffee's troops and reached Jackson's line at its weakest point had not Pakenham ordered a general retreat. The British general was influenced too much by what had happened to the column closest to the river. He wrongly assumed that the column on the right was suffering the same destructive mauling. In the action, Americans lost nine killed and eight wounded. As for the British, they now had a healthier respect for American firepower. Their attack had failed. Pakenham then decided to move his line farther back. He took a position two miles from the rampart and threw up two advance redoubts.[50]

Later Jackson was asked by his biographer and friend, John H. Eaton, what he would have done had the British succeeded in their attack and broken his line. "I should have retreated to the city, fired it, and fought the enemy amidst the surrounding flames. There were with me men of wealth, owners of considerable property, who, in such an event, would have been among the foremost to have applied the torch to their own buildings, and what they had left undone I should have completed. Nothing for the comfortable maintenance of the enemy would have been left in the rear. I would have destroyed New Orleans, occupied a position above on the river, cut off all supplies, and in this way compelled them to depart from the city."[51]

Having failed in his frontal attack, Pakenham decided to treat the American position as a fortification and, therefore, he erected breeching batteries to knock out their guns. For the next three days, while the redoubts were being built, heavy naval cannons were dragged across the bayou. It was a monumental task as four 24-pound carronades and ten 18-pounders were ferried from the ships, floated up a canal, and then transferred to carts that were pulled by sailors across a swamp nearly half a mile long and put in place.

While this horrendous task was under way, Jackson used the time to reinforce the rampart. The ditch was deepened and the mud bank heightened. At the suggestion of Jean Lafitte, the general extended his line from the cypress woods into the swamp, thus strengthening what had been the weakest point of the entire line.

Jackson now realized that the invasion was before him. There was no need to keep a power watch on Chef Menteur. So he ordered the Tennessee troops to join him. The number of artillery emplacements along the rampart was increased from 5 to 12. Cotton bales were sunk into the ground and wooden platforms built on top of them to hold the 32- and 24-pounders and prevent them from miring into the ground. Across the river, on the west bank of the Mississippi, Patterson placed a 24-pounder and two 12-pounders behind the levee just opposite the British batteries, at a distance of three-quarters of a mile. A defensive line was erected, and General Morgan and the Louisiana militia were assigned to defend the line and protect Patterson's batteries. Pakenham's three-day interruption of the invasion gave Jackson just enough time to strengthen his defenses on both sides of the river. But the west bank still needed further strengthening, and this failure almost resulted in the loss of the battle for the Americans. And the fault was clearly Jackson's, although he would never admit it.

The British commander completed his preparations for bombarding the American position by the evening of December 31. His batteries were strung out between the river and the swamp in five places and were protected by barrels of sugar found on the nearby plantations. Sandbags would have been preferable, but they were not available in this swampy area. These batteries were capable of unloading 300 pounds of lead per salvo compared to the 224 pounds the Americans were capable of throwing. When the preparations had been completed, Pakenham moved his army forward and took cover about 500 yards from the rampart, waiting for their artillery to breach the American line the following morning.

On New Year's day, 1815, a thick fog rose from the river and covered the entire plain, reducing visibility to just a few yards. It just so happened that Jackson had decided to conduct a grand review of his entire army on the open ground between the rampart and his headquarters at the Macarté House. The British meanwhile waited for the fog to lift. About ten o'clock the fog slowly evaporated and the redcoats were amazed to see troops in ranks, mounted officers riding through the ranks, bands playing, and flags flying in the air. It was a brilliant scene that ended suddenly and swiftly when the main British artillery began firing. Congreve rockets screamed their alarm as the Americans scattered in every direction. Lines of smartly dressed regulars came apart, visiting dignitaries and magistrates and ladies from the city became a frightened mob. Had the British charged the line or used antipersonnel ammunition rather than demolition ammunition, they might well have broken the line and seized the ditch.

The British aimed first at the Macarté House, which they knew served as Jackson's headquarters. The general and his staff were just finishing breakfast when the house was shaken by the crash of rockets. Mortar shattered masonry and ripped the plaster from the walls. Miraculously no one was hurt, "though for ten minutes after the batteries opened, not less than a hundred balls, rockets and shells struck the house."[52]

Jackson himself rushed to the rampart where his troops were assembling to return the artillery fire after their initial confusion. "Don't mind these rockets," he cried, "they are mere toys to amuse children." Later the British admitted that the American army was the first "that was not thrown into confusion by their rockets"—or so John Reid later reported.[53] Within minutes the ditch barked out an artillery response to the British attack. For the next hour and a half the cannonading was constant, and the entire delta shook from the impact of the explosions. Dominque You, brother of Jean Lafitte, stationed at the end of the embankment, called to his gunners to fire more rapidly and cram their pieces to the mouth with chain shot, ship canister, and any other destructive missile they could find. Captain Humphrey, commanding the number-one battery, watched as his shots fell and adjusted the range so that subsequent shots would fall right on target. Patterson's naval batteries were particularly accurate, and they destroyed the British artillery mounted on the levee. "Too much praise," wrote Jackson to Monroe, "cannot be bestowed on those who managed my artillery."[54]

But the British also inflicted substantial damage on the American line. The carriage of one of Dominique You's 24-pounder was broken, and the 32- and 12- pounders were destroyed. Two caissons, one of which contained 100 pounds of ammunition, blew up, which caused the British troops to let out a great cheer in the mistaken belief that the American line had been breached.

Indeed, the enemy had again failed in its objective, despite its professionalism. Many sugar casks stacked around the gun emplacements for protection burst and disabled the guns. Some batteries had bad flooring, and after a few salvos the guns were driven into the mud and out of operation. By noon the British slackened their fire; then the guns on the left and right fell silent, followed at three o'clock by the levee guns. All told, the British lost 44 killed and 55 wounded, while the Americans suffered 11 dead and 23 wounded.[55] As night fell, it started to rain, and the British were forced to drag their guns back to their camp through the mud. Unwisely, Jackson did not attempt to capture those guns (or drive the British away from them), which he could have easily done without exposing his men to the numerically superior enemy. He was extremely cautious and fearful of suffering greater casualties.

Pakenham's failure to breach Jackson's line with his artillery infuriated him. And it was probably useless to try that tactic again. So he decided that the only way he could take New Orleans was with a direct assault on Jackson's position. But that would take many thousands of troops in a direct frontal attack. He would overwhelm the Americans by sheer numbers. And he believed he could do it because he expected reinforcements to arrive at any moment. Specifically, one Major General John Lambert was bringing with him the crack Seventh Fusiliers and the Forty-third Regiment. As a matter of fact, they had already reached the fleet anchorage and were on their way across the lake to join the main force. They arrived in the camp on January 6.

In planning his operation of a frontal assault, Pakenham decided to set up a situation that would catch American army in a crossfire. He proposed to send Colonel William Thornton and 1,500 troops across the river to the west bank, capture Patterson's guns, and turn them on the rampart. This enfilade, timed to coincide with the assault of the main force on the river's east bank, would rake Jackson's line in a withering fire that would wipe it out.

But transporting 1,500 men across the Mississippi required a small fleet of boats, which Pakenham did not have. Barges were available, but they lay moored in Bayou Bienvenu and could not reach the river. Admiral Cochrane suggested widening and deepening Villeré's canal to provide a navigable route from the bayou to the river. Once the operation had been completed and the levee breached, the barges could move rapidly from their base to the river and across the Mississippi.

The plan was excellent. An enfilade would surely wipe out Jackson's defense. And because the American position on the west bank was perilously weak because of Jackson's failure to provide sufficient troops, it could easily be captured, especially if hit quickly and with strength. The brilliant leadership of Colonel Thornton would surely provide all the skill necessary to overwhelm the Americans. Once Patterson's guns were taken and turned on Jackson's line, a murderous crossfire would result and punch one hole after another into Old Hickory's position.

Widening and deepening the canal took many days of arduous labor that not only delayed the invasion but again gave Jackson additional time to strengthen his defense. Unfortunately, he thought only of the rampart, not the west bank. The ditch was further widened and heightened. By now the line of defense ran for more than half a mile from the river to the swamp and extended into the swamp for a short distance, then turned in a right angle toward the city. The rampart itself averaged 5 feet in height. In some places it was 20 feet thick, but in others it was so thin that a cannonball would have no trouble puncturing it. For example, on the left side, the breastwork was thick enough only to withstand musket fire. With some reluctance, Jackson agreed to build an advance redoubt near the river, but it was still under construction when the main battle took place. He also ordered construction of two additional lines of defense behind the rampart, one closer to the city by two miles and the other closer still by one mile and a quarter. Most of the work on these constructions was done by slaves, a labor force Pakenham needed but did not have.[56]

In the time it took for the British to work on the canal, the American force steadily increased in number. On January 4 more than 2,000 Kentucky militiamen arrived, but only a very few of them had guns. The need for guns and ammunition had occasioned Jackson to appeal to Monroe for help. Since August he had requested rifles; they arrived in mid-January, after the major battle had been fought. He warned Washington that if he suffered a military disaster, it would be the fault of the government. "Depend on it," he ranted at Monroe, "this supineness, this negligence, this *criminality* let me call it, of which we witness so many instances in the agents of government, must finally lead, if it be not corrected, to the defeat of our armies & to the disgrace of those who superintend them."

The Kentucky troops had just arrived, he told Monroe, "but not more than one third of them are armed, & *those* very indifferently. I have none here to put into their hands, & can, therefore, make no very useful disposition of them."[57] He assigned half of the new recruits to Brigadier General John Adair to support General Carroll's Tennesseans in the center. The rest he held in reserve or sent over to the west bank to reinforce Patterson's position.

Jackson should have sent the entire Kentucky contingent to the west bank. Although he ordered Brigadier General Morgan to abandon his post at the English Turn and take a position on the river's west bank, Jackson did not provide enough troops to maintain a defensive line and an advance. Half of the few Kentucky soldiers he sent were unarmed. Thus the force on the west bank was undermanned and underarmed. But Jackson did not believe the British would strike from across the river since it would take many boats to move the troops, and they would be seen in sufficient time to take appropriate action.

By January 7 the canal the British built was ready to receive the barges. On an inspection tour, Pakenham noticed that only one dam had been constructed to hold back the river. He asked his engineers about the advisability of building a second dam as a precaution in case the first dam collapsed. They assured him the dam would hold, but to their astonishment it did collapse, delaying the operation even further and in the process negating Pakenham's plan to set up a crossfire.

That same day Commodore Patterson walked along the west side of the river and stopped at a point directly opposite the British camp. For several hours he watched what the enemy was doing, and their actions sent chills down his spine. He could see that they were extending the canal to the river, breaching the levee, and loading cannons aboard barges. Already several of these barges had entered the Mississippi. Then Patterson inspected Morgan's weak position and the number of men assigned to defend it. He panicked. Straightaway he dispatched Richard S. Shepherd to Jackson's headquarters to beg the general to provide Morgan with more troops.[58]

Shepherd arrived at the headquarters at one on the morning of January 8, 1815, and found Jackson lying on a sofa, trying to get a few hours' sleep. He conveyed Patterson's request, ending with Morgan's information that the main attack would come on the west bank.

"Hurry back and tell General Morgan that he is mistaken," Jackson replied. "The main attack will be on this side, and I have no men to spare. He must maintain his position at all hazards."

Shepherd left and Jackson roused his sleeping aides. "Gentlemen," he said, "we have slept enough. Arise. The enemy will be upon us in a few minutes; I must go and see Coffee."[59]

Jackson was correct in his assessment of the situation. There was too much activity in front of him to call into question his belief that the main assault would come on the east side of the river. What he did

Tecumseh, a Shawnee Indian Leader who planned to unite Indian tribes and drive the white intruders out of their country. He died at the Battle of Thames on October 5, 1813, during the War of 1812.

The Massacre of Fort Mims on August 30, 1813.

William McIntosh, a Creek ally of General Andrew Jackson during the Creek Wars against the Red Sticks, who fought for the United States during the First Seminole War.

Menawa, a leader of the Creek Red Sticks and participant in the Battle of Horseshoe Bend on March 27, 1814.

Creek leader of the Red Sticks, William Weatherford, surrenders to Andrew Jackson after the Battle of Horseshoe Bend on March 27, 1814.

Portrait of Major General Andrew Jackson painted by artist Thomas Sully.

General Andrew Jackson commands his troops on horseback against the British under General Pakenham in January of 1815.

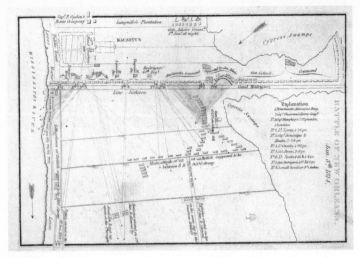

British and American troop positions during the Battle of New Orleans, January 8, 1815.

The Death of British General Edward Pakenham on the battlefield during the Battle of New Orleans.

Map of Spanish Florida in 1820.

Billy Bowlegs, the prominent leader of the Seminole Indians during Seminole Wars against the United States in Florida. Photograph by Arthur P. Lewis

not appreciate was the possibility that while the principal attack would indeed come on the east side, the British could set up a crossfire by taking the west side, a crossfire that could wipe him out.

So he felt he was ready for what the British would throw at him. He had about 4,000 men (600 of whom were regulars) on the front line with another 1,000 held in reserve.[60] The artillery was set up in three groups—river, center, and swamp—and his front line consisted of the Seventh Regiment, under Colonel George Ross, at the river, next to them a battalion of the city's militia, commanded by Major Jean Plauché, then the battalions of free blacks under Lacoste and Daquin, then the Forty-fourth Regiment, the Tennesseans under Carroll, supported by Adair's Kentuckians, and Coffee's cavalry on the left with Choctaw Indians scouting in the swamp.

Against this formidable line, Pakenham prepared to send a column of 2,200 men, consisting of the Fourth, the Twenty-first, and the Forty-fourth regiments and three companies of the Ninety-fifth, all under the command of General Sir Samuel Gibbs. They would hit Jackson's line a little left of center. A second column of 1,200 men, consisting of the Ninety-third and three companies of the Ninety-fifth, led by Major General Keane, would attack the American position along the river. At the same time a West Indian regiment of 520 soldiers would skirmish in the swamp to distract Coffee and punch a hole in the line on Jackson's extreme left. Meanwhile, Thornton and his troops, having crossed the river, would capture Morgan's guns as Gibbs and Keane began their assault and turn the batteries against Jackson. A third column of 1,500 men, made up of the Seventh Fusiliers and the remainder of the Forty-third, under Major General Lambert, was held in reserve near the center of the field.[61]

At 3 A.M., after several delays because of cave-ins along the banks of the canal, Thornton and a third of his force entered the barges and started across the Mississippi. According to Pakenham's plan, they were expected to land three miles below the American line, move up swiftly along the bank, and seize Morgan's position.

But as soon as the boats entered the river, they were caught in a current that swept them a mile and a half farther downstream and put them off schedule by several hours. It was nearly daylight when they finally reached the west bank. Thornton realized at once that, try as he might, he could never capture the American batteries before the general attack began. Then, suddenly, he saw the flashes of gunfire across the river and knew the main attack had already begun.

+≈≈+

At 4 A.M. on the east side of the river, a column of redcoats from the Forty-fourth Regiment, led by a particularly incompetent officer by the name of Lieutenant Colonel the Honorable Thomas Mullins, third son of Lord Ventry, stole within half a mile of the mud rampart. These redcoats, an advance of Gibbs's column, were instructed to carry fascines and ladders as they crept forward. The fascines were bundles of sugarcane to be thrown in the ditch in front of the American line to fill it up. The 16 ladders assigned to the operation were needed to scale the rampart. The fascines and ladders had to be in place before the column could move forward and begin the attack.

The redcoats moved quickly but silently, and they almost reached their goal when they suddenly realized their blunder.

Damn! They had forgotten the fascines and ladders.

Quick time to the rear to gather them and then race back into position before the signal to attack.

Too late! The battle for New Orleans had begun.[62]

+≈≈+

January 8, 1815, had dawned with a thick mist covering the plain separating the two armies. But as the day brightened, the mist slowly evaporated to reveal a splendidly arrayed and professional British army stretched two-thirds of the way across the field. All at once a Congreve rocket shot up into the air near the swamp, followed by a second rocket next to the river. They announced with a screaming voice that the battle to take the city had begun.

Drums beat a steady rhythm as Gibbs's column charged forward, aimed at Jackson's left near the swamp. Old Hickory, standing behind the line in the center, immediately called the reserve in the rear to move quickly to the rampart.

"Stand to your guns," cried Jackson, and remember, "don't waste your ammunition—see that every shot tells."[63]

All along the ditch American guns shot up and over the embankment, and in a moment produced a devastating blaze to challenge the invaders. The New Orleans Battalion Band struck up with "Yankee Doodle" as small arms, rifles, and cannons exploded in the faces of the advancing British. No sooner had one round of firing found its mark than a second round followed moments later. The American ranks rotated, first one line, then the next, followed by a third. The first line stepped back after firing, while the second line rushed forward and delivered their collective rebuke to the redcoats. When they backed away, the third line took their place. There was no intermission in the constant discharge of musket fire.[64]

Gibbs's column came to within 100 yards of the rampart but, without the fascines and ladders, the blast from the embankment stopped them in their tracks. Instead of rushing across the ditch, as planned, and scaling the rampart, they paused and returned the fire. Mullins' advance also paused, threw down the ladders and fascines, and started shooting too. It was a ghastly mistake. They were sitting ducks, and the American sharpshooters picked out their targets and blasted away. Volley after volley from Jackson's line smashed into the column, and dozens of redcoats crumbled to the ground. The advance now disintegrated into a confused and reeling army that did not know what to do. It verged on total disarray.

"Give it to them, my boys," shouted Jackson as he walked along the left of his line, encouraging his men to show the redcoats what American soldiers could do. "Let us finish the business to-day."

"Fire! Fire!" ordered General Carroll to the Tennessee and Kentucky marksmen in response to Jackson's command. And these sharpshooters let out an enthusiastic shout as they emptied their guns at the British column. The firepower of the American line was devastating. In fact, the smoke became so thick from the explosions that General Adair asked batteries 7 and 8 to cease fire temporarily until the air cleared.[65]

The Americans knew they had found their mark as they watched scores of enemy soldiers drop to the ground, many of them falling on top of one another. Major Harry Smith, an aide to Pakenham, said he had never seen a more destructive fire poured upon a single line of men.[66]

British officers rushed forward and screamed at their troops to advance. The disciplined troops responded to the command as ordered and headed toward the rampart. A few of them did reach and scramble into the ditch, but since they lacked ladders, they could not mount the rampart.

"Where are the Forty-fourth?" they cried. "If we get to the ditch we have no means of scaling the line."

Gibbs saw their plight and tried to help. "Here come the Forty-fourth," he shouted, as though his command could make it happen. "Here come the Forty-fourth."

Reassured, the column again moved forward. But the Forty-fourth did not come—at least not in the numbers necessary to scale the rampart. The few who did arrive did not have enough ladders and fascines. Again the column halted. And again the American line poured shot and shell into their ranks.

Then it happened: the psychological disintegration of the attack. The British troops lost their nerve. "The horror before them was too great to be withstood." They could no longer face that "flashing and roaring hell" in front of them. They recoiled and began a general retreat as Gibbs commanded them to re-form the line and advance. They paid him no heed and kept retreating. In that moment the battle was lost for the British and won for the Americans.[67]

Pakenham rode forward from his position in the rear. "For shame," he cried, "recollect that you are British soldiers. This is the road you ought to take," as he pointed toward the rampart.

Gibbs ran up to him and exclaimed in a voice choking with emotion, "The troops will not obey me. They will not follow me."[68]

Pakenham galloped to the head of the retreating column, pleading with them to turn around and follow him. At that moment a shower of balls from the rampart struck him, shattering his arm and killing his horse. He then mounted his aide's black Creole pony and pursued his soldiers, calling on them to halt and re-form their line.

This time they not only heard but heeded him. Having withdrawn out of range of the Tennessean and Kentucky rifles they halted and turned around. And to their amazement, they saw the magnificent tartan-trousered Highlanders, commanded by General Keane, marching rapidly toward them to strengthen their column. These 900 Highlanders had made a successful feint on the right side of Jackson's line and then were ordered to cross the field and come to the rescue of Gibbs's column on the left. As they executed an oblique turn to the right, exposing a flank to the enemy, the bagpipes started playing the regimental charge, "Monymusk," whereupon the Highlanders started to run. As they did the Americans peppered them with rifle, musketry, grape, round, and buckshot. The entire Highlanders line was raked, fore and aft, the front as well as the left flank. The carnage was frightful.

Seeing the Highlanders charge restored the courage of Gibbs's column. The troops dropped their knapsacks, re-formed their line, and headed back toward the ditch. Once they came within range the rampart spat out its rebuke. One round followed another straight into the faces of the on-coming redcoats. One 32-pounder, loaded to the muzzle with musketballs slammed into the head of the column at point-blank range and leveled it to the ground. Some 200 men were killed or wounded in this single salvo.

"Order up the reserve," Pakenham shouted to an aide. Then he called over to the Highlanders with the wave of his hat and the cry

"Hurra! Brave Highlanders!"[69] The rampart also sent its salute with its big guns, and everyone standing near the commanding general was struck down by the blast. Pakenham was hit in the thigh, his horse was killed, and both were thrown to the ground. Aides rushed to his side and started to lift him to his feet when another shot pierced his groin and he instantly lost consciousness. He was carried back out of the range of the American sharpshooters and propped up under an oak tree in the center of the field. He had suffered a mortal wound and within a few minutes he died.[70]

In addition to Pakenham, Gibbs and Keane were both struck down in the blast. They were carried from the field. Gibbs lingered for another day before he too expired. The entire high command of the British army in the forward position had been wiped out, and the effect on the troops was devastating. It "caused a wavering in the column which in such a situation became irreparable," reported Lambert.[71] The brave Highlanders came within 100 yards of the ditch before they halted as round after round decimated their ranks, leaving 500 wounded or dead lying on the ground. Those still standing finally turned and ran. "Before they reached our small arms," said General Coffee, "our grape and cannister mowed down whole columns, but that was nothing to the carnage of our Rifles and muskets."[72]

Even so, a few British soldiers did manage to reach the ditch and get across. Major Thomas Wilkinson, followed by Lieutenant John Lavack and 20 men, mounted the rampart, using what ladders were available. When Wilkinson got to the top he called out, "Now, why don't the troops come on? The day is our own." A hail of bullets greeted him and he fell forward. The Tennesseans and Kentuckians were so taken by his heroism that they lifted his body and moved it to the rear.

"Bear up, my dear fellow," said one of the Americans, "you are too brave a man to die." Wilkinson nodded and said, "I thank you from my heart. It is all over for me. You can render me a favor. It is to communicate to my commander that I fell on your parapet, and died like a soldier and a true Englishman."

Lavack scrambled his way to the top of the breastwork and demanded the swords of two American officers standing close by. "Oh, no," one of them responded, "you are alone, and, therefore, ought to consider yourself *our* prisoner." Lavack looked around and saw that he was indeed alone, so he calmly surrendered.[73]

Far to the rear of the British attacking force, General Lambert received word of the death of Pakenham and the mortal wounding of Gibbs. As Keane was also wounded, Lambert took command. He ordered the reserve troops forward, but they could do no more than cover the retreat of the fleeing columns.

Throughout, Jackson took a position on a slightly elevated ground near the center of the line so that he could observe the action and if necessary issue commands. But he trusted his officers and allowed them full authority in directing their troops. This was an important part of his ability to command loyalty and respect, and a vital aspect of his talent as a leader. He looked absolutely calm and seemed to have no doubt as to the outcome of the battle. Few spoke to him. But once the British began their retreat, Colonel Thomas Hinds of the Mississippi Dragoons came up to him and asked permission to pursue the fleeing redcoats. It was all too tempting. Still, Jackson realized it could invite disaster, so he refused permission. The risk taker of the Creek War had matured. And a wise decision it was because the Dragoons would have run head on into Lambert's powerful reserve unit.

Still, the British did have some success in attacking Jackson's line. The brigade closest to the river crept up on the American outpost so quickly after the rocket signaled the beginning of the battle that the defenders had to scramble for their lives. The British, lead by Colonel Robert Rennie, pursued them, and soon they were engaged in hand-to-hand fighting. They were so intermingled that Captain Humphrey, the commander of the number-one battery on Jackson's line, had to withhold his fire lest he hit his own men. The American outpost finally made it to safety when they raced over a plank across the ditch to the rampart. At once Humphrey's battery opened up on the British, but Rennie and two of his men managed to mount the parapet, although they were immediately cut down. Had Keane's column followed quickly behind Rennie's successful advance, they might have breached Jackson's line. But Pakenham ordered Keane to support Gibbs, and Keane led his men across the field to their subsequent destruction.[74]

On Jackson's extreme left, where Coffee and his men guarded the cypress swamp, a detachment of British West Indian troops moved close to his position but became mired in the mud or were drowned or captured.

The Americans also suffered a stinging defeat, one Jackson himself should have prevented. He seemed oblivious of the danger on the opposite side of the river, and this defeat on the west bank of the Mississippi was as total as the victory on the east side. Not only had he failed to provide enough soldiers on the west side, but he apparently never visited the site during the period when the British first started to move toward the city. Even worse, he failed to have boats ready to cross the river should reinforcements be necessary.

What happened was tragic. To prevent a British landing on the west bank, Major Jean Arnaud and 120 Louisiana militiamen were sent three miles below Morgan's line of defense. They took up their position and then went to sleep, leaving one sentry on guard. Thornton and his 600 men landed at daybreak about one mile downstream of Arnaud's encampment. Using three gun barges manned by 100 sailors to cover his flank, Thornton rushed forward and almost captured the sleeping militiamen. But they awoke at the sentry's alarm and quickly retreated.[75] They met up with a detachment of Kentuckians sent to assist them. Together they tried to halt Thornton's advance, but he easily turned their right and sent the Louisianians fleeing into the swamps. He then routed the Kentuckians who rushed back to Morgan's position, with the British close behind.[76]

Morgan's line behind a sawmill race was too long for the number of troops available to defend it. And many of the men were inadequately armed or not armed at all. The right side of this line was particularly weak, so the poorly armed Kentuckians were assigned to it. Thornton quickly determined the weakness of the American position and sent two columns against it, one at the center and the other at the right side. The Kentuckians fired what few guns they had and then abandoned their position. Morgan chased after them on horseback but could not get them to return. The British rushed over the millrace, scaled the parapet, attacked the left side of the line, and forced it to retreat.

Patterson's batteries, which were 300 yards to the rear of Morgan's line, were now in jeopardy. The commodore ordered the guns to be spiked, and the ammunition thrown into the river. But his orders were not carried out, for the British were able to restore half his guns to action. The American gunners boarded the *Louisiana* and sailed it into the river. Patterson himself managed to escape to the rear.

Thornton tried to get the guns repaired as quickly as possible in order to enfilade Jackson's line. And his men completed the task just as they received the news of the disaster on the east side of the river from General Lambert. Thornton and his men were ordered to retire, recross the river, and join the main army.[77]

It was then 10 A.M. The battle in front of the rampart had ended an hour and a half earlier. The principal attack had lasted only 30 minutes.

+≈≈+

Once the battle ended, Jackson walked down the line with his staff, stopping at each command to congratulate the men on their bravery and skill. At the same time the band played "Hail Columbia." Then for the first time the entire line burst forth with loud and prolonged cheers for their general. And it continued for quite some time. But the cheers soon turned to stunned silence when the troops mounted the rampart and wandered around the battlefield. What they saw shocked them profoundly. The ground, reported one man, was "covered with dead and wounded lying in heaps, the field was completely red."[78] The area in front of the rampart was so strewn with the dead, the dying, and the wounded that "you could have walked a quarter of a mile to the front on the bodies of the killed and disabled."[79] Some 40 dead and over 100 wounded lay in the ditch. "Some had their heads shot off, some their legs, some their arms. Some were laughing, some crying, some screaming."[80] Many had hidden behind the pile of dead for protection, and now began to move. "I never had so grand and awful an idea of the resurrection as on that day," Jackson later wrote. "After the smoke of the battle had cleared off somewhat, I saw in the distance more than five hundred Britons emerging from the heaps of their dead comrades, all over the plain, rising up, and still more distinctly visible as the field became clearer, coming forward and surrendering as prisoners of war to our soldiers. They had fallen at our first fire upon them, without having received so much as a scratch, and lay prostrate, as if dead, until the close of the action."[81]

There were many cries for help. The American soldiers assisted the wounded by helping them to the area behind the rampart where they could receive medical attention. Some British soldiers lying in the ditch did not understand "the language of the free men of color" who tried to help them and, thinking they were about to be murdered by the blacks, killed or wounded several of them. In fact, one modern writer argues that more American casualties occurred after the battle than during it.[82]

Later Jackson reported to Secretary Monroe that he suffered 7 killed and 6 wounded. But these were battle losses, not the later casualties among the free men of color or those injured during the minor skirmishing that continued for the next several days. On January 14 Jackson received a full report that claimed 13 Americans killed, 39 wounded, and 19 missing in the action on January 8.[83]

The British admitted to 2,037 casualties: 291 killed, 1,262 wounded, and 484 captured or missing.[84] A great many people, including Jackson, had trouble believing these figures, particularly the staggering number of British losses compared to those of the Americans. The British loss, the general reported to Monroe, "[were] immense. I had at first computed it at 1500, but it is since ascertained to have been much greater. . . . My loss was inconsiderable. . . . Such a disproportion in loss, when we consider the number and the kind of troops engaged must, I know, excite astonishment, and may not, every where, be fully credited; yet I am perfectly satisfied that the amount is not exaggerated [*sic*] on the one part, nor understated on the other."[85]

Immediately upon the British withdrawal from the battlefield, Lambert wrote Jackson complementing him on the care given to the wounded, requesting a return of casualties, and asking that an unarmed party be permitted to bury the dead and tend to the wounded. Jackson agreed. Lambert then asked for a truce, fully intending to withdraw rather than renew the attack, perhaps with the intention of striking Mobile, the original site of the invasion plan. But it was not until midnight of January 18 that he and his army quietly decamped, leaving behind 80 seriously wounded men under medical attendance. Also left behind were 2 officers, 14 pieces of heavy artillery, and a considerable amount of shot. They had destroyed the powder before they departed. They carried the body of General Pakenham in a hogshead of rum to be shipped to the Caribbean for later reshipment to London.[86]

The following day, January 19, Jackson inspected the British camp. He was tempted to pursue the enemy and deliver a knockout blow, but his sense of caution held him back. Furthermore, his aide, Edward Livingston, advised against it. "What do you want more?" he asked. "Your object is gained. The city is saved. The British have retired."[87]

What Livingston said was true. Jackson had his victory, one he earned and richly deserved. He was a determined, brave, untutored but innately skillful commander who inspired his men to perform acts of courage and valor. He radiated confidence and implacable resolution. He inspired his men. He made mistakes; but he was lucky, as he himself admitted, and he demonstrated remarkable leadership. He made the right decision to fight the British on the east bank, and he set up a defense so formidable that the greatest professional army in the world could not fight their way through it.

On January 25, what remained of the British army finally dragged itself through the bayous to the fleet on Lake Borgne and sailed away. They captured Fort Bowyer on February 11 with the intention of taking Mobile, but then official word arrived announcing that a peace treaty between England and the United States had been signed on December 24, 1814, and the war was over. Early in March the ill-fated expedition sailed back to England.

CHAPTER 4

The First Seminole War

VIRTUALLY OVERNIGHT GENERAL ANDREW JACKSON BECAME a national hero. When news of this stupendous victory reached Washington on February 4, 1815, the city exploded out of its long nightmare of military defeat. The city went "wild with delight." Crowds gathered and surrounded the President's mansion, the homes of the cabinet officers, and other war activists to express their joy and shout words of congratulation. The mayor issued a proclamation calling for the illumination of the city. Newspapers proclaimed this "ALMOST INCREDIBLE VICTORY!!! Enemy . . . beaten and repulsed by Jackson and his brave supporters with great slaughter. The Glorious News . . . has spread around a general joy, commensurate with the brilliance of this event, and the magnitude of our Victory."[1]

"Glory be to God," shouted *Niles' Weekly Register,* "that the barbarians have been defeated. Glory to Jackson . . . Glory to the militia . . . Sons of freedom . . . benefactors of your country . . . all hail!"[2]

As the news of the victory spread from city to city, it kindled "everywhere the maddest enthusiasm." In Philadelphia parades were quickly organized and transparencies constructed to depict the battle as best they could conceive it. One person made a transparency showing Jackson on horseback at the head of his staff, pursuing the British, with the motto "This day shall ne'er go by, from this day to the ending of the world, but He, in it, shall be remembered."[3]

Then, nine days later, just as the ecstatic joy over the victory was sinking into the national consciousness, news arrived from Europe that the commissioners in Ghent had signed a treaty ending the war and would go into effect after both Great Britain and the United States had ratified it. The news electrified the American people, coming on the heels of the victory at New Orleans. Men ran through the streets, screaming "Peace! Peace!" With lighted torches and lamps they marched through the avenues at night, weeping with pride and happiness that this horrible war was at last over.

Over! And the knowledge that an American army had not simply beaten a professional British army but pulverized it prodded citizens into fully appreciating what it meant to be a citizen of the United States. What a spurt it gave to nationalism. Hereafter patriots were not simply Virginians, Tennesseans, New Yorkers, New Englanders, whatever, but *Americans.* "The last six months is the proudest period in the history of the Republic," insisted *Niles' Weekly Register.* "We . . . *demonstrated* to mankind a capacity to acquire a skill in arms to conquer 'the conquerors of all' as Wellington's *invincibles* were modestly stiled. . . . *Who would not be an American? Long live the Republic! . . . Last asylum of oppressed humanity! Peace is signed in the Arms of Victory!"*[4]

The pride the American people now had about their country, their faith and confidence in it, had all been restored by Andrew Jackson. The nation had entered this war, in part, to prove its right to independence, but the last two years had produced nothing but one military disaster after another, including the burning of the White House and the Capitol. Some said that the country's failure to defend itself proved that the United States was only a temporary experiment in freedom, that its independence was not deserved. But then along came Andrew Jackson and his heroes who slaughtered a magnificent British army and repelled the greatest armada in history. It demonstrated to the world the nation's right to be free. No longer did the American people have to prove to themselves or anyone else that their independence was deserved. Now they could go about the business of building a nation. Indeed, wrote one early Jackson biographer, "from that time on the Union had less of the character of a temporary experiment. The country had also won respect abroad, and was recognized in the family of nations as it had not been before."[5]

In the public mind, all this was the result of the incredible victory that Andrew Jackson had achieved at New Orleans, and since it was followed almost immediately by the news of a peace treaty, they pictured him in their minds as a special messenger of the Almighty who had come to rescue His people and preserve their freedom. No wonder he was hailed as the "Hero of New Orleans." He remained a hero to the nation for the remainder of his life and well beyond. Not until the civil rights movement of the 1960s did his reputation change, because of the removal of the Indians that occurred when Jackson was president. But at the beginning of the nineteenth century, his popularity exceeded even that of George Washington, Benjamin Franklin, and Thomas Jefferson. He was "The Hero."

Congress, of course, immediately passed a series of resolutions commending the Hero and his army. Representative George M. Troup of Georgia congratulated the House "on the glorious termination of the most glorious war ever waged by any people. To the glory of it, General Jackson and his gallant army have contributed not a little. I cannot, sir, perhaps language cannot, do justice to the merits of General Jackson . . . ; it is a fit subject for the genius of Homer."[6]

Most states also passed resolutions to thank Jackson for what he had accomplished. "We consider your defence of . . . New Orleans," read one, "as the most illustrious among illustrious deeds." President

Madison sent his congratulations. Soon songs were written to commemorate the victory, the most popular of which was "Jackson Is the Boy":

> And sing a song of joy!
> Let party spirit cease,
> Here's "Victory and Peace."
> And here's "Immortal Jackson."[7]

It has often been incorrectly noted in textbooks that the war ended on December 24, 1814, when the commissioners in Ghent signed the peace treaty, and therefore the Battle of New Orleans occurred after the war had concluded. Actually the treaty specifically stated that not until both Great Britain and the United States had ratified the treaty would the war end. It took weeks for the treaty to reach the United States. The Senate immediately ratified it in mid-February, a month after the battle took place in New Orleans. That was the moment when the war officially ended.

⊹⊱══⊰⊹

Back in New Orleans, Jackson held off withdrawing his army from the rampart until January 21, feeling it would be imprudent to move them any earlier. But first he contacted the Abbé Guillaume Dubourg, the apostolic administrator of the diocese of Louisiana and the Floridas, and said that the return of the army to the city should be celebrated with a religious ceremony of thanksgiving to be performed in the cathedral. "The signal interposition of heaven," the general wrote, "in giving success to our arms against the Enemy . . . . must excite . . . emotions of the liveliest gratitude." The Abbé agreed totally and assured Jackson that he would make the arrangements necessary so that "the brightest ornament . . . will certainly be yourself, General, surrounded by your brave army."[8]

On January 23 the ceremony took place. A temporary arch, supported by six Corinthian columns, was erected in the public square opposite the cathedral. A huge crowd filled the square; balconies and rooftop were alive with spectators. Then the Hero strode into the square accompanied by his staff while people screamed their delight at seeing him. They called to him by name while salvos of artillery announced his presence. He was asked to walk to the cathedral through the path prepared for him. As he passed under the arch, two children standing on a pedestal lowered a laurel crown to his head. Then a ballad was sung to the tune of "Yankee Doodle."

When Jackson reached the cathedral, the Abbé was waiting for him on the porch. After the welcoming speech, the Hero thanked the Abbé for his prayers and then turned to the crowd and wished wealth and happiness to the city in recognition of its courage and endurance. Inside the church a *Te Deum* was sung, after which a guard of honor attended Jackson and accompanied him to his quarters. In the evening the curfew was temporarily suspended, the city was fully illuminated, and the people gave themselves over to feasting and merry-making.[9]

The following morning the people awoke from their debauch to find that martial law had been reimposed. They had expected that all the regulations and restrictions on their liberty and daily life would be lifted. But they did not understand the character and will of their Hero. After all, as far as he knew, the war was still in progress, and the British might return to launch a second attempt to capture the city. Jackson was there to safeguard New Orleans and the entire Mississippi Valley, and he was determined to maintain military preparedness. That meant that the militia must remain under arms and the people must continue to submit to martial law.

Within days the Hero of New Orleans turned into the "Tyrant of New Orleans." Discontent mounted in the city, and grumbling about the despot rose from whispers to shouts. One legislator by the name of Louis Louaillier wrote an article in the local newspaper demanding that the laws resume their function and that "the citizens of this State should return to the full enjoyment of their rights." Jackson had him immediately arrested, whereupon Louaillier hired a lawyer who went to Dominick A. Hall, the U.S. district judge, and obtained a writ of habeas corpus. When informed of this action, Jackson had Hall arrested and put in jail. Later, on March 12, the general had the judge marched out of town under guard and set free four miles from the city. This high-handedness about individual legal and constitutional rights, especially in light of the many rumors that the war had ended, was outrageous if not bizarre.

It was not until March 13 that official word and copies of the ratification of the peace treaty arrived from Washington. Martial law was revoked immediately and those persons held in confinement for military crimes were released. Louaillier was discharged from prison and Hall returned to the city. The judge promptly held Jackson in contempt and fined him $1,000, which Jackson paid himself, refusing to accept money raised by popular subscription. He asked that the money already collected be distributed among the families of the soldiers who died in defense of the city.[10]

Jackson had style. He always did have.

It is one of the remarkable contradictions in Jackson's character that at one moment he could ruthlessly seize and exercise absolute power and at the next walk away from it without a single regret or sense of loss. He knew and at all times performed his duty as he understood it. He knew what he had to do and how to go about achieving it. Never for a moment did he believe he was doing something wrong. Martial law was dictated by the invasion of an enemy and was the only way the general felt he could insure order among the many different ethnic groups that inhabited the city.

Jackson's final days in New Orleans were spent peacefully with his wife, Rachel, and their adopted son, Andrew, both of whom had arrived in the Crescent City a few days after the announcement of peace. As it turned out, their journey back home to Nashville was one long and exhilarating ovation as town after town held celebrations to honor him. "He is everywhere hailed as the saviour of his Country," reported John Reid. He has been "feasted, caressed & I may say idolized. They look upon him as a strange prodigy; & women, children, & old men line the road to look at him as they would at the Elephant. This is a sort of business in which he feels very awkwardly . . . . He pulls off his hat—bows graciously but as tho his spirit were humbled & abashed by the attention which is shown him."[11]

The Hero and his party arrived back in Nashville on May 15. and he enjoyed a grand parade, a regal reception, and a gala dinner attended by Governor Blount and other dignitaries. To the many orations of welcome home he responded simply: "I am at a loss to express my feeling. The approbation of my fellow citizens is to me the richest reward. Through you, sir," he said to Representative Felix Gundy, who served as chairman of the festivities and had just delivered a long speech extolling Jackson and the outcome of his several campaigns, "I beg leave to assure them that I am *this day* amply compensated for every toil and labor."[12]

Jackson played the modest hero to the hilt, and he became quite proficient in responding graciously and humbly to the extravagant praise showered on him. And virtually everywhere he went he was presented with medals, even decorated swords.

In the late fall, after Congress had reconvened, Jackson journeyed to Washington to be feted and feasted and entertained at the President's mansion. Even Thomas Jefferson went out of his way to greet the general and present a toast during the Hero's brief trip to Lynchburg, Virginia. "Honor and gratitude," said the former President in his toast, "to those who have filled the measure of their country's honor."[13]

So universal was the praise heaped on Jackson that he was told that there could be "little doubt, that with the proper management of your friends that you might be elected to the highest Office in the American Government."[14]

⊹━━⊹

The war having ended, the American army was reorganized in the spring of 1815 and reduced to 10,000 men in the northern and southern divisions and commanded by two major generals: Jacob Brown commanding in the North and Andrew Jackson commanding in the South. The new secretary of war, Alexander J. Dallas, notified Jackson of his appointment on May 22, 1815, and told him that the Division of the South included not only the southern states but most of the Northwest. The administration, said Dallas, wished to begin a policy of "civilizing the Indians, by the establishment of competent posts on a lower route, from Chicago along the Illinois river, to St. Louis . . . [and] is committed to your special care, as falling within the duties of your command."[15]

The government also permitted Jackson to set up his headquarters at his home, the Hermitage, outside Nashville, and this allowed him the luxury of attending to his military duties while managing his plantation and other private affairs. He was paid a salary of $2,400 a year, along with $1,652 in allowances, which provided a very comfortable and dependable income. His staff lived with him and at various times included Sam Houston, Richard Keith Call, Andrew Jackson Donelson, Robert Butler, James Gadsden, John and Samuel Overton, his personal physician Dr. James C. Bronaugh, and John H. Eaton.

Jackson's primary concern in commanding the Southern Division was the protection of the southern frontier, a task complicated by the continued hostility of the Creeks, especially those operating out of Spanish Florida, and the presence of such British military officers as Colonel Edward Nicholls and Captain George Woodbine. Besides arming the Creeks, the British encouraged them to believe that the land they had surrendered in the Treaty of Fort Jackson would be returned, since the Treaty of Ghent dictated the restoration of all Indian property as of 1811.

Jackson had no intention of restoring the lands he had won in the Creek War, so his first concern was seeing to it that the boundary line between Indian and U.S. territories was marked out. He received regular reports from subordinate officers about Indian activities, and since the West had been committed to his "special care," he also communicated with the territorial governors of Illinois and Missouri, Ninian Edwards and William Clark, who were serving as commissioners negotiating treaties with Indians along the Mississippi River. Not until the tribes "are made to smart by our arms, and taught to disregard the *talks* . . . of bad men, agents of British mercenaries," he wrote to these governors, will there be "peace, tranquility and perfect security. . . . Keep me well advised of the Disposition of the Indians on your frontier."[16]

In accordance with his determination to run the boundary line established by the Treaty of Fort Jackson, the general saw to it that his friend and colleague General John Coffee was named one of the three commissioners appointed to undertake the task. He could count on Coffee to execute his wishes. And those wishes were not concealed, as he made quite clear to the secretary of war. "I have no hesitation in believing that it is all important to the tranquility of the south that the line should be run without delay."[17] That meant that those Creeks living in what was now U.S. property would have to move.

Jackson became even more determined after receiving a letter Colonel Nicholls in Florida wrote to Benjamin Hawkins, who forwarded it to the general. In it Nicholls protested the "complete breach of the 9th Article" of the Treaty of Ghent. He went on to remind Hawkins that "if your Citizens break through the laws of a free and independent [Creek] Nation guaranteed as such by my Sovereign it must be at their peril."[18]

The sheer audacity of Nicholls in writing this letter, coupled with his presence in Florida where he could continue to arm and incite the Indians, drove Jackson wild. "Nothing ever surpassed or equaled the bare-faced effrontery of Col. Nichol [*sic*]," he ranted. The Colonel should be seized and punished. "The Creek line *must* be run, and with as little delay as possible."[19]

Further complicating the matter was the fact that Cherokees and Chickasaws claimed that some of the land taken under the Treaty of Fort Jackson was theirs. And the Cherokees submitted their complaint to Washington.

Meanwhile Coffee informed Jackson that he had assumed his duties as an Indian commissioner and had begun the task of running the northern boundary line. "I am aware of the importance and necessity of finishing this business," he wrote, "and as such, have determined to act, alone, if I am not joined by the other Comrs. delay with me at this late date is inadmissible." So, without further ado, Coffee succeeded in extending the line to the Cherokee boundary and was about to run it to the "Chickasaw and Choctaw lines."

Elated by the news, Jackson told Coffee to conclude the business as quickly as possible. Just remember, he said, the Indian will "claim every thing and any thing."[20] Indeed, the general had a number of fixed ideas about how to treat Indians. First of all, they are subject to the sovereignty of the United States and "have only a possessory right to the soil, for the purpose of hunting and not the right of domaine." Therefore, Congress has "full power, by law, to regulate all the concerns of the Indians." They occupy more land than they really need, and they should be limited to that amount necessary to feed, clothe, and house the tribe. Their extensive landowning only foments wars with whites. "Their territorial boundary must be curtailed," he insisted. Furthermore, Coffee must remember that "[a]n Indian is fickle, and you will have to take the same firm stand and support it and you are sure of success." Moreover, the "Treachery of the Indian character will never justify the imposing of confidence in their professions." Finally, "it may be necessary . . . to make the chiefs some presents" to help in the negotiations. But always be sure to have the necessary authority to offer these bribes and know precisely where the money is coming from.[21]

Jackson hated having to bribe the chiefs, but he did it all the time. In January 1815, for example, some $60,000 worth of goods was sent to him to distribute in the best way he knew how. Fortunately, he himself was scrupulously honest. But bribery stuck in his craw. "It is now discovered," he informed the secretary of war, "that nothing can be done without corrupting their Chiefs. This is so inconsistent with the principles of our Government that it is high time the Legislature should exercise its function and pass all laws for the regulation of the Indians. If they have too much land circumscribe them. Furnish them with the means of agriculture, and you will thereby lay the foundation of their civilization by making them husbandmen. Treat them humanely and Liberally but put an end to treating with them and obtaining the Country by corrupting their Chiefs which is the only way by which a Treaty can be obtained."[22]

In dealing with the Indians, Coffee reported that the Creeks insisted that in ceding all their lands west of the Coosa River, some of it overlapped with Cherokee and Chickasaw claims to land south of the Tennessee River and with Choctaw claims to land east of the Tombigbee River. Worse, it seems the Cherokees had protested to the then secretary of war, William H. Crawford, and convinced him of the legitimacy of their argument, namely that the Creek Treaty violated their property rights. So Crawford signed a new treaty with the Cherokees on March 22, 1816, in which a 50-mile-wide strip in the northwestern part of the Creek cession from the Coosa to the Mississippi line was awarded to the Cherokee Indians, along with $25,500 to pay for damages by the Tennessee militia during the Creek War.

Jackson exploded. That land of 4 to 5 million acres belonged to the United States, he stormed, and will not be returned. He protested to James Monroe, then secretary of state and former secretary of war, and assured him that the people of the West would not tolerate the loss of territory they fought for and of "incalculable Vallue to the U States."[23]

Crawford added to Jackson's fury when he reminded the general that the March 22 treaty had been "approved by the Senate and House of Representatives, and is the supreme law of the land. Submission to it is a duty which will not be neglected." The Hero then shot back that the militia would not assist in surrendering the land to the Cherokees. "Political discussion," he boldly told the secretary, "is not the province of a military officer. As a man, I am entitled to my opinion, and have given it freely.[24]

Jackson was clearly insubordinate when he spoke to the secretary in this way, especially in declaring what the military would or would not do. But he was determined to force the administration into adopting his interpretation of his treaty with the Creeks. The peace treaty at Ghent did not apply to his treaty, he argued, since it pertained to a separate military action. Besides, the "the real Indians, the natives of the forest are little concerned" about "our" acquisition of land. It is the "designing half-breeds and renegade white men" among them who protest our actions, to say nothing of the British murderers who reside in Florida and constantly incite the Indians to take up arms against us.

Half-breeds, renegade white men, and British—they are the enemies of the country and of peace. Moreover, he said, think about the effect of the March 22 treaty on American citizens living close to the frontier. "The people of the west will never suffer any Indian to inhabit this country again," he declared. And he was right. Westerners were furious that the administration surrendered any territory back to the Indians.

Sure enough, the clamor of protests from the West, plus the danger of antagonizing the Hero of New Orleans, was sufficient to convince the politicians in Washington to repudiate the March 22 treaty and appoint several commissioners to persuade the tribes to accept the Treaty of Fort Jackson as written. Coffee, the Choctaw agent Colonel John McKee, and Congressman John Rhea of Tennessee were appointed to treat with the Choctaws, while Jackson, General David Meriwether of Georgia, and Jess Franklin of North Carolina were chosen to treat with the Cherokees and Chickasaws. Crawford told Jackson that the commissioners, in their negotiations with the Cherokees, Chickasaws and Choctaws, were expected to get them to sign new treaties by which they relinquished their previous land claims.[25]

The suggestion was not lost on Jackson and over the next several years, using verbal appeals, threats of violence, bribery, and sometimes actual force, he succeeded in signing a series of treaties with these tribes by which the United States acquired vast holdings of land in the present states of Tennessee, Florida, Georgia, Alabama, and Mississippi. Starting with the Creek cession in the Treaty of Fort Jackson, he went on to sign treaties with the Cherokees on September 14,

1816, and again on July 8, 1817; then he signed treaties with the Chickasaws on September 20, 1816, and again on October 19, 1818; and on October 18, 1820 he signed a treaty at Doak's Stand with the Choctaws.[26]

Jackson was very anxious that the land be put up for sale very quickly so that American settlers could occupy it and thereby strengthen the defense of the frontier. As "soon as the lands are sold," he explained to Coffee, "the Legislative authority will have the right to lay off counties, Establish which American citizens could inhabit and develop Towns &c &c."[27] And, as general of the Southern Division, he made it his business to see to it that Indians did not occupy lands ceded to the United States—or whites occupy land the Indians rightly owned. Of course, he fervently believed that all the tribes in the Southeast should be moved beyond the Mississippi River as a matter of national security. As long as they stayed where they were, they constituted a potential threat to American safety.

One of Jackson's most important undertakings as general of the U.S. Army was the planning and construction of a military road through the heart of what had been hostile Indian country. Coffee assisted, and in the process surveyed about 100 townships by July 1817. The road itself was built under Jackson's direction between July 1817 and January 1819, and he selected the areas where military posts would be established. As finally completed, the road extended 483 miles from Nashville to Madisonville on Lake Pontchartrain, enabling the rapid movement of troops to the Southwest when necessary and shortening mail service between Washington and New Orleans to 17 days.[28]

But Jackson's biggest land haul came as the result of the First Seminole War, when land was acquired not only from the Seminole tribe but from Spain as well. And it brought about the final expulsion of British intruders along the Gulf Coast.

The First Seminole War had been brewing for some time. As early as the spring of 1816, during the final year of James Madison's presidency, Jackson had to contend with the existence of the Negro Fort in

Spanish Florida, not far from the Gulf of Mexico. This fort attracted runaway slaves who had escaped bondage throughout the entire Southeast, from the Carolinas to the Mississippi. Extending over two acres, it was built in a square and its ramparts and parapets made of hewn timber filled with dirt. Nine to 12 pieces of cannon were mounted on it, along with mortars and howitzers. Inside the fort were several large stone houses and barracks. According to reports from General George Pendleton Gaines, some 300 runaway slaves lived in the fort, wore red coats, and had been supplied with "a large quantity of British muskets, Powder and other supplies."[29]

An infuriated Jackson asked the secretary of war for permission to cross the border and destroy the fort. But the reply was typical of the Madison administration. Instead of destroying the fort, it read, just contact the Spanish governor, Mauricio de Zúñiga, and notify him of what is going on. "The principles of good government," wrote Secretary Crawford, require that Zúñiga be invited "to put an end to an evil of so serious a nature." If the governor fails to act on the suggestion, he went on, then the President would decide what to do next.

Which meant to do nothing, sniffed Jackson. But he obeyed the instruction and wrote to Zúñiga that the fort had to be leveled. Failure to do so "will compel us in self Defence to destroy" it and the "Banditti" within it. Zúñiga replied that he realized a problem existed and he would be happy to cooperate. So if the renowned General Jackson would like to participate in the reduction of the fort, he would be proud to serve under him![30]

Taking no chances with the ability or readiness of the governor to handle the problem, Jackson gave Gaines discretionary authority to invade Florida, but he sent him a clear signal that he wanted the fort obliterated. "If the fort harbours the Negroes of our citizens or friendly Indians living within our Territory," he said, "or hold out Inducements to the Slaves of our Citizens to desert from their owner's service, this fort must be destroyed." He added that "you possess the power of acting on your Discretion, which I hope you will exercise on this."[31]

Gaines hardly needed much encouragement. Constantly troubled by the Florida situation, he immediately sent troops to reduce the Negro Fort. At the same time a naval squadron from New Orleans reached the mouth of the Apalachicola River on July 10, 1816, and provided support for the land operation. On July 27 the gunboats opened fire on the fort, using hot shot, and on the very first volley hit the fort's magazine. A terrific explosion occurred, which killed 270 individuals and wounded another 61. A number of black leaders in the fort were captured and turned over to the Indians to be tortured and killed.[32]

That settled one problem for Jackson, but another remained. He continued to receive reports in the following months that the situation along the Georgia–Florida border had worsened. One such report from Gaines related an incident in which a party of Seminole Indians had attacked a "defenceless family and massacred a woman (Mrs. Garrot) [Mrs. Obediah Garrett] and her two children—the woman and the eldest child were scalped, the house robbed and set on fire." These butchers then retreated to the safety of their sanctuary in Spanish Florida, believing they would not be pursued by avenging Americans. Gaines documented his report by forwarding incriminating letters, one of which was signed by Alexander Arbuthnot, a British trader from the West Indies. This villain, said Gaines, was "one of those *self-styled Philanthropists* who have long infested our neighboring Indian villages, in the character of British agents—fomenting a spirit of discord (calculated to work the destruction of the deluded savages) and endeavoring by pretended care and kindness, to effect the destruction of these wretched savages."[33]

The Seminoles were actually part of the Creek Confederation and had welcomed the Red Sticks who had fled to their country following the Creek War. Seminoles were Hitchitee people and received their name from the Creek Muskogees who called them "Seminoles," which roughly translates as "frontiersmen" or "people of distant fires." Actually, the Seminoles did not constitute a single tribe but rather an alliance of earlier tribes, such as Apalachicolas, Yamasces, and Uchess, along with newer groups like the Tallahassees, Oconees, and Mikasukis. Americans lumped them all together and called them Seminoles, probably as a convenience in negotiating treaties.[34]

Gaines continued to alert Jackson to the fact that the Seminoles and their Red Stick allies were taking suggestions on what to do and how to behave from Alexander Arbuthnot, "the prime director on the part of the seminole Indians in the adjustment of our affairs." Worse, he had arrogantly disputed Jackson's insistence that the peace treaty of Ghent did not in any way invalidate the Hero's Treaty of Fort Jackson.[35]

When Gaines learned that Captain George Woodbine had promised British aid to over 2,000 Red Sticks and Seminoles and 400 runaway slaves from Georgia who had congregated in and around the area of Fowltown, located just north of the Florida border, he decided to act. He had also learned that the chief of the village, Neamathla, claimed land that had been ceded to the United States. He therefore dispatched a force of 250 soldiers of the First Brigade from Fort Scott to arrest the chief and his warriors. If they resisted, they were to be treated "as Enemies."

When the force arrived outside the town, they were fired upon. They returned the fire and succeeded in to driving off the inhabitants. Obviously, the number of Red Sticks and Seminoles in the area had been exaggerated. In fleeing, the Indians left behind four dead warriors, one dead woman, and several other wounded men. The soldiers then completed their assignment by burning Fowltown. Among the many artifacts found in Neamathla's house before it was consumed by flames were a British coat with gold epaulettes and a certificate signed by a captain of marines stating that Neamathla was a "faithfull friend to the British." Gaines notified Jackson that he was convinced "that nothing but the application of force, will be sufficient to ensure a permanent adjustment of this affair."[36]

The burning of Fowltown is usually cited as the beginning of military action by the American army that precipitated the First Seminole War. And the killing continued when, nine days later, a "very considerable" number of Seminoles fanned out over 150 yards along the shore of the Apalachicola River, a mile below the juncture of the Flint and Chattahoochee rivers that form the Apalachicola, and ambushed a boat commanded by Lieutenant Richard W. Scott. It carried 40 soldiers, 7 women, and 4 children. The Indians killed all but 6 soldiers, who escaped, 4 of whom were wounded. The 7 women, wives of the soldiers, were taken captive or executed. The children were seized by their heels and had their brains splattered as their heads were slammed against the sides of the boat.[37] For the Seminoles it was an act of revenge for the destruction of Fowltown.

And that did it. Jackson immediately forwarded this information to John C. Calhoun, the newly appointed secretary of war in the administration of President James Monroe. In his letter Jackson pointed out that Spain was required by treaties to keep the Indians from invading the United States. Clearly Spain was incapable of fulfilling this responsibility. Thus, if the Seminoles were using Florida as a "sanctuary"—which they were—then, said Jackson, it is incumbent upon us to "follow the mauraders and punish them in their retreat." Spain must be given "due notice," naturally. "The War Hatchet having been raised . . . [the] frontier cannot be protected without entering their country."[38]

Instead of getting the pusillanimous response he usually received from Washington, this time he heard posthaste—and he was ordered to take action. On December 26, 1817, Calhoun ordered him to proceed immediately to Fort Scott and take command of American forces in the district. A reported 2,700 Seminoles regularly threatened the frontier, said Calhoun, and he wanted Jackson to "terminate a conflict" that Monroe had hoped to avoid "but which is now made necessary by the "Settled hostilities" of the Seminoles. Meanwhile, Gaines was informed that it was President Monroe's wish that he consider himself "at liberty to march across the Florida line," if he felt that he had adequate forces, and attack the Seminoles "within its limits, should it be found necessary, unless they shelter themselves under a Spanish fort. In the last instance, you will immediately notify this department."[39]

By this time Jackson had come to believe that it was necessary to not only put a stop to the incursions of the Seminoles but to seize East Florida. The Madison administration had already taken possession of West Florida, on the assumption that it was part of the Louisiana Purchase. Now, thought the general, was the time to absorb the rest of the peninsula. Already Gaines had captured Amelia Island on December 23 from pirates and slave traders, after first receiving the administration's permission to do so. Jackson wrote to President Monroe, bypassing the secretary of war, and suggesting that since permission had already been given to take Amelia Island, why not seize "simultaneously the whole of East Florida" and hold it as an indemnity "for the outrages of Spain upon the property of our citizens"? It would also "save us from a war with Great Britain" or any other European power intent on attacking us.

Recognizing that if the administration acted on his suggestion, it might create a international uproar, Jackson went on to explain how it could be accomplished without directly "implicating the Government." Simply "let it be signifyed to me," he wrote, "through any channel (say Mr. J[ohn] Rhea), [Tennessee representative Rhea had been in recent communication with Jackson] that the possession of the Floridas would be desirable to the United States & in sixty days it will be accomplished."[40]

This letter, dated January 6, 1818, should have caused Monroe to take immediate action. He was being asked to authorize an illegal action against a foreign country, an action that could cause all sorts of domestic and international complications. What Jackson proposed was tantamount to a declaration of war. Knowing the general's reputation for acting on his own—his invasion of Florida in 1814 without the approval of the administration was just one example of his rash impetuosity—Monroe should have given him a direct and immediate order not to seize Florida if that was in fact his intention. And it had to come from him personally. After all, the letter was addressed to him, not the secretary of war. Sending such an order through Calhoun would most likely have been dismissed by Jackson if he felt it was in the country's interest to do so.

But Monroe did nothing of the kind. Instead, on January 30, he told Calhoun to write Jackson and instruct him "not to attack any post occupied by Spanish troops, from the possibility, that it might bring the allied powers on us."[41] At the very least, knowing Jackson's past history, Monroe should have checked with Calhoun to be sure he sent the order. But he did not. And the secretary never sent it. Why was it not sent? Surely Calhoun would not disobey a direct order from the President. Could it be that Monroe never gave such an order?

If true, the President never gave it because he really did want Jackson to seize Florida—considering his past enthusiasm to obtain the entire territory—but in his position he could not say so explicitly or even provide the slightest hint that the action had executive authority. Monroe later claimed he was ill when he received Jackson's request. After showing it to Calhoun and William H. Crawford, now secretary of the treasury, he forgot about it until it all blew up in his face when the invasion took place. Both Calhoun and Crawford said that they told the President that the letter was about Florida and required an answer. Did he really forget about it? And if it can be imagined what Calhoun thought, knowing he had been bypassed by the general in seeking this authorization.

Jackson always insisted that he had the President's approval and that he received it though John Rhea. Supposedly Rhea assured the general that Monroe had given his consent. Rhea's response was received in mid-February 1818 and destroyed a year later at the President's request, a request that was conveyed to the Hero by Rhea—or so Jackson contended.[42] Actually there is a letter in the Jackson papers by Rhea dated January 12, 1818, in which he says: "I expected you would receive the letter you alluded to, and it gives me pleasure to know you have it, for I was certain it would be satisfactory to you, you see by it that the sentiments of the President respecting you are the same."[43] The only problem with using this letter to prove Jackson's contention is the fact that it was written before Monroe had received Jackson's request. The general's letter was dated January 6 and Rhea's, January 12. They most probably crossed in the mail.

Exactly what Rhea was alluding to is unclear but surely, on reading it, Jackson must have been convinced that his intention regarding Florida was exactly the same as Monroe's. Even more convincing was an actual letter from Monroe dated December 28, 1817, in which he writes: "This days mail will convey to you an order to repair to the command of the troops now acting against the Seminoles," obviously referring to Calhoun's order of December 26. These Indians, Monroe continued, have "long violated our rights & insulted our national character. The mov'ment will bring you, on a theatre, when possibly you may have other services to perform depending on the conduct of the banditti at Amelia Island and Galvaston [*sic*]."

Other services to perform! What could Monroe have been thinking of? Driving the pirates from the island? But Gaines had already captured the island on December 23. What else could the President have intended if not the seizure of Florida, especially given Monroe desire for the entire territory? If Jackson needed further convincing, it surely came with the concluding section of the President's letter: "This is not a time for you to think of repose. Great interests are at issue, and until our course is carried through triumphantly & every species of danger to which it is exposed is settled on the most solid foundation, you ought not to withdraw your active support from it."[44]

"Great interests are at issue"! What great interests, if not the completion of the absorption of the entire territory of Florida?

"Every species of danger to which it is exposed is settled on the most solid foundation." Every species would include the Indians, of course, and the British, and the Spanish. The Spanish were not themselves much of a danger militarily, except that they could not control the Seminoles and keep them from attacking Americans. Only if Spain was completely removed from Florida could that danger be settled on the "most solid foundation."

Surely Jackson felt authorized to accomplish what he had proposed to Monroe when he received a letter from Calhoun dated February 6, in which he said, "I have the honor . . . to acquaint you with the entire approbation of the President of *all the measures* which you have adopted to terminate the rupture with the Indians. The honor of our arms, as well as the interest of our country requires, that it should be speedily terminated as practicable, and the confidence reposed in your skill and promptitude assures us that peace will be restored on such conditions as will make it honorable and permanent."[45]

Jackson always believed that the only way to achieve a "permanent" peace in the South was to drive out all foreigners from the region. He now felt he had the strong support of the Monroe administration to do exactly that. Even the Spanish understood what the Americans were about. Luis de Onís, the Spanish minister to the United States, complained that the policy of seizure began in 1810 and 1812 when West Florida, including Mobile and the Baton Rouge district, were claimed as part of the Louisiana Purchase. In his *Memoirs,* Onís stated that the President insisted "that as all these territories belonged to the United States as an integral part of Louisiana, he considered it expedient to occupy them." What followed was predictable. "To these publick acts of aggression and violence were afterwards added General Jackson's march . . . in East Florida . . . . I protested in the name of the king, against all and each of these excesses, but the cabinet in Washington refused to reply to me, and inflexibly adhered to their system of policy"[46]

When Jackson did invade and seize Florida, the incident created, as might be expected, an international furor, and he was threatened with censure by Congress. Rhea protested the action on the floor of the House of Representatives and insisted that Old Hickory had informed Calhoun of his intended actions and had received a reply on February 6 "acquainting him of the entire approbation of the President of all the measures he had adopted to terminate the war."[47] Unquestionably that was Jackson's belief, one he communicated to Rhea, who relayed it to the members of the House.

Having made up his mind, having received what he believed was proper approval, Jackson now prepared to move into East Florida and expel whatever Spanish authority still operated within the colony. He wrote to a group of eight officers who had served with him in the Creek War and asked them to assemble a group of Tennessee volunteers to join his army and march with him into Florida. "The Seminole Indians have raised the war hatchet," he informed them. "They have stained our land with the blood of our Citizens; their war spirit must be put down; and they ought to know that their safety depends upon the friendship and protection of the U. States." To accomplish this mission, he wanted 1,000 mounted "Gun men" armed and equipped to serve for the duration of the campaign. "Your General who led you to victory on the plains of Talledega, Emuckfau, and Tahopek, asks you to accompany him to the heart of the Seminole Towns, and there aid in giving peace and safety to the Southern Frontier."[48]

One of the eight officers leaked the information that Jackson had called for volunteers; when it reached the Congress, several members did not hesitate to express their outrage. Jackson had assumed congressional authority to raise troops. Who gave him leave to do this? No one, they cried. It was just another example of his contempt for lawful authority and readiness to take the law into his own hands.

Abner Lacock of Pennsylvania in the Senate and Henry R. Storrs of New York in the House issued reports from their respective military committees recommending appropriate action to rein in this out-of-control general. He must be taught a lesson, they declared, one that other officers in the service needed to learn as well.

When Jackson heard about these reports, he immediately responded by arguing that he had done nothing improper. For the information of the congressmen, he lectured, volunteers were the equivalent of militiamen and were raised in accordance with state law and established military practice. He did what he did to save time, since he believed he was dealing with an emergency situation. Furthermore, in Calhoun's letter to him of December 26 in which he was assured of 800 regulars and 1,000 Georgia militia, the secretary said he could call on neighboring governors for additional militia if he felt the need. And Jackson always liked to have a numerical superiority of troops when he went into battle. It was one of his hard and fixed principles.[49]

On January 22, 1818, General Jackson departed his headquarters at the Hermitage and headed for Fort Scott. As he proceeded through Tennessee, he was delighted to find that volunteers were "flocking to the standard of their country, with that patriotic zeal which has uniformly characterised the Citizens of that state." He calculated that he would have at least two regiments of mounted "Gun men" who would be mustered into service at Fayetteville by February 1 and could be "assembled if called for." He himself arrived in Huntsville on January 26 and reported to Calhoun that the only problem "was the want of arms . . . . The arms which had been distributed to the militia for their service in the last War have already disappeared" and are possibly now in the hands of the "very savages who have been excited to war against us." Thus it is very important, he went on, to build a "national Depot, with an Armory, Foundery [*sic*], & every facility for fabricating Weapons of War: being established in the South West."[50]

Jackson reached Hartford, Georgia, on February 12 after a long journey slowed by heavy rain that turned roads into quagmires. There he met General Gaines, just returned from his seizure of Amelia Island, who described the terrible conditions that existed at Fort Scott. The soldiers guarding the fort, he said, suffered from dwindling supplies and low morale[51]—proof that Jackson needed to hurry and reach the fort as soon as possible. So, with hardly a pause, he resumed his march, again experiencing nothing but "bad roads, high waters, & constant rain." He pressed on "through a wilderness of sixty miles, with various large water courses unusually high to pass." He received several dispatches from the commander at Fort Scott informing him of "his determination to abandon that post in a few days if supplies did not reach him."[52]

When he finally arrived at Fort Scott, just north of the Florida border, at 7 P.M. on March 9, 1818, it had taken him 46 days to travel 450 miles. He told his wife that it was a matter of pride that he had not lost a single man "by sickness or any other casualty" and that the troops were in relatively good health. His army now consisted of 3,000 regulars and volunteers and an additional force of 2,000 Indians, mostly friendly Creeks.

And they took a few prisoners. General William McIntosh, a mixed blood who commanded the friendly Creeks, captured Red Ground, an Indian village, and a party consisting of 53 warriors and 180 women and children. What is more, he did it without firing a single shot. But the chief of that town, along with 30 warriors, escaped. The Red Sticks had a special hatred for McIntosh. He had "caused much blood to be spilt, for which," decreed an assembled council of Muskogee chiefs, "we denounce him to the whole nation, and will give the usual reward of the brave, to anyone who may kill him."[53]

Anxious to attend the business of punishing the Seminoles, Jackson resumed his march on March 10, and the invasion of Florida began in earnest. He slammed into the peninsula and hurriedly moved down the east side of the Apalachicola River and linked up with ships, commanded by Captain Isaac McKeever, which had arrived from New Orleans on March 25, "laden with supplies." These ships were anchored in the bay at the mouth of the Apalachicola. The captain agreed to cooperate with Jackson, which, said the general, "will ensure me supplies along the coast, & capture such of the enemy who may attempt to make their Escape to the smaller islands bordering on our coasts."[54]

On March 15 Jackson reached the site of the Negro Fort and ordered it rebuilt, placing Lieutenant James Gadsden of the engineering corps in charge. Gadsden did such an excellent job that Jackson renamed the site Fort Gadsden. Jackson always showed great appreciation for superior work done by his subordinates and went out of his way to acknowledge it. This was an important reason why he won the respect and loyalty of his men.

Although Jackson knew he must hunt and kill the savage Indians who murder "our Citizens," he did not forget that the Seminoles received help to commit these crimes from the Spanish and especially the British. The Indians had been seeking help ever since the Americans began their "lawless incursions to drive us from our lands," as they termed it. Two chiefs wrote to the Bahamian governor, Charles Cameron, and pleaded for assistance.

Our brethren are now fighting for the lands they inherited from their forefathers, for their families and friends. But what will our exertions do, without assistance. To whom can we look up to for protection and support, but to those friends who have at former times held forth their hands to uphold us, and who have sworn in their late treaty [of Ghent] with the Americans, to see our just rights and privileges respected and protected from insult and aggression.

We now call on your excellency, as the representative of our good father, King George, to send us such aid in ammunition, as we are absolutely in want of. . . . We have applied to the Spanish officer at the fort of St. Marks; but his small supply prevent his being able to assist us." Please, your excellency, send us not only ammunition but "an officer, or person to lead us."[55]

On this last request, chiefs "in full council assembled" petitioned King George directly to see to it "that British officers should be constantly kept among us" so that we shall not "be driven to the desert sands of the sea, from the fertile fields of our forefathers." As "our good father, king George" knows, "we have found and bled for him against the Americans, by which we have made them our bitter enemies." Surely, then, he will "not forget the suffering of his once happy children here."[56]

The Indians actually did have one British individual who tried to help them, but he was not an officer or an official of the British government. Alexander Arbuthnot was a 70-year-old Scottish trader who came to Florida from the Bahamas in the spring of 1817 to trade with the Indians, exchanging blankets, rum, knives, guns, tomahawks, powder, beads, and paint for skins, beeswax, and corn. He got along so well with the Seminoles that they gave him their power of attorney to act on their behalf. With him came two other Englishmen: Captain George Woodbine of the Royal Marines, who had helped organize Indian attacks in Florida against the Americans during the War of 1812, and Robert Ambrister, a dashing young officer of the Royal Marines, who had lost his commission by engaging in an illegal duel and had come with Woodbine to Florida in the hope of finding adventure and a way back into the service.

At the start of the American incursion into Florida, Ambrister sought to aid the Indians by inviting British military officers to send help. He singled out Colonel Edward Nicholls in making his requests since Nicholls had been sent to Pensacola in 1814 by Admiral Cochrane and had armed some 4,000 Creek and Seminole warriors. Nicholls had also assured the Indians that the British government would protect them after the war. Now Ambrister demanded that Nicholls make good on his promise. The Indians cry out for help, he said, while the Americans encroach on their territory, slaughter them, and burn their villages. "They complain of the English government neglecting them, after having drawn them into a war with America, that you, sir, have not kept your promise, in sending people to reside among them, and that if they have not some person or persons, resident in the nation to watch over their interest, they will soon be driven to the extremity of the peninsula."[57]

Actually Jackson would have liked nothing better than to drive the Indians out of Florida altogether, and when he heard what the British had promised, he felt it provided irrefutable proof that both Spain and England were intent on perpetuating warfare along the American frontier. It justified his invasion of Florida and the punishment he intended to mete out to the Indians.

Once his troops had rested and had their fill of the food supplied by McKeever's ships, the general ordered his soldiers to resume their march and head for the center of the Seminole country. They moved out on March 26 and headed northeast from Fort Gadsden in the general direction of St. Marks. Five days later they were joined by McIntosh and the Creek allies and a detachment of Tennessee volunteers.

As the army approached the hostile village of Mikasukian, Jackson's advance corps of spies ran into a party of Indians and attacked them. The Indians fought back hard. The army rushed forward, and, as usual, the general extended his flank columns in an encircling action in order to surround the hostiles and wipe them out. But the Indians, seeing what was about to happen, quickly retreated before the encircling columns could be joined. Frustrated but still determined, Jackson began a systematic hunt for Mikasukian towns, and each one he found he burned to the ground. He estimated that over 300 dwellings were put to the torch. He also hunted for supplies in order to starve the Indians, his men confiscating "the greatest abundance of corn cattle &c" which they "brought in." In addition, he destroyed all the Negro plantations he found in the area, especially along the Apalachicola River.

In the council house of the leading chief of the Mikasukians, Jackson found more than 50 scalps. Worse, "in the center of the public square, the old red stick's standard, *A Red Pole,* was erected, crowned with scalps, recognized by the hair, as torn from the heads of the unfortunate companions of [Lieutenant Richard W.] Scott," who had commanded the boat the Indians ambushed along the shore of the Apalachicola River at the start of the war.[58] What further proof was necessary, Jackson asked, that the Red Sticks who escaped from Horseshoe Bend had come to Florida to renew their war against the United States than the presence of *"A Red Pole?"* In coming to Florida, the Red Sticks fully expected the Seminoles to join with them in their ongoing struggle.

Jackson continued his advance and headed directly for St. Marks, sloughing through a wet and swampy terrain and arriving outside the town on April 6. The first thing he did was write to the commandant of the fort in the town, Don Francisco Caso y Luengo, that he had invaded Florida with the president's permission "to chastise a Savage foe" and had "penetrated to the Mekasukian Towns & reduced them to ashes." From information gained from Colonel José Masot, the governor of Pensacola, to two "of my Captains, [John] Gordon and [Richard K.] Call, I was induced to believe" that the "Barbarians" who escaped from the Mikasukian towns "had fled to St. Marks for protection." The governor further stated that these savages "had demanded of you large supplies of munitions of war, with the threat in the event of a refusal, of taking possession of your fortress." As proof, Jackson stated that the wife of the Indian chief, Chenubbee, who was presently a captive in his camp, assured him that "Hostile Indians & Negroes obtained their supply of ammunition from St. Marks. To prevent the recurrence of so gross a violation of neutrality & to exclude our savage Enemies from so strong a hold as St. Marks I deem it expedient to garrison that fortress with American Troops untill the close of the present war." This necessary action, Jackson said, can be justified "on that universal principal of self defence." He needed St. Marks as a depot to ensure the success of his operation. "I came not as an the Enemy but as the Friend of Spain. Spanish rights, and property will be respected."

Since "our mutual savage enemies" were gathering their forces "near or on the Sewaney," Jackson asked for a prompt reply with an English translation "as neither myself or staff are acquainted with the Spanish."[59] His letter was delivered by Lieutenant James Gadsden.

It is interesting to note that the general liked to pretend that the Americans and Spanish were somehow allied in the war against the "savage enemies." He presumed, of course, that Spain would do everything in its power to help him defeat their common foe. In assuming control of the fort, it was typical of Jackson to put a legal face on his illegal action.

In his response, Luengo congratulated the American general on his success in destroying the Mikasukian towns and emphatically contradicted the claim of Chief Chennabee's wife that Indians and Negroes had obtained ammunition at St. Marks "since I was advised to keep a strict & perfect neutrality." As for Jackson taking control of the fort, the commandant begged leave "to state to you what difficulties I should involve myself in with my Government if I were to conform with what your Excellence proposes . . . without first receiving orders to that effect which I shall immediately solicit." Until he received such authority, he hoped "your Excellency will desist from your intention."[60]

The very same day he received Luengo's refusal, Jackson fired back his reply. "The occupation of St Marks is essential to the accomplishment of my campaign." Once I leave the vicinity, the Indians will seize the fort and the retaking of it will "cost me more American blood than I am disposed should be shed. Success to my operations requires dispatch; you will excuse me, therefore, in refusing your request" to wait until you receive the proper authority from your government. St. Marks must "be immediately occupied by American troops."[61]

Luengo asked for time "to reflect," which was granted. Then a "negotiation ensued, and an effort made to protract it to an unreasonable length." In the conversations between the commandant and Gadsden, it became clear to Jackson that the Spaniard was stalling. "I hesitated no longer," the general explained to Calhoun, "and as I could not be received in friendship I entered the Fort by violence." Two light companies of the Seventh Infantry and one of the Fourth under the command of Major Twigs was ordered to advance and lower the Spanish colors and "hoist the Star Spangled banner on the ramparts of Fort St Marks." The order was executed promptly, and the Spanish garrison offered no resistance.[62]

On entering the fort, Jackson found what he called "evidence of the duplicity & unfriendly feelings of the commandant." He also discovered that "savage Enemies of the U. States" had access to the town and that chiefs held council meetings in the commandant's "own Quarters." Furthermore, cattle plundered from American citizens "had been contracted for & purchased by the Officers of the Garrison." Worse, foreign agents had free access within the walls of St Marks," in particular one Alexander Arbuthnot, who was "an inmate of the family of the Spanish commandant." This "fiend," Arbuthnot, had been captured and slapped in irons, reported Jackson, awaiting trial once the necessary evidence had been gathered.

Besides that of Arbuthnot, another capture took place when Captain Isaac McKeever, while cruising along the coast on April 3, lured two important Red Sticks chiefs, Josiah Francis (or Hillis Hadjo) and Himollemico, aboard his ship by flying the British flag. Josiah Francis carried with him a commission as brigadier general in the British army, a rifle, and a snuffbox presented to him by the Prince Regent. Himollemico reportedly led the expedition that slaughtered the Scott party. Both hostiles thought they had found refuge aboard the ship. Instead they found a rope. They were both hanged on Jackson's orders on April 8.

After they were cut down, Jackson was asked if the bodies should be thrown into the river. "No," he responded, "they have ceased to be enemies, let them be buried as decently as our means will admit of. See that it is done."[63]

On the very day the two Red Stick chiefs were hanged, some 60 Indian men, women, and children entered Fort St. Marks and surrendered to Jackson. It was an encouraging sign, but it did not satisfy him. A much larger number of hostiles lived in and around Bowlegs Towns on the Suwannee River, which lay 100 miles to the east of Fort St. Marks, and the general decided to march his army to that location and destroy the town. So he dispatched Luengo and his family to Pensacola and told his wife that "Sodom and Gomorrow [sic] are destroyed."[64] On the morning of April 9, Jackson swung his army out of Fort St. Marks, carrying only eight days' rations, and began what he hoped would be the end of the Seminole War.

Chief Bowlegs, a Hitchitee warrior leader and brother of the Seminole chief, King Payne, who was killed in 1812, led his people from the area around present-day Gainesville to the Suwannee River site at the conclusion of the Patriot War of 1812–1813, when Americans from Georgia unsuccessfully attempted to seize East Florida. It was Jackson's understanding that Bowlegs was recognized as the principal chief of all the towns in the Suwannee region and that the towns sheltered many slaves who had escaped from the United States, along with a large contingent of Indians who belonged to the powerful Alachua branch of the Seminole alliance.

As Jackson's army moved eastward, the soldiers tramped through wet and swampy grasslands. It took time and effort to make any headway but on the morning of April 12, the army came upon a party of

Indians along the rim of a swamp at a place called the Natural Bridge on the Ecofina River. The friendly Creeks and the Tennessee volunteers attacked and routed the Seminoles, killing 37 warriors and capturing 6 men and 97 women and children. Among the captives was one of the women who had been taken prisoner "at the massacre of Scott." In addition, a number of horses and about 500 cattle were seized. Jackson had hoped to capture Peter McQueen, the son of a Scot trader and Tallassee woman, who was a so-called prophet and one of the most daring and intrepid leaders of the Red Sticks, but the general was repeatedly disappointed. McQueen had been captured at Tallapoosa but managed to escape. Then an old Indian woman offered to exchange the prophet for the right of her people to be "carried to the upper tribes of the Creek nation, and there provisioned until they could raise their own crops." Jackson foolishly agreed and freed the woman. She was never heard from again. McQueen continued to avoid capture and probably died sometime around 1820.[65]

Since the towns along the Suwannee were still his principal objective, Jackson pressed on, despite the swamps and "the continued sheets of water" that slowed his progress. On the morning of April 15 his scouts came upon another but smaller party of Indians and killed one warrior and captured a man, a woman, and two children. Jackson was now about 12 miles from the Bowlegs Towns.

That night he made camp and issued a general order to his troops that accompanied his plan for capturing the villages. In the order, he said he wanted every man to act as a soldier and not willfully kill women or children but "to recollect we war with savages who have without mercy torn the locks from the head of the aged matron down to the infant babe. These are the wretches who should feel the avenging rod." In addition, he forbade any soldier from touching "any of the supplies in the enemy's towns until the attack shall have closed, when they will be collected, and an equal distribution made."[66]

Early the next morning the army broke camp and moved on, expecting to reach its objective by 1 P.M. Unfortunately by 3 p.m. the army was still about six miles away from the Bowlegs Towns when it suddenly came upon a "remarkable pond." Jackson could have camped for the night but six mounted Indians discovered their presence and managed to escape capture. Presumably the warriors alerted the towns to their approaching danger. So the general was forced to continue the march.

They arrived at their objective at sunset, and Jackson immediately formed his lines. On his left flank were the Second Regiment of Tennessee volunteers, commanded by Colonel Thomas Williamson, and a portion of the friendly Creeks, led by Colonel Noble Kennard. They were ordered to initiate the attack. Jackson commanded the center, consisting of regulars, the Georgia militia, and the Kentucky and Tennessee guards. They would bear the full brunt of the assault. The First Regiment of Tennessee volunteers, headed by Colonel Robert H. Dyer, and part of the friendly Creeks under McIntosh, made up the right flank and were expected to cut off the hostiles' retreat at the western side of the river.

The attack was swift and not as successful as Jackson hoped. The left flank moved forward and engaged the hostiles. Then the center struck, followed by the right flank. Several hundred Negro warriors, their backs to the river, put up a stiff resistance but could not match the firepower of the Americans and soon retreated and crossed the river. Most of the Seminoles, "having been previously informed of our force," fled the area. The Americans chased them and Jackson figured that Colonel Dyer and the friendly Creeks "did them considerable injury." The next day nine Negroes and two Indians were found dead, and two other Negroes were captured. Foraging parties were sent out and they found a considerable quantity of corn and cattle.[67]

Having obtained several small crafts, Jackson ordered General Gaines "with a strong detacht & to [*sic*] days provision" to cross the river and continue the pursuit of the Indians. For the next several days they scoured the swamps for six miles beyond the river without finding the main body of hostiles.

Most probably the Seminoles scattered into the wilderness and found hiding places in remote areas. Eventually they migrated to the lakes in north-central Florida or around Tampa Bay.

Although the troops failed to destroy the Seminole tribe, Jackson was very proud of them and reported their bravery and skill to the secretary of war. "Every officer & soldier under my command when danger appeared," he wrote, "shewed a steady firmness which convinced me that in the event of a stubborn conflict they would realized the best hopes of their country and General."[68]

Jackson then proceeded to loot and burn the Bowlegs Towns. Over 300 were put to the torch. Then, on the evening of April 18, while the troops gathered around several fires, who should come charging into the camp but the swaggering former Royal Marine, Robert Ambrister, along with Peter Cook, a recently dismissed employee of Arbuthnot, and several others, but not Woodbine. They were totally unaware that the Indians had decamped and that General Jackson and his army now occupied the site. Before they could realize their situation, they were seized. One of them had a letter from Arbuthnot to his son John, who worked in his father's store on the river. The letter warned the son of Jackson's approach. Now the general understood how the Seminoles knew his intentions and managed to elude him and escape with their families and much of their belongings.

Realizing the seriousness of their situation, both Ambrister and Cook decided to cooperate with Jackson in the hope of winning clemency. They told him that Arbuthnot's schooner, *Chance,* lay moored at the mouth of the Suwannee River, preparing to sail for Tampa Bay. At the suggestion of his aide, Gadsden, the general agreed to send him and a detachment of soldiers downriver to capture the ship and get it ready to transport the sick and wounded soldiers back to St. Marks.

Gadsden had little trouble seizing the schooner. He also discovered a number of documents that convinced Jackson, when he read them, that both Arbuthnot and Ambrister were involved in "corrupt transactions" and should be tried for their crimes by a "Special Court of Select officers." Several documents also "involved the British Government in the Agency . . . . and was well advised of the measures which they had adopted to excite the Negroes & Indians in East Florida to war against the U States."[69]

By this time Jackson honestly felt he had ended the war. After all, he had burned the Bowlegs Towns and the Mikasuki village near Tallahassee, destroyed hundreds of houses, confiscated a great deal of food-supplies, executed Josiah Francis and Himollemico, taken possession of Fort St. Marks—"the hot bed of the war," he called it[70]—and driven the Seminoles into the swamps. There were no hostile Indians around to fight. It was time to go home. Besides, he was very ill and told Calhoun that he needed to return to his home at the Hermitage in order to "regain my health." He had already sent the Georgia militia back to Hartford, where they were to be paid for their service and discharged. It was now May and already the weather had turned unbearably hot and humid. The "sickly season," as he called it, had begun.[71]

But first he must return to St. Marks and see to the trial of the two "notorious villains," Arbuthnot and Ambrister. So Jackson and his army pulled up stakes, departed the burned-out Bowlegs Towns, and headed for his base, which he reached in five days, a distance of 107 miles.[72]

No sooner did Jackson arrive back in St. Marks than he arranged for the convening of a court-martial to try the Scot trader and the former Royal Marine. The court was made up of 12 officers, General Gaines presiding. This action was very precipitous and Jackson should have consulted with the administration before taking such a step. He could have waited but he was so anxious to have the men punished that he set aside any thought of delaying their trial. The question immediately arose as to whether this court had any legal validity. There were legal questions involved, especially when the prosecution argued that in helping the Indians, the defendants had forfeited their allegiance to Great Britain, had become outlaws, and therefore should be executed. An international incident was sure to erupt if the legal rights of these two foreign nationals were not properly respected.

The court convened on April 26 and heard three charges against Arbuthnot: "exciting and stirring up the Creek Indians to war against the United States"; serving as a spy for the Indians and supplying them with arms; and "exciting the Indians to murder two American traders, William Hambly and Edmund Doyle." The court denied that it had jurisdiction on the third charge, which was dropped. In support of the other two charges, evidence was presented to prove that Arbuthnot had advised the Creek chief Little Prince not to comply with the Treaty of Fort Jackson; that he supplied the Seminoles with ammunition to be used against American settlers; that he communicated with British officials as the Indians' agent; and that his letter to his son John had been shown to the hostiles in Bowlegs Towns, thereby assisting their escape from Jackson's army.[73]

Arbuthnot spoke in his own defense. He was respectful and dignified. He dismissed the evidence involving him with Little Prince as hearsay. The letter to his son was meant to get him out of harm's way and allow him to save as many skins, books, and other important items as possible. He instructed his son to "tell my friend Bowleck that he is throwing away his people to attempt to resist such a powerful force." But he admitted selling 10 kegs of power to Bowlegs at Suwannee so that the chief's people could hunt and feed themselves, not kill Americans. The 10 kegs were meant to help them stave off hunger, nothing more. "May it please this honorable court," Arbuthnot concluded, "I close my reply to the charges and specifications preferred against me, being fully persuaded that, should there be cause of censure, my judges will, in the language of the law, lean to the side of mercy."[74]

It was an able defense and well argued. But it did not convince this jury. To them, trafficking with Indians meant killing Americans, and Arbuthnot's efforts to help the Seminoles was misinterpreted. On April 28, after a short deliberation, two-thirds of the court pronounced him guilty of both charges and ordered that between the hours of eight and nine in the morning he be "suspended by the neck, with a rope, until he is *dead*."

Next came Ambrister, who faced two charges: first, "aiding, abetting, and comforting the enemy, supplying them with means of war," and second, "leading and commanding the Lower Creeks in carrying on a war against the United States." The evidence against him was quite strong. Documents were submitted, several in his own hand. One of them was a letter to Governor Cameron in which he said that Josiah Francis and "all the Indian chiefs" had asked him to tell the Prince Regent in England "that they are at war with the Americans" and "ask for his assistance." They "beg your excellency will be as expeditious as possible. Your excellency is the only dependence they have, and who the Prince Regent told them would give them every assistance that lay in your power." In another letter, again in his own hand, Ambrister acknowledged that he had sent a party of warriors to attack the Americans.

Ambrister pleaded not guilty to the first charge and "guilty with justification" to the second. He really did not have much to offer by way of a defense and so he threw himself on the mercy of the court. The jury rather liked his soldierly manner and his readiness to admit his guilt, but they were forced to acknowledge that he had aided in a war against the United States. So they ordered that he "be shot to *death*" at the same hour that Arbuthnot was hanged.[75]

Then one member of the court requested a reconsideration of the verdict, resulting in a change of the punishment to "fifty stripes on his bare back" and confinement "with a ball and chain to hard labor for twelve calendar months." The American officers who served on the court-martial were most probably influenced by the fact that, like them, Ambrister was (or at least had been) an officer in the armed forces.[76]

Whatever the reason for this change, General Jackson would have none of it. The same day, April 28, that the verdict was handed down, he approved the sentence of Arbuthnot and the first sentence of Ambrister. Both men were to be executed. As far as Jackson was concerned Ambrister was the "successor" of "that unfeeling monster," George Woodbine, who was responsible for the murders of so many American women and children. Having participated in a war against the United States, Jackson felt, Ambrister had forfeited his allegiance to Great Britain, and become nothing but an outlaw and therefore deserved to be shot to death. And so, at the appointed hour of April 29, the executions were carried out, Arbuthnot hanged and Ambrister shot.[77]

Jackson's behavior throughout this extraordinary incident reflected frontier bigotry, fear, and hatred at its worst. He had already declared the Seminole War at an end, and yet here he was executing two foreign nationals when he did not have the legal authority to do so. The "special court" had even less authority. True, Ambrister had pleaded guilty to one charge, but the court decided a punishment of 50 lashes and 12 months of hard labor was sufficient penalty. What gave Jackson the right to reverse it? That question was raised repeatedly in the months following the announcement of the executions.

Jackson felt fully justified in acting so precipitously "The proceedings of the Court martial in this case," he informed Calhoun, "with the volume of Testimony justifying their condemnation, presents scenes of wickedness, corruption, and barbarity at which the heart sickens." There is no doubt, he continued, that the government of Great Britain "had knowledge" that Ambrister and Arbuthnot were its "authorized Agents" and "was well advised of the measures which they had adopted to excite the Negroes & Indians in East Florida to war against the U States." Jackson went on to express the hope that the execution of these "[t]wo unprincipled villains will prove an awful example to the world, and convince the Government of Great Britain as well as her subjects that certain, if slow retribution awaits those unchristian wretches who by false promises delude & excite a Indian tribe to all the horrid deeds of savage war."[78]

As these two English nationals lay dead on the ground a group of Indians came to the fort to sue for peace and were struck dumb at the sight of their executed friends. It made a profound and lasting impression on them. They and others like them found that deep inside General Andrew Jackson lay a terrible, vindictive enemy against whom the Indians would only find their graves and the confiscation of their property.

In some political circles there was genuine fear that the country had produced another Napoleon who would in the future extinguish liberty in the country and abrogate the rights of American citizens. When members of Congress learned what had happened at St. Marks, both the Senate and House agreed to look into the matter and have their appropriate committees investigate and report their findings.

In its report of January 12, 1819, the House Committee on Military Affairs disapproved the proceedings of the special court and condemned the executions. The Senate report of February 24, 1819, declared that the court proceedings were a departure from normal forms of justice and "calculated to inflict a wound on the national character."[79]

But Jackson had not finished outraging and frightening certain segments of American society. The Spanish had yet to be chastised. After all, they were equally guilty of allowing the Indians to war against the United States by their inability to properly police Florida and prevent the "savages" from obtaining ammunition and supplies in their towns. Initially Jackson had decided to return home and try to recover his health now that the Seminole War was over. But he changed his mind. It was fully four months since Monroe had intimated that he wanted Jackson to take Florida. There were "great interests" at issue, the President wrote to Jackson, and you should not "withdraw your active support from it" until they were settled on "the most sold foundation."

Indeed not. So the general decided to act. On the day the two British nationals were executed, Old Hickory marched his army of 1,200 regulars and volunteers out of St. Marks and headed for Fort Gadsden, the old Negro Fort. He left 200 troops to garrison St. Marks. After he arrived at Fort Gadsden, he and the army rested a few days. He wrote to Calhoun, giving a full account of his activities and informing him that he intended "to make a movement to the West of the Apalachicola" and strike at Pensacola. Hostile Indians had free access to Pensacola and from that quarter are kept advised "of all our movements." He also told Calhoun that he had written to the governor of Pensacola, José Masot, and asked that supply ships from New Orleans be permitted to pass freely up the Escambia River to Fort Crawford. Masot refused, and so, said Jackson, "Pensacola must be occupied with an American force. The Governor treated according to his deserts or as policy may dictate." It is my duty to tell you, the Hero continued, that "so long as Spain has not the power, or will . . . to preserve the Indians within her territory at peace with the U States, no security can be given to our Southern frontier without occupying a cordon of Posts along the Sea Shore . . . The Moment the American Army retires from Florida, The War Hatchet will be again raised, & the same scenes of indiscriminate murder with which our frontier settlers have been visited, will be repeated."[80]

Jackson also wrote to Masot and reiterated his complaints, announcing that he deemed it "politic and necessary to occupy Pensacola." Again he cited "the immutable principles of self defence" as justification. This action will be the third time American troops have been compelled to take the town, he continued. "This time it must be held until Spain has the power or will to maintain her neutrality." If "peacable surrender" is refused, "I shall enter Pensacola by violence and assume the Government." He ended by calling Masot an aggressor on whom the blood that was sure to be shed "will rest on your head."[81]

But Masot was not to be bullied by Jackson. The day before Jackson wrote his letter, Masot dispatched his own list of grievances to the general. American troops under your command, he wrote, invaded Florida and by so doing insulted the King of Spain. "In his name" I demand that you leave this territory. "If you will proceed contrary to my expectations I will repulse you force to force. The results in this case will be an effusion of blood," and you, Andrew Jackson, will be "responsible before God & Men for the consequences."[82]

Jackson blasted back, saying that "the first shot from your Fort must draw down upon you the vengeance of an irritated Soldiery. . . . I applaud your feeling as a Soldier in wishing to defend your Post, but where resistance is ineffectual & the opposing force overwhelming—

The sacrifice of a few brave men is an act of wantonness for which the Commanding Officer must be accountable to his God."[83]

Weary and annoyed with this senseless bickering, Jackson headed for Pensacola after a short stay at Fort Gadsden. He and the army of 1,200 regulars and volunteers arrived outside the town on May 24. Masot had retreated to the rebuilt Fort Carlos de Barrancas outside Pensacola, where he hoped to make a stand, placing Luis Piernas in command of the town. Jackson easily swept aside the Spanish commandant's token effort of resistence by the Spanish commandant and lowered the Spanish flag.

Just before entering the town, he sent a note to Piernas stating that he had been informed of orders to fire upon his troops seeking to obtain supplies from an American ship anchored in the bay. "I wish you to understand distinctly," he wrote, "that if such orders are carried into effect, I shall put to death every man found in arms."[84] And he meant it.

Next he ordered Masot to surrender Barrancas. The Spaniard refused, whereupon Old Hickory dragged forward his single nine-pound cannon and five eight-inch howitzers, aimed them at the fort, and opened fire. He kept up the firing throughout the morning of May 27 and intermittently during the afternoon. He was about to bring forward his ladders and mount the walls when a white flag broke out over the fort, signaling capitulation. Jackson found that 300 Spanish soldiers guarded the fort. With that number of Americans, he sneered, he "could have kept it from combined Urope."[85]

Masot marched his troops out of the fort. "All I regret," Jackson reportedly said, "is that I had not stormed the works, captured the Governor, put him on his trial for the murder of Stokes and his family [Americans recently killed in an Indian raid] and hung him for the deed."[86] But this was so much Jacksonian bombast, since under the terms of the capitulation, the Spanish garrison was permitted to retire from the fort with full military honors. In addition, these troops were to be transported to Cuba, and Spanish property and rights guaranteed. Jackson was pleased with the terms. They amounted, he told

Calhoun, "to a complete cession to the u states of that portion of the Floridas hitherto under the government of Don Jose Masot."

Not only had this First Seminole War ended in triumph, as far as Jackson was concerned, but the authority of Spain to any part of Florida had now been completely extinguished. He told Calhoun on June 2, 1818 that the "Seminole War may now be considered at a close."[87]

CHAPTER 5

The End of Military Service

JACKSON WENT OUT OF HIS WAY TO ASSURE THE RESIDENTS of Pensacola that his seizure of the province did not emanate from a desire by the United States to expand its territory at the expense of the Spanish, nor out of any hatred for the Spanish people or their government. In a proclamation to the citizens, he claimed that it was a war to end "the horrors of savage massacre." The Spanish authority could not control the Indians so the United States had to do it. He reaffirmed his commitment to protect Spanish property and rights, and Spanish laws would continue to operate. Moreover, he pledged "free toleration to all religions."

Then he announced the formation of a provisional government with Colonel William King as civil and military governor of Pensacola to enforce U.S. revenue laws, and James Gadsden, now a captain, as tax collector. Also, the archives of the province would be brought under American control.[1]

With the capture of the Negro Fort, Fort St. Marks, and Fort Carlos de Barrancas; the burning of hundreds of Indian villages and the killing of many of the Seminole chiefs; the executions of Josiah Francis, Himollemuco, Arbuthnot, and Ambrister; the destruction of Spanish authority in Florida; and the establishment of a provisional government for the province, Jackson believed he had fulfilled the assignment as ordered by Calhoun and Monroe. East Florida was now a possession of the United States. "I view the Possession of the Floridas," he wrote the President, "Essential to the peace & security of the frontier, and the future wellfare [*sic*] of our country." Now the only vestige of Spanish presence in Florida was Fort St. Augustine. Cuba, he thought, was also essential to "the security of our southern frontier and to our commerce in a state of war, and can be taken by a Coup de Main whenever thought necessary." Give me the Fifth Infantry and a twenty-two gun brig and I will capture Fort St. Augustine in short order. Give me another regiment and a frigate, Jackson said, and "I will insure you cuba in a few days."[2]

Calhoun responded by saying that "I entirely agree with you, as to the importance of Cuba to our country. It is, in my opinion, not only the first commercial and military position in the world, but is the Key stone of our Union. No American statesman ought ever to withdraw his eye from it. . . . Should our relations with Spain end in a rupture, we ought to be prepared immediately . . . to seize on it, and to hold it for ever." For the moment, however, "we ought, at first, to limit our operations to Florida, and rest there for the present."[3]

Cuba! American statesmen still have their eyes on it, but they missed several opportunities to seize it and "hold it for ever."

Jackson was satisfied with the administration's response, but now he needed to go home. He told Rachel he was emaciated, completely exhausted, had a bad cough from being exposed to so much "wading waters" and from traveling on foot some 25 miles each day. Still, he reveled in the fact that his men were all healthy. He boasted that "we have lost but three in Battle, one by Sickness, two by drowning & one shot by accident in the whole campaign." Most of all he was proud of the fact that "I have destroyed the babylon of the South, the hot bed of the Indian war & depredations on our frontier." We have suffered deprivation, "but we have met them like Soldiers."[4]

On reaching Columbia, Tennessee, on June 26, he discharged the volunteers. Then he moved on to Nashville, where he was welcomed by extravagant celebrations. To England and Spain he had demonstrated the military might of the United States, and the American people could not begin to tell him how much that meant to them. Andrew Jackson had proved to the world that Americans were strong and united and could defend their rights against the greatest powers on earth.

But Jackson had also created an international uproar that could have resulted in open conflict with England or Spain or both. He tried and executed English nationals without proper legal authorization. The British minister to the United States, Charles Bagot, informed Secretary of State John Quincy Adams that his government would make a formal response to the executions of its nationals and requested a copy of the trial proceedings. Bagot said he could not imagine any "possible circumstance which would warrant their execution," but he was willing to withhold further comment until he had the chance to examine the transcripts. Adams, in response, assured the minister that the United States had not authorized the trial or executions. They were, he said, "totally unexpected."[5]

Jackson had also seized Florida, established a provisional government, and installed military officers to run what rightly belonged to Spain. Luis de Onís, the Spanish minister to the United States, peppered Adams with protests over Jackson's actions. He assured the secretary that his country felt its honor had been deeply offended by this most "unfortunate incident." Even the French minister, Hyde de Neuville, called on the secretary and "in a very grave tone, shaking his head," said "it was a very disagreeable affair."[6]

President Monroe felt caught in a singularly ugly situation. On the one hand, he faced a very proud, opinionated, sensitive, and extraordinarily popular general who took offense at any criticism of his military record; and on the other, he faced the representatives from two foreign nations who were demanding explanations for the illegal acts committed against their citizens. So what did he do but duck away from the tempest and hide out on his farm in Loudoun County, Virginia. He did not return to Washington until mid-July

According to Secretary Adams, the secretary of war was "extremely dissatisfied with General Jackson's proceedings in Florida." Calhoun said he believed that the general meant to initiate a war with Spain and then command "an expedition against Mexico." It was all part of Jackson's expansionist ambitions. Something had to be done, Calhoun argued, to remind the general that not only did civilian authority run the country, but it decided if war was to be declared, in which case it would oversee the operation of the conflict. He felt that at the very least Jackson should be censured, and he had the support of the other cabinet members—all, that is, except Adams.[7]

When the full cabinet met after Monroe's return to the White House, Adams defended the general and his actions, arguing that he was justified in everything he had done. Once the meeting ended, the President had a choice: either repudiate what happened in Florida and censure Jackson, or retain what had been seized and defend the general.

But Monroe preferred another course of action. He had no intention of defending Old Hickory or assuming responsibility for what occurred in Florida. What he did was draft a note to the Spanish minister acknowledging that Jackson had exceeded his instructions, although insisting that the general had been guided by military necessity in seizing St. Marks and Pensacola and by Spain's inability to police its colony and prevent Indian deprivations against Americans along the frontier.

Then he decided to write to Jackson himself. It was now six months since Jackson had asked him to use Rhea as a conduit for authorization to seize Florida. Monroe knew Jackson's temperament, and he had to be careful to assure the general that he supported him and his actions. He failed miserably. On July 19 he wrote that his position required him to take a "comprehensive view of the whole subject," examine all the circumstances, and all the "dangers to which this measure is exposed . . . and all the good" that might result from it.

Then he told Jackson flatly that he had exceeded his instructions and assumed authority he did not have. "In transcending the limit prescribed by [your] orders, you acted on your own responsibility, on facts and circumstances which were unknown to the government, when the orders were given, many of which occurred afterward, and which you thought imposed on you the measure, as an act of patriotism, essential to the honour and interests of your country." In attacking the Spanish authority in St. Marks and Pensacola you, in effect, declared war against Spain, a power reserved exclusively to Congress under the Constitution.[8]

Jackson had no problem in accepting responsibility for his actions. "Responsibility is not feared by me," he told the President in reply, "if the General good requires its assumption. I never have shrunk from it, and never will." But he denied that he had transcended his orders. The order of December 26, 1817, gave him full authority to conduct the campaign as he felt necessary. You ought to know, he sarcastically added, that "*all the acts* of the inferior are the acts of the Superior—and in no way, can the subordinate officer be impeached for his measures."[9]

While this contretemps was taking place between the general and the President, John Quincy Adams used his considerable diplomatic skills to convince the Spanish that holding on to Florida only invited future depredations by the Indians against Americans and military responses from the United States when its citizens were murdered. It was obvious to all, he said, that Spain could not properly police Florida. Better to sell the colony to the United States and spare itself any future affronts to Spanish honor. Besides, he told the Spanish minister, the president "will neither inflict punishment, nor pass a censure upon General Jackson" for his conduct, the motives for which were prompted by the "purest patriotism" and "self defense." Then he hit home with a powerful argument: "Spain must immediately make her election, either to place a force in Florida adequate at once to the protection of her territory, and to the fulfilment of her engagements, or cede to the United States a province, of which she retains nothing but the nominal possession, but which is, in fact, a derelict, open to the occupancy of every enemy, civilized or savage, of the United States, and serving no other earthly purpose than as a post of annoyance to them."[10]

And that did it. On February 22, 1819, Spain agreed to cede to the United States all its territories east of the Mississippi River known as East and West Florida for $5 million in assumed American claims against Spain. Both Adams and Onís signed the document. But it took until October 24, 1820 before King Ferdinand VII agreed to the cession and returned the document to the United States, where it awaited Senate ratification since Congress was not in session.

As for the British, they were easily placated by the evidence the U.S. minister in London, Richard Rush, spread before Lord Castlereagh concerning the guilt of Arbuthnot and Ambrister in aiding the Indians to kill American citizens. More important, England was anxious to cultivate the friendship of the United States and exploit the ever-growing American market. It made more sense to look the other way. So the British lodged no protest and did not demand satisfaction in any form for the executions of its nationals.

But in Congress prior to the signing of the Adams-Onís Treaty, any number of members took serious offense over what Jackson had done, especially in exercising powers that were reserved exclusively to the House and Senate. Their respective military committees investigated the charges and responded with recommendations that the general be censured. The House committee submitted its report on January 12, 1819.

Alarms about what was about to happen in Congress flashed back to the Hermitage, and the hero was urged to drop everything and hasten to Washington to assist in his defense. There was "much intrigue . . . on foot," he was told, by those who wish to sully your reputation and demean your accomplishments as a military officer.

Still other friends advised him to stay put, fearing he would lose his temper and say and do something that would only prove the charges against him.

Never one to run away from a fight, Jackson dismissed the naysayers and rushed to Washington. He would confront his enemies and provide needed information to his friends at the capital who would defend him. "Major," he told his friend and neighbor William B. Lewis, "there's a combination in Congress to ruin me. I start for Washington to-morrow morning."[11]

Jackson raced through the wintry countryside and arrived in Washington on January 23, 1819. Just in time. The House was continuing its debate on motions put forward by Representative Thomas W. Cobb of Georgia to disapprove the seizure of St. Marks and Pensacola and forbid the execution of any captive taken in time of peace or in an Indian war without the consent of the President.

The House debate lasted over a month, reaching its high point when the Speaker, Henry Clay, surrendered the chair, moved to the well of the House, and began a personal assault on General Jackson. He warned of the dangers of allowing a military person to wage war and execute foreign nationals on his own authority. He realized that the public adored Jackson for his services to the country, but he reminded his colleagues that as elected officials, they must act independently and intelligently and according to the rule of law, not the passing whims of an uncomprehending public. The representatives "may even vote the general the public thanks; they may carry him triumphantly through this House. But, if they do, in my humble judgment, it will be a triumph of the principle of insubordination—a triumph of the military over the civil authority—a triumph over the power of this House—a triumph over the constitution of the land. And I pray most devoutly to Heaven that it may not prove, in its ultimate effects and consequences, a triumph over the liberties of the people."[12]

From that moment on Andrew Jackson conceived a hatred for Henry Clay that lasted for the rest of his life, and he did everything in his considerable power to block the Speaker's great ambition to become the President of the United States. "The hypocracy & baseness of Clay," he roared in a letter to Major Lewis, "make me despise the Villain. I hope the western people will appreciate his conduct accordingly."[13]

Jackson's presence in the capital, where he was closeted with his friends and defenders to plan strategy, strengthened the pro-Jackson forces in the House. Their strategy was to take control of the debate and remind the public over and over of the general's heroism, especially at New Orleans. Speakers were scheduled according to a precise order, and they rebutted every accusation put forward by the anti-Jackson forces. Richard M. Johnson of Kentucky, Alexander Smyth of Virginia, George Poindexter of Mississippi, and others paraded the general's military victories before the public, how he had defeated an overwhelming British army and restored the nation's confidence in itself. "And shall we see him depart from this city in disgrace; censured and dismissed from office by Congress?" asked Smyth. "No; it cannot be. Forbid it, every power that guards the protectors of innocence. Forbid it, policy. Forbid it, gratitude. Forbid it, peace!" Poindexter capped the series of speeches with a ringing declamation of how Jackson had brought the nation a full measure of military glory.[14]

On February 8, 1819, the House—meeting as a committee of the whole—voted on each of the resolutions introduced by Cobb. On the charge that the House disapproved the executions of Arbuthnot and Ambrister, the vote was 54 yes, 90 no. On condemning the capture of Pensacola as unconstitutional, the count was 65 yes, 91 no. On drafting a law to forbid the invasion of a foreign country without the approval of Congress, the tally was 42 yes, 112 no.

This complete victory for Jackson was immediately followed by three formal votes by the entire House itself. By a vote of 108 to 62, it refused to condemn the trials and executions of the two British nationals; by a vote of 107 to 63, it refused to censure Jackson; and by a vote of 70 to 100, it declined to characterize the seizure of Florida as unconstitutional.[15]

Jackson could not have asked for a more complete vindication. He was fully exonerated. Of course, the members of the House knew full well how the public felt about Old Hickory and were not about to jeopardize their political careers by voting against him. In fact, the public loved their hero even more because he had endured and triumphed over this insulting agony. "From the earnestness with which the company pressed around him," noted Adams at a presidential reception, "the eagerness with which multitudes pushed to obtain personal introductions to him, and the eye of respect and gratitude which from every quarter beamed on him, it has as much appearance of being his drawing-room as the President's."[16]

Following this total victory, Jackson returned home. Then when Monroe learned that the King of Spain had approved the treaty and was sending it to Washington for ratification by the Senate, he wrote to Jackson and asked him to agree to serve as governor of Florida, now that it was part of the United States. "The climate will suit you," he cooed, having heard that at the time the general was in ill heath with a severe cold. Indeed, Jackson lay prostrate. The bullets in his chest and shoulder had produced "violent pain." He could barely think or work. Tired and worn out, he gave serious thought to resigning his army commission. Once before, when the Florida treaty was first signed, Monroe had invited Jackson to take the post and was turned down. Now he tried once again to coax him into accepting his offer. "It will give me pleasure to place you in that trust," he said. As a follow-up, Secretary Calhoun urged him to accept, arguing how the general's "talent and experience" were essential in establishing the government in Florida. "It will require a military eye," he declared, "as its defences ought to receive early and prompt attention." Since you are intimately connected with Florida, only you, "at the outset," could put the government on a "respectable footing."

But in his weakened condition, Jackson was in no mood to go back to Florida and start working again. His initial reaction was to reject the offer once more. "My fortune and constitution," he wrote in reply, "have already been much impaired in the service of my country." But his friends in Washington and at home begged him to accept and tried to enumerate all the benefits that would accrue from his acceptance. Slowly he began to realize that by accepting, he could "quicken the organization of the Government and tend to draw to that country a respectable population" whose presence would enhance the security of the nation. So he wavered. Then his Washington friends, led by Tennessee senator John H. Eaton, argued that the appointment would validate everything he had done previously in Florida.

And that argument struck home. Jackson accepted the appointment on condition that "I may resign as soon as the Government is formed and in full operation."[17]

In making this offer to Jackson, the President had another and perhaps more compelling reason to pressure the Hero. The country was still feeling the effects of the financial Panic of 1819, and the government wished to reduce the size of its army. This necessitated the demotion of one of its two generals, either Jackson or Jacob Brown, both highly sensitive and difficult men to handle. But Brown had the active support of William Crawford, the secretary of the treasury. Therefore, in getting Jackson to accept the Florida position and thereby resign his army commission, which he had been threatening to do for years, Monroe would find a solution to his dilemma. Thus, when he emphasized the importance of the assignment, the Hero of New Orleans agreed to take it.

On February 13, 1821, the Adams–Onís Treaty was submitted to the Senate for its approval. Six days later it was ratified with only four dissenting votes. Immediately Monroe appointed General Andrew Jackson as governor of East and West Florida with powers of a "captain general and intendant of Cuba and commissioner" to receive the territory from Spain.[18] He received a salary of $5,000 plus expenses. On June 1, 1821, Andrew Jackson resigned his commission as major general of the U.S. Army. His military career ended as his political career was about to take off. And the American people could not wait to show him how much they loved and admired him and wanted him to lead this nation as President of the United States.

CHAPTER 6

The Military Legacy

ANDREW JACKSON'S MILITARY CAREER HAS NEVER BEEN FULLY evaluated. Was he a great commander? Should his exploits on the battlefield constitute a matter of interest by Americans today? The answer to both questions can be found in the results of his actions. And they provide evidence that he was indeed a truly outstanding general who achieved something quite remarkable for the American people. He won victory after victory over his country's enemies. The argument that Americans never won a great victory on the battlefield during the Revolution was now refuted by the overwhelming result of the Battle of New Orleans. The casualty list alone spoke volumes about the meaning of the victory and why Americans at the time desperately needed it. They reveled in the British defeat and now boasted about being a citizen of this free country. As for the defeat of the Spanish in Florida, that effort was hardly a test of Jackson's military skill since

Spain offered only a token force to oppose him. The Indians constituted a more difficult task because they could withdraw and hide and later return to renew their assaults on Americans living on the frontier.

In deploying his troops, Jackson usually, but not always, relied on a simply technique: He extended his left and right flanks and then had them come together in a pincer movement to encircle the enemy. Unfortunately, it did not always work. Even at New Orleans he attempted it without success.

One thing Jackson did know that helped him enormously and that was how to use his spies effectively in gathering information and providing suggestions about how to use it. He regularly devised operations for them. When successful, they provided him with the data he needed in planning his attacks. And he learned how essential it was to outnumber his opponents, especially when fighting Indians.

Why and how, then, did he become a general? Why? Ambition. He became a general because the rank would lift him into the social class that he aspired to. He probably had no overwhelming desire for soldiering. He was simply ambitious, and the rank of major general would make a world of difference in the society in which he lived. The rank provided a title and prestige within his social class. Besides, on the frontier young men were expected to serve in the militia to protect the community from Indian attack. Since such service was obligatory, why not serve at the highest rank available? And all it took was an election by other officers, a political campaign that proved relatively easy since, over the years, he had been running for office and winning elections.

Jackson's ability as a commander resulted from the simple fact that he was a born leader of men. Senator John McCain of Arizona, a former navy pilot during the Vietnam war, argued in 2008 that there are two kinds of military leaders: the "organizer of victory type," such as Generals George Marshall and Dwight Eisenhower, and the more "inspirational" type, those "who are gifted at leading men into battle." Andrew Jackson was distinctly the "inspirational" type.[1] Moreover, his mere presence drew attention. When he walked into a room, people took notice. He was tall and thin and carried himself with military stiffness. More than anything else in determining his success as a military commander was the fact that he cared about his troops, about their needs and comfort, and they knew it. He was tough, but his soldiers followed him, trusted him, loved him, and knighted him affectionately with the nickname, "Old Hickory." He suffered with his men during the many hardships they both endured in the wilderness, surrendering his horses to the sick, for example, when he himself was fainting from exhaustion. He publicly recognized the successes of others and went out of his way to reward them. Junior officers were intensely loyal to him; and not one of them ever betrayed him or conspired against him. He always asked his men to act like soldiers who were proud of their calling.

And he was driven by a fierce determination to succeed. Defeat was something he could not abide. He demanded victory, and his soldiers did everything in their power to achieve it for him.

When it came to higher authority, Jackson could be insubordinate. He had no problem in bypassing his immediate superior, the secretary of war, if he felt he needed presidential authority for an intended action, such as the seizure of Florida. He was opinionated and so self-confident that he could not understand or accept any opinion that differed with his own. He would obey an order if he agreed with it. Otherwise he would dismiss it and claim that he acted for the good of his country, a belief that was sincere however wrong-headed it might be.

Most of all—and Jackson himself understood it and commented on it—he was lucky. He was in the right place at the right time when opportunities developed that could advance his career, such as the outbreak of the Creek War and the arrival of the invading British along the Gulf of Mexico just when he had defeated the hostile Indians. He was also lucky when the consequences of his mistakes were erased by the mistakes of his enemies.

As for his relevance today as a military commander, Jackson did something that has reverberated with succeeding generations of Americans. When he established martial law in New Orleans and refused to lift it after the battle on January 8, 1815, had successfully ended, he triggered a dispute between those who fear the loss of civil rights and those who insist that strong measures must be invoked to protect the country during periods of extreme crisis. It is a dilemma that has risen repeatedly in this country between those who insist that national security must be maintained at all costs and those who argue that this nation is grounded in individual freedom that must never be abrogated.

Jackson labored for years to have the fine of $1,000 imposed on him by Justice Hall rescinded, but not until 1843 did Congress oblige him. The Jacksonian Democrats argued that he should not be punished for doing what he believed was essential to protect the United States when invaded by a hostile army, while their political opponents at the time, the Whigs, insisted he had undermined personal liberties.[2]

During the Civil War, President Abraham Lincoln felt it necessary to suspend the writ of habeas corpus. This time the Democrats objected on the grounds that he violated the Constitution, while those who defended the President's action, many of them former Whigs, took the position that his action was necessary in order to save the Union.

This difference of opinion has come down to the present day. Essentially it is a dispute between those who defend civil rights and those whose main concern is the protection of the United States from the hostile acts of its enemies. Probably the latest example of this problem occurred during the presidency of George W. Bush, who approved actions, such as the torture of suspected terrorists, in the name of national security. No doubt this argument will continue well into the future.

+>=—=<+

So grateful were the American people for what Andrew Jackson had done that they elected him President of the United States, despite the fact that he did not have the education or the public service that could compare to those who had preceded him. A new expression was devised to characterize his career: self-made man. He was an orphan born in poverty, without the advantages so many of his contemporaries enjoyed, and yet he rose to the highest office in this land. He fulfilled the American dream. Like his soldiers, the American people trusted and loved him, and he did not disappoint them. Rather than the Napoleon so many feared he would become, Andrew Jackson turned out to be the great advocate for equality. As President, he helped this country evolve from a republic into a democracy.

And many of the qualities that made him a great general also aided him in becoming a great President. For decades his predecessors faced the problem of dealing with unrelenting clashes between whites and Native Americans. The first thing Jackson as President accomplished was passage of the Indian Removal Act over stiff congressional opposition. The Trail of Tears was a terrible price to pay for this legislation but, as Jackson predicted, the Cherokee, Chickasaw, Creek, Choctaws, and Seminole tribes are alive today. They were not annihilated like the Yamassee, Mohawks and Pequots, and other eastern tribes.

He showed the same determination in forcing foreign nations to pay what they owed when they were responsible for damages to property belonging to Americans. During the Napoleonic Wars of the early nineteenth century, Americans had suffered many commercial losses, not only at the hands of the French and British but by such nations as Russia, Denmark, Portugal, the Netherlands, and the Kingdom of the Two Sicilies. Previous administrations had tried to bring about a settlement of these claims but the demands were rudely brushed aside. Then Andrew Jackson became President and he made it clear that he would accept nothing less than full payment from these European nations. In short order Russia, Portugal, and Denmark paid what was owed. He used a display of military might to bring the Kingdom of the Two Sicilies to terms, and with France it took the threat of war to force that country to pay what was due. His goal, he said, had always been "to demand the respect of all Europe."[3] And this he did.

Jackson also faced down South Carolina when it adopted an Ordinance of Nullification by which the tariffs passed by Congress were declared void within that state. He warned them that he would not allow the laws of the United States to be disobeyed. The nullifiers were engaged in treason, he said, and he promised military action if they persisted in their defiance. A compromise tariff was finally worked out, and South Carolina repealed its ordinance.

At the start of his administration Jackson asked for changes in the Second National Bank of the United States, a central bank chartered by Congress. The opposition in Congress passed a bill rechartering the Bank even though its present charter was not due to expire for four more years. Jackson vetoed the bill, and in so doing expanded the powers of the presidency by insisting on his right to void any legislation he felt was not in the public interest. In the past the veto power was only used if the legislation was deemed unconstitutional. Jackson put forward the idea that he could go beyond that reason and veto what he disliked. This action, in effect, made him an equal partner in the legislative process. The question of the Bank bill was finally taken to the people to decide in the presidential election of 1832 and the people sided with Jackson and reelected him. Shortly thereafter he removed the government's deposits from the Bank and within a few years the Bank went bankrupt.

And most important of all, President Jackson paid off the national debt. The one and only time the nation was without a debt. Not a penny was owed to anyone, foreign or domestic. A national debt, he wrote in 1824, is "a national curse, [and] my vow [if I become President] shall be to pay the national debt."[4] He achieved that goal in January, 1835. At a "banquet of extraordinary magnificence" held at Brown's Hotel in Washington, Senator Thomas Hart Benton rose to address a gathering of 250 persons. "This month of January, 1835," he cried, "in the fifty-eighth year of the Republic, ANDREW JACKSON being President, the NATIONAL DEBT IS PAID! and the apparition, so long unseen on earth, a great nation without a national debt! Stands revealed to the astonished vision of a wondering world!"

The crowd let out a lusty cheer.

Then Benton proposed a toast. "PRESIDENT JACKSON: *May the evening of his days be as tranquil and as happy for himself as their meridian has been resplendent, glorious, and beneficent for his country.*"[5]

Jackson had quite a career, all made possible by his success as a military commander in defeating his country's enemies, both "savage and civilized." Few generals before or since could match what General Andrew Jackson accomplished. In the present age the American people should still be grateful for what he did.

Notes

Introduction

1. Jackson to Winchester, October 4, 1806, in Harold D. Moser and Sharon Macpherson, eds., *The Papers of Andrew Jackson* (Knoxville, TN, 1984), II, p. 111. Hereafter cited as Jackson, *Papers*.

Chapter 1

1. John Trotwood Moore, *Taylor Trotwood Magazine* (May 1907): 142–143.
2. Susan Alexander, "The Fugitives from the Waxhaws," *National Intelligencer,* August 1, 29, 1845, reprinted in William A. Graham, *General Joseph Graham and His Papers on North Carolina Revolutionary History* (Raleigh, NC, 1904), p. 71. I am grateful to Dr. Hendrik Booraem for informing me of this source.
3. Ibid., pp. 72–73.
4. James Parton, *The Life of Andrew Jackson* (New York, 1861), I, pp. 64–65. Hereafter cited as Parton, *Jackson.*
5. Alexander, "Fugitives from the Waxhaws," p. 73; Amos Kendall, *The Life of Andrew Jackson* (New York, 1844), p. 14. Hereafter cited as Kendall, *Jackson.*
6. Parton, *Jackson,* I, 72; Kendall, *Jackson,* p. 25; Robert V. Remini, *Andrew Jackson and the Course of American Empire* (Baltimore, MD, 1998), pp. 16–17. Hereafter cited as Remini, *Jackson.*
7. Kendall, *Jackson,* p. 45. Jackson described his suffering in Camden in a letter to Sam Houston, July 1824, Jackson Papers, Library of Congress (Hereafter cited as LC).

8. James McLaughlin to Amos Kendall, January 2, 1843, Jackson Papers, LC.

9. Parton, *Jackson,* I, pp. 104–105.

10. Ibid.

11. Ibid. p. 121.

12. Ibid., I, pp. 123–124.

13. Ibid.

14. J. G. M. Ramsey, *The Annals of Tennessee to the End of the Eighteenth Century* (Charleston, SC, 1853), p. 484.

15. Ibid.; John Reid and John H. Eaton, *The Life of Andrew Jackson* (1817; reprint University, AL, 1975), p. 16.

16. Albigence W. Putnam, *History of Middle Tennessee* (Nashville, 1859), pp. 317–318.

17. Robert V. Remini, *Andrew Jackson and His Indian Wars* (New York, 2001), pp. 27–29.

18. Jackson to Smith, February 13, 1789, Jackson, *Papers,* I, p. 16.

19. Jackson to John McKee, May 16, 1794 in ibid., I, pp. 48–49.

20. Ramsey, *Annals of Tennessee,* pp. 602–617; Putnam, *History of Middle Tennessee,* p. 478 note.

21. Ramsey, *Annals of Tennessee,* p. 648.

22. Remini, *Jackson,* I, pp. 76–85.

23. *Annals of Congress,* 4th Congress, 2nd Session, pp. 1738–1739.

24. Ibid., p. 2155.

25. Claiborne to Jackson, July 20, 1797, Jackson, *Papers,* I, p. 148.

26. Jackson to Major James Ore, March 4, 1797, ibid., I, p. 128.

27. Parton, *Jackson,* I, p. 227

28. Sevier to Jackson, May 8, 1797, in John Spencer Bassett, ed., *The Correspondence of Andrew Jackson* (Washington, DC, 1926–1933), I, p. 31. (Emphasis in original; hereafter cited as Jackson, *Correspondence.*)

29. Jackson to McKinney, May 10, 1802, in Jackson, *Papers,* I, pp. 294–295.

30. Ibid.

31. Jackson to Winchester, May 10, 1802, in ibid., I, pp. 295–296.

32. Ibid.

33. Jackson to George W. Campbell, October 15, 1812, in ibid., II, pp. 335.

34. For these treaties, see Charles C. Royce, *Indian Land Cession in the United States* (Washington, DC, 1904), pp. 648–651, 652–653.

35. Blount to Jackson, December 28, 1809, Jackson, *Papers,* II, pp. 226–227

36. Jackson to Blount, June 4, 1812, in ibid., II, pp. 301–302

37. Jackson to Colbert, June 5, 1812, in ibid., II, pp. 302–303.

38. Jackson to Blount, July 3, 1812, in ibid., II, p. 307.

39. Ibid.
40. H. S. Halbert and T. H. Ball, *The Creek War of 1813–1814* (Chicago, 1885; reprint University, AL, 1969), pp. 100, 103
41. Remini, *Jackson,* I, pp. 173–174.
42. Jackson to Armstrong, March 13, 15, 1813, Jackson Papers, LC; Parton, *Jackson,* I, p. 378.
43. Jackson to Grundy, March 15, 1813, Jackson, *Papers,* II, p. 385; Jackson to Lewis, April 9, 1813, in Jackson, *Correspondence,* I, p. 304.
44. Jackson to Rachel Jackson, March 15, 1813, Jackson, *Papers,* II, p. 187.
45. Parton, *Jackson,* I, p. 382; Kendall, *Jackson,* p. 149.
46. Parton, *Jackson,* I, pp. 384, 486.
47. Ibid.
48. General Order, September 10, 1813, Jackson Papers, LC; Reid and Eaton, *Jackson,* p. 33.

Chapter 2

1. Jackson to William B. Lewis, October 24, 1813, Jackson Papers, LC.
2. Message to the Troops, October 24, 1813, in ibid.
3. Davy Crockett, *Life of Davy Crockett* (New York, 1854), p. 75.
4. Jackson to Blount, November 4, 1813, in Jackson, *Correspondence,* I, p. 341.
5. Jackson to Rachel, December 29, 1813, in Jackson, *Papers,* II, p. 516.
6. *United States Telegraph,* July 3, 1828.
7. Jackson to Blount, November 11, 1813, in John Brannan, ed., *Official Letters of the Military and Naval Officers During the War with Great Britain in the Years 1812, '13, '14 and '15* (Washington, DC, 1823), p. 265.
8. Jackson to Blount, November 15, 1813, Jackson Papers, LC.
9. Reid and Eaton, *Jackson,* p. 60.
10. Parton, *Jackson* I, pp. 446.
11. Address of Officers, November, 1813, Jackson Papers, LC.
12. Reid and Eaton, *Jackson,* p. 63.
13. Ibid., pp. 65–66.
14. Ibid., p. 68.
15. Jackson to Blount, November 29, 1813, Jackson Papers, LC.
16. Reid and Eaton, *Jackson,* pp. 68–71.
17. Coffee to John Donelson, December 22, 1813, in *American Historical Magazine* 6 (April 1901): 178 (hereafter cited as *AHM*).
18. Jackson to Coffee, December 9, 1813, Jackson Papers, LC.
19. Jackson to Rachel, December 14, 1813, in Jackson, *Correspondence,* I, pp. 391–392.

20. Jackson to Rachel, December 29, 1813, in Jackson, *Papers,* II, 515.

21. Herbert J. Doherty, Jr., *Richard Keith Call: Southern Unionist* (Gainesville, FL, 1961), p. 7; John Reid to Nathan Reid, October, 1813, John Reid Papers, LC.

22. Coffee to Jackson, December 20, 1813, Jackson Papers, LC.

23. Jackson to Coffee, December 31, 1813, in Jackson, *Correspondence,* I, p. 431.

24. Jackson to Pinckney, January 29, 1814, in ibid., p. 448.

25. Reid and Eaton, *Jackson,* p. 128.

26. Ibid., p. 129.

27. Jackson to Pinckney, January 29, 1814, in Jackson, *Correspondence,* I, pp. 448–450.

28. Ibid., p. 451.

29. Reid and Eaton, *Jackson,* p. 136.

30. Pinckney to John Armstrong, February 6, 1814, quoted in Parton, *Jackson,* I, 498.

31. Jackson to Pinckney, February 12, 1814, Jackson Papers, LC.

32. John Reid to Nathan Reid, October 17, November 6, 1813, Reid Papers, LC.

33. Parton, *Jackson,* I, p. 508.

34. General Order, March 12, 1814, in Jackson, *Correspondence,* I, p. 479.

35. Reid and Eaton, *Jackson,* pp. 142–143.

36. Jackson to Pinckney, March 14, 1814, Jackson Papers, LC; H. S. Halbert and Hall, *The Creek War of 1813–1814* pp. 246–247.

37. Reid and Eaton, *Jackson,* pp. 148–149.

38. Jackson to Blount, March 31, 1814, in Jackson, *Correspondence,* I, p. 479; Jackson to John Armstrong, April 2, 1814, National Archives.

39. Jackson to Pinckney, March 28, 1814, in Jackson, *Correspondence,* I, 488–489.

40. Reid and Eaton, *Jackson,* p. 150.

41. Jackson to Blount, March 31, 1814, in Jackson, *Correspondence,* I, 491; Jackson to Blount, April 1, 1814, Jackson Papers, LC.

42. This is the tradition about Montgomery. But, according to Coffee, Montgomery reached the breastwork, thrust his rifle through a porthole, and killed an Indian. He in turn was shot through the same porthole and died. Coffee to John Donelson, April 1, 1814, 6 *AHM* (April 1901): 183.

43. Jackson to Rachel, April 1, 1814, in Jackson, *Papers,* III, p. 54.

44. Halbert and Hall, *Creek War,* pp. 276–277.

45. Amos Kendall, *The Life of Andrew Jackson* (New York, 1944), p. 282/

46. Jackson to Blount, March 31, 1814, in Jackson, *Correspondence,* I, pp. 491–492

47. Ibid.

48. Jackson to Rachel, April 1, 1814, in Jackson, *Papers,* III, 55.

49. Jackson to Rachel, April 14, 1815, Jackson Papers, LC.

50. Reid and Eaton, *Jackson,* pp. 155–157.

51. Anne Newport Royall, *Letters from Alabama, 1817–1822* (University, AL, 1969), p. 91; George Cary Eggleston, *Red Eagle and the Wars with the Creek Indians of Alabama* (New York, 1878), pp. 334–347; Reid and Eaton, *Jackson,* pp. 165–167.

52. Ibid.

53. Ibid., p. 168.

54. Ibid.; Jackson to Pinckney, April 18, 1814, in Jackson, *Correspondence,* I, p. 504.

55. Armstrong to Pinckney, March 17, 20, 1814, *American State Papers, Indian Affairs,* VI, p. 338, Washington, D.C. (hereafter cited as *ASPIA*); Pinckney to Jackson, March 7, 1814, in Jackson, *Correspondence,* I, pp. 496–497; Jackson to Pinckney, May 18, 1814, in ibid., II, pp. 1–2, Jackson to John Williams, May 18, 1814, in Jackson, *Papers,* III, 74–75.

56. Reid and Eaton, *Jackson,* pp. 173–176.

57. Armstrong to Jackson, May 22, 28, 1814, Jackson to Armstrong, June 8, 1814, Jackson Papers, LC.

58. Jackson to Rachel, September 22, 1814, in Jackson, *Papers,* III, p. 145.

59. Jackson to Rachel, August 10, 1814, in ibid., III, p. 114.

60. The original instructions to Pinckney can be found in Armstrong to Pinckney, March 17, 20, 1814, *ASPIA,* I, pp. 836–837.

61. Jackson to Armstrong, June 27, 1814, in Jackson, *Papers,* III, p. 83.

62. Armstrong to Jackson, July 18, 1814, in ibid., III, p. 90.

63. John Armstrong, *Notes of the War of 1812* (New York, 1840), I, p. 16, note 1.

64. Jackson to Hawkins, July 11, 1814; Jackson to Coffee, July 17, 1814, Jackson Papers, LC.

65. Reid and Eaton, *Jackson,* p. 186.

66. Jackson talk in Jackson, *Papers,* III, pp. 109–110.

67. Reid and Eaton, *Jackson,* pp. 173, pp. 190–191; Jackson to Coffee, August 10, 1814, in Jackson, *Papers,* III, 113.

68. Pinckney to Hawkins, April 23, 1814, in *ASPIA,* I, p. 858.

69. Hawkins to Pinckney, August 16, 1814, in ibid., VI, p. 341.

70. Jackson to Armstrong, August 10, 1814, in ibid., III, 792.

71. Jackson to Rachel, Jackson, *Papers,* III, 114.

72. Jackson to Overton, August 20, 1814, in Claybrooke Collection, Tennessee State Library, Nashville.

73. Jackson to Armstrong, August 10, 1814, in *American State Papers, Military Affairs,* III, 792. Jackson to Rachel, August 23, Jackson to Coffee, August 10, 1814, in Jackson, *Papers,* III, pp. 117, 113.

74. Jackson to Rachel, August 5, 1814, in Jackson, *Papers,* III, p. 105.

75. Jackson to Manrique, August 24, 1814, in ibid., III, p. 121.

Chapter 3

1. Reginald Horsman, *The War of 1812* (New York, 1969), p. 227; Frank L. Owsley, Jr., "Role of the South in the British Grand Strategy in the War of 1812," *Tennessee Historical Quarterly* 31 (Spring, 1972): 29–30.

2. Pigot to Cochrane, June 8, 1814, in Public Record Office Admiralty, I/506, London; Robin Reilly, *The British at the Gates* (New York, 1974), pp. 130–131; John K. Mahon, "British Command Decisions Relative to the Battle of New Orleans," 6 *Louisiana History* (Winter 1965): 53.

3. Jackson to Armstrong, August 5, 1814, Jackson Papers, LC.

4. Manrique to Ruiz Apodaca, September 10, December 6, 1814, Jackson to Manrique, August 30, 1814, Papeles de Cuba, legajos 1795, Archivo General de Indias, Seville, Spain (hereafter cited as AGI).

5. William Lawrence to Jackson, September 15, 1814, in Brannan, *Official Letters,* pp. 424–425; Reid and Eaton, *Jackson* pp. 214–215; James Parton, *Jackson* I, p. 108; Horsman, *War of 1812,* pp. 232–233.

6. Monroe to Jackson, October 10, 1814, in Jackson, *Correspondence* II, p. 71.

7. Jackson to Monroe, October 21, 1814, Monroe to Jackson, October 26, 1814, in ibid., II, pp. 82–83, 79.

8. Jackson to Manrique, November 6, 1814, Papeles de Cuba, legajos 1795, AGI. A subsequent letter was written and delivered, and the terms were rejected by the governor's council.

9. Parton, *Jackson,* I, p. 620.

10. Jackson to Monroe, November 14, 1814, in Jackson, *Correspondence,* II, 97.

11. Jackson to Rachel, November 15, 1814, in Jackson, *Papers,* III, pp. 186–187.

12. Jackson to Monroe, November 14, 1814, in Jackson, *Correspondence,* II, p. 99

13. Jackson to Manrique, November 9, 1814, Papeles de Cuba, legajos 1795, AGI.

14. Manrique to Jackson, November 9, 1814, in ibid.

15. Jackson to Rachel, November 15, 1814, in Jackson, *Papers,* III, p. 187.

16. Jackson to Winchester, November 22, 1814, *Miscellaneous Jackson Papers,* New York Historical Society, New York City.

17. Louise Livingston Hunt, *Memoir of Mrs. Edward Livingston with Letters Hitherto Unpublished* (New York, 1886), pp. 53–54.

18. Alexander Walker, *Jackson and New Orleans* (New York, 1856), pp. 17–18.

19. Monroe to Jackson, December 10, 1814, in Jackson, *Correspondence,* II, 110.

20. Vincent Nolte, *Fifty Years in Both Hemispheres* (New York, 1854), p. 207.

21. Manrique to Jackson, July 26, 1814, Jackson, *Papers,* III, 96.

22. Jackson to Claiborne, September 30, 1814, in ibid., III, 151.

23. Lafitte to Lockyer, September 4, 1814, and Lafitte to Claiborne, no date, in A. Lacarriere Latour, *Historical Memoir of the War in West Florida and Philadelphia* (Philadelphia, 1816); Charles B. Brooks, *The Siege of New Orleans* (Seattle, 1961), pp. 40–47.

24. Resolutions of the Louisiana Legislature Concerning the Baratarians, December 14, 1814, in Jackson, *Correspondence,* II, 114; Latour, *Historical Memoir,* p. 71.

25. See Jackson's Proclamation to the People of Louisiana in Jackson, *Correspondence,* II, p. 58.

26. Latour, *Historical Memoir,* p. 71.

27. Jane L. DeGrummond, *The Baratarians and the Battle of New Orleans* (Baton Rouge, 1961), pp. 65–71.

28. Jackson to Claiborne, September 21, 1814, in Jackson, *Papers,* III, 144.

29. To the Free Coloured Inhabitants of Louisiana, in Jackson, *Correspondence,* II, 59.

30. Jackson to Waters Allen, December 23, 1814, in Jackson, *Papers,* III, 216.

31. Jackson to Coffee, December 11, 1814, Jackson *Papers,* LC.

32. Brooks, *Siege of New Orleans,* pp. 92–96; Horsman, *War of 1812,* pp. 238–239.

33. Jackson to Coffee, December 16, 1814, Jackson, *Papers,* III, p. 205.

34. Charles Gayarré, *History of Louisiana* (New York, 1855), IV, p. 419

35. Walker, *Jackson and New Orleans,* pp. 143–144.

36. Gayarré, *History of Louisiana,* IV, p. 419

37. Walker, *Jackson and New Orleans,* p. 126.

38. Ibid., p. 150.

39. Ibid., p. 151; Latour, *Historical Memoir,* p. 88.

40. Nolte, *Fifty Years,* pp. 109–110.

41. Jackson to Monroe, December 27, 1814, in Jackson, *Correspondence,* II, p. 127.

42. Ibid.

43. Report of Killed, Wounded and Missing . . . December 23, 25, Jackson Papers, LC: Latour, *Historical Memoir,* p. 112.

44. Ibid.

45. DeGrummond, *Baratarians,* p. 101.

46. Reid to Nathan Reid, December 30, 1814, John Reid Papers, LC.

47. Sir John Fortescue, *History of the British Army* (London, 1899–1930), X, 161.

48. DeGrummond, *Baratarians,* pp. 97–103

49. Latour, *Historical Memoir,* p. 128; Walker, *Jackson and New Orleans,* p. 227

50. DeGrummond, Baratarians, pp. 106–107; Latour, *Historical Memoir,* p. lix.

51. Parton, *Jackson,* II, p. 143.

52. Walker, *Jackson and New Orleans,* p. 256.

53. Ibid.; John Reid to Elizabeth Reid, February 10, 1815, Reid Papers, LC.

54. Jackson to Monroe, January 2, 1815, Jackson Papers, LC.

55. Latour, *Historical Memoir,* p. lix.

56. DeGrummond, *Baratarians,* p. 115.

57. Jackson to Monroe, January 3, 1815, in Jackson, *Papers,* III, p. 228.

58. Paterson to Jackson, January 7, 1815, Jackson Papers, LC; Morgan to Jackson, January 7, 1815, Jackson, *Papers,* III, pp. 234–235.

59. Walker, *Jackson and New Orleans,* pp. 318–319.

60. Jackson to Monroe, February 13, 1815, Jackson Papers, LC.

61. Ibid.; Lambert to Lord Bathurst, January 10, 1815, in Latour, *Historical Memoir,* p. cl; Horsman, *War of 1812,* pp. 245–246.

62. Reilly, *British at the Gates,* p. 295.

63. Walker, *Jackson and New Orleans,* p. 327.

64. Reid and Eaton, *Jackson,* p. 339.

65. *Niles' Weekly Register,* February 11, 1815; Walker, *Jackson and New Orleans,* p. 327; Parton, *Jackson,* II, 207.

66. Sir Harry Smith, *The Autobiography of Lieutenant General Harry Smith* (London, 1902), I, p. 236.

67. Reid and Eaton, *Jackson,* p. 339; Parton, *Jackson,* II, p. 197; Wilbert S. Brown, The Amphibious Campaign for West Florida and Louisiana (University, AL, 1969), p. 49.

68. Parton, *Jackson,* II, 197; Brooks, *Siege of New Orleans,* p. 239. For the British account of the battle, see John Henry Cooke, *A Narrative . . . of the Attack on New Orleans in 1814 and 1815* (London, 1835), pp. 234–235.

69. Walker, *Jackson and New Orleans,* p. 330; Reid to Abram Maury, January 9, 1814, Reid Papers, LC; Reilly, British at the Gates, p. 299.

70. Lambert to Lord Bathurst, January 10, 1815, in Latour, *Historical Memoir,* p. cli.

71. Ibid.

72. Coffee to John Donelson, January 25, 1815, in *American Historical Magazine* 6 (April 1901): 186.

73. Parton, *Jackson,* II, 199.
74. Walker, *Jackson and New Orleans,* p. 332; Brown, *Amphibious Campaign,* p. 148.
75. Reid and Eaton, *Jackson,* p. 345.
76. Patterson to the secretary of the navy, January 13, 1815, in Latour, *Historical Memoir,* pp. lx-lxiv.
77. Lambert to Lord Bathurst, January 10, 1815, in ibid., p. clii.
78. *Raleigh* (North Carolina) *Star,* February 10, 1815; *Niles' Weekly Register,* February 25, 1815.
79. Walker, *Jackson and New Orleans,* p. 341.
80. "A Contemporary Account of the Battle of New Orleans by a Soldier in the Ranks," *Louisiana Historical Quarterly* 9 (January 1926): 14.
81. Parton, *Jackson,* pp. 208–209.
82. Walker, *Jackson and New Orleans,* p. 343.
83. Jackson to Monroe, January 13, 1815, Jackson Papers, LC; Latour, *Historical Memoir,* p. lx; A. P. Hayne to Jackson, January 13, 1815, in Brannan, *Official Letters,* p. 459.
84. Lambert to Lord Bathurst, January 10, 1815, in Latour, *Historical Memoir,* p. cliii; Lambert to Bathurst, January 28, 1815, in Public Record Office, War Office, 1/141, London.
85. Jackson to Monroe, January 13, 1815, Jackson Papers, LC.
86. Lambert to Jackson, January 8, 1815, in Jackson, *Correspondence,* II, pp. 133–134; Jackson to Lambert, January 8, 1815, in Jackson, *Papers,* III, 235.
87. Nolte, *Fifty Years,* p. 224.

Chapter 4

1. *Washington National Intelligencer,* February 7, 1815.
2. *Niles' Weekly Register,* February 14, 1815.
3. John Binns, *Autobiography,* quoted in Parton, *Jackson* II, pp. 248.
4. February 18, March 4, 1814.
5. William Graham Sumner, *Andrew Jackson* (Boston, 1882), p. 51.
6. *Annals of Congress,* 13th Congress, 3rd Ses., p. 1155.
7. A copy of this song can be found in the Jackson Papers, LC.
8. Parton, Jackson, II, p. 270; Dubourg to Jackson, no date, in Jackson, *Correspondence* II, p. 150 note 1.
9. Latour, *Historical Memoir,* pp. 197–198, 199–200; Parton, *Jackson,* II, pp. 273–274.
10. "Andrew Jackson and D. A. Hall," *Louisiana Historical Quarterly* 5 (October 1922): 511.
11. Reid to Sophia Reid, April 20, 1815, Reid Papers, LC.
12. Parton, *Jackson,* II, p. 329.

13. Ibid., p. 334.
14. Andrew Haynes to Jackson, October 24, 1815, Jackson Papers, LC
15. Dallas to Jackson, May 22, 1815, in Jackson, *Correspondence,* II, p. 206.
16. Jackson to Edwards and Clark, June 27, 1815, in Jackson, *Papers,* III, pp. 367–368.
17. Jackson to Dallas, June 20, 1815, in Jackson, *Correspondence,* II, p. 21; Jackson to Dallas, July 11, in Jackson, *Papers,* III, p. 372.
18. Nicholls to Hawkins, June 12, 1815, Jackson, *Correspondence,* II, p. 211, note 2.
19. Jackson to Hawkins, August 14, 1815, in ibid., II, p, 214.
20. Coffee to Jackson, January 21, February 3, 1816, in ibid., II, 225, 232; Jackson to Coffee, February 2, 13, 1816, Jackson, *Papers,* IV, pp. 6–7, 11.
21. Jackson to Monroe, March 4, 1817, Monroe Papers, New York Public Library, New York; Jackson to Coffee, September 19, 1816, Coffee Papers, Tennessee Historical Society; Jackson to Henry Atkinson, May 15, 1819, in W. Edwin Hamphill, ed., The *Papers of John C. Calhoun (Columbia, 1963–),* IV, p. 63; Jackson to William H. Crawford, July 20, 1816, *American State Papers, Indian Affairs,* II, p. 103
22. Jackson to Calhoun, August 25, 1820, Jackson Papers, LC.
23. Jackson to Monroe, May 12, 1816, ibid.
24. Crawford to Jackson, May 20, June 19, 1816, Jackson Papers, LC; Jackson to Crawford, June 10, 1816, Jackson, *Correspondence,* II, p. 248.
25. Crawford to Jackson, July 1, 1816, in Jackson, *Correspondence,* II, p. 251.
26. For a complete discussion of Jackson's activities as Indian commissioner, see Robert V. Remini, *Andrew Jackson and His Indian Wars* (New York, 2001), pp. 94–129.
27. Jackson to Coffee, August 12, 1817, Jackson, *Papers,* IV, p. 132.
28. Jackson to George Graham, an interim secretary of state, June 11, 1817, *American State Papers, Indian Affairs,* II, 142; William A. Love, "General Jackson's Military Road," *Publications of the Mississippi Historical Society* 9 (1910): 402–417.
29. Gaines to Jackson, May 14, 1816, in Jackson, *Papers,* IV, p. 31.
30. Zúñiga to Jackson, May 26, 1816, ASPIA, I, pp. 714–715; Captain Ferdinand Amelung to Jackson, June 4, 1816, Jackson, *Correspondence,* II, pp. 242–243.
31. Jackson to Gaines, April 8, 1816, Jackson, *Correspondence,* II, p. 239.
32. James W. Silver, *Edmund Pendleton Gaines* (Baton Rouge, 1949), p. 63.
33. Gaines to Jackson, April 2, 1817, in ibid., IV, 107.
34. R. S. Cotterill, *The Southern Indians* (Norman, OK, 1954), p. 8.

35. Gaines to Jackson, July 10, 1817, in Jackson, *Correspondence,* II, pp. 305–306.

36. Gaines to Jackson, November 21, 1817, *ASPIA,* I, p. 686.

37. Gaines to Jackson, December 2, 1817, in Jackson, *Papers,* IV, pp. 153–154.

38. Jackson to Calhoun, December 16, 1817, in ibid., p. 161.

39. Calhoun to Jackson, December 26, 1817, Calhoun to Gaines, December 16, 1817, in Jackson, *Correspondence,* II, pp. 141–142 and note 2.

40. Jackson to Monroe, January 6, 1818, in ibid., II, pp. 345–346.

41. Monroe to Calhoun, January 12, 1818, in Jackson, *Papers,* IV, p. 165.

42. Actually the existence of this letter can probably never be proved, according to the editor of the Jackson *Papers,* IV, p. 166, but David S. Heidler and Jeanne T. Heidler in their book *Old Hickory's War: Andrew Jackson and the Quest for Empire* (Mechanicsburg, PA, 1996), p. 121, insist that there was no letter and that Jackson lied about it.

43. Rhea to Jackson, January 12, 1818, in Jackson, *Correspondence,* II, p. 348.

44. Monroe to Jackson, December 28, 1817, Monroe Papers, New York Public Library, New York.

45. Calhoun to Jackson, February 6, 1818, in *American State Papers, Military Affairs,* I, p. 697 (hereafter cited as *ASPMA*).

46. Luis de Onís, *Memoria* (Madrid, 1820), p. 18. An English translation was later prepared by Tobias Watkins in 1821.

47. *Annals of Congress,* 15th Congress, 2nd Ses., p. 863.

48. Jackson to Robert Henry Dyer et al, January 11, 1818, in *ASPMA,* I, p. 767.

49. The reports are in ibid., I, p. 740, II, pp. 99–103; Jackson's Memorial to the Senate, February 23, 1820, *Annals of Congress,* 15th Congress, 2nd Ses., Appendix, pp. 2320–2324.

50. Jackson to Calhoun, January 27, 1818, Jackson, *Papers,* IV, p. 172.

51. Jackson to Calhoun, February 10, 26, 1818, in *ASPMA,* I, pp. 697–698.

52. Jackson to Rachel, March 26, 1818, in Jackson, *Papers,* IV, 183–185.

53. Chief of the Muskogee Nation to the King of England, in *The United States and the Indians,* 11th–15th Congress, 1810–1819 (Washington, DC, 1820), Supplement, XIV, pp. 45–47.

54. Jackson to Rachel, March 26, 1818, in Jackson, *Papers,* IV, pp. 183–185.

55. Cappachemicco and Boleck to Cameron, no date, in United States and the Indians, Supplement, XIV, p. 134.

56. Muscogee chiefs to the King of England, in ibid., pp. 45–47.

57. Arbuthnot to Nicholls, August 26, 1817, in ibid., XIV, pp. 133.

58. Jackson to Calhoun, April 8, 1818, in Jackson, *Correspondence,* II, pp. 358–359.

59. Jackson to Caso y Luengo, April 6, 1818, in Jackson, *Papers,* IV, pp. 186–187.

60. Luengo to Jackson, April 7, 1818, in ibid., IV, pp. 188–189.

61. Jackson to Luengo, April 7, 1818, in *United States and the Indians,* Supplement, XIV, p. 114.

62. Jackson to Calhoun, May 5, 1818, in Jackson, *Papers,* IV, p. 198.

63. *Niles' Weekly Register,* August 21, 1819.

64. Jackson to Rachel, April 6, 1818, in Jackson, *Correspondence,* II, p. 359.

65. Jackson to Calhoun, April 20, 1818, in Jackson, *Papers,* IV, pp. 193–195.

66. General Order, April 15, 1818, in ibid., IV, p. 192.

67. Jackson to Calhoun, April 20, 1818, in ibid., IV, pp. 193–195.

68. Ibid.

69. Jackson to Calhoun, May 5, 1818, in ibid., IV, p. 199.

70. Jackson to Rachel, April 8, 1818, in Jackson, *Correspondence,* II, p. 357.

71. Jackson to Calhoun, May 5, 1818, in Jackson, *Papers,* IV, p. 199.

72. Jackson to Calhoun, April 26, 1818, in *ASPMA,* I, p. 701.

73. Ibid., I, p. 734.

74. Arbuthnot to his son, John, April 18, 1818, in ibid., I, pp. 712, 734.

75. Ambrister to Cameron, March 20, 1818, "Minutes of the Proceedings," April 26–28, 1818, in ibid., I, pp. 721–734.

76. Ibid., I, p. 734.

77. *Niles' Weekly Register,* June 6, 1818.

78. Jackson to Calhoun, May 5, 1818, in Jackson, *Papers,* IV, 199.

79. Both reports and a minority House report can be found in *ASPMA,* I, pp. 735–743.

80. Jackson to Calhoun, May 5, 1818, in ibid., IV, pp. 199–200.

81. Jackson to Masot, May 23, 1818, in ibid., IV, pp. 207–209.

82. Masot to Jackson, May 22, 1818, in ibid., IV, pp. 205–206.

83. Jackson to Masot, May 25, 1818, in ibid., IV, p. 211.

84. Jackson to [Piernas], May 24, 1818, in Jackson, *Papers,* IV, 210.

85. Jackson to George W. Campbell, October 5, 1818, in Jackson, *Correspondence,* II, p. 397.

86. Parton, *Jackson,* II, 492–493.

87. Jackson to Calhoun, June 2, 1818, in *American State Papers, Foreign Affairs,* IV, pp. 602–603.

Chapter 5

1. Jackson to Calhoun, June 3, 1818, in *American State Papers, Foreign Affairs,* IV, p. 603 (hereafter cited as ASPFA).

2. Jackson to Monroe, June 2, 1818, in Jackson, *Papers,* vol. IV, p. 211.

3. Calhoun to Jackson, January 23, 1820, in ibid., IV, p. 352.

4. Jackson to Rachel, June 2, 1818, in ibid., IV, pp. 212–213.

5. Charles Francis Adams, ed., *Memoirs of John Quincy Adams* (Philadelphia, 1874–1877), IV, pp. 102–103.

6. Ibid., IV, p. 105.

7. Ibid., IV, p. 107.

8. Monroe to Jackson, July 19, 1818, in *Monroe, Memoirs, Writings of James Monroe,* VI, (New York, 1903) pp. 54–61.

9. Jackson to Monroe, August 19, 1818, Jackson, *Correspondence* II, pp. 389–390.

10. Adams to Onis, July 23, 1818, in *ASPFA,* IV, pp. 497–499.

11. Robert Butler to Jackson, December 15, Eaton to Jackson, December 14, 1818, in Jackson, *Correspondence,* II, 413; Poindexter to Jackson, December 12, 1818, Jackson Papers, Library of Congress; Parton, *Jackson* II, p. 533.

12. *Annals of Congress,* 15th Congress, 2nd Ses., pp. 631–655.

13. Jackson to Lewis, January 25, 30, 1819, *Jackson-Lewis Papers,* New York Public Library, New York.

14. *Annals of Congress,* pp. 518–527, 655–703, 936–986.

15. Ibid., pp. 1136–1138.

16. Adams, *Memoirs,* IV, p. 243.

17. Jackson to Calhoun, November 13, 1820, Calhoun to Jackson, January 25, 1821, in Calhoun, *Papers,* V, pp. 434, 572–573, Jackson to Monroe, February 11, 1821, in Jackson, *Papers,* V, p. 10.

18. Calhoun to Jackson, March 31, 1821, in Calhoun, *Papers,* V, p. 706.

Chapter 6

1. *Newsweek,* February 11, 2008, p. 30.

2. On this point see Matthew Warshauer, *Andrew Jackson and the Politics of Martial Law* (Knoxville, TN, 2006).

3. Jackson's Address to the foreign ministers, April 6, 1829, in U.S. Presidents. A. Jackson, New York Public Library.

4. Jackson to William S. Fulton, July 4, 1824, in Jackson, *Correspondence,* III, 259.

5. *Washington Globe,* January 12, 14, 1835.

Index

Adair, John, 109, 111, 114
Adams, John Quincy, 167–70, 173–4
Adams-Onís Treaty, 170, 174
Alabama, 16, 34, 37, 39, 50, 65, 67, 72–3, 80–3, 85–9, 121, 134, 143
    See Mobile
Alexander, Susan, 6–7
Ambrister, Robert, 148, 155–9, 166, 170, 172
Amelia Island, 140, 145
American Revolutionary War, x, 1, 6–7, 10, 19, 23, 76, 97, 103, 175
Arbuthnot, Alexander, 137–8, 147, 151, 155–9, 166, 170, 172
Armstrong, John, 33–4, 39, 50, 54, 66–8, 70–1, 75, 81
Arnaud, Jean, 118

Bagot, Charles, 167
Bahamas, 146–7
Barataria Bay privateers, 90–3
Baton Rouge, Louisiana, 86, 94–5, 143

Battle of Emuckfaw Creek, 51–3, 62
Battle of Enotachopco Creek, 52–3
Battle of Fort Bowyer, 82–3
Battle of King's Mountain, 23
Battle of Lake Borgne, 88–95
Battle of Horseshoe Bend, 56–62, 68, 149
Battle of New Orleans, xi–xii, 6, 71, 85, 92–4, 108–21, 124–6, 175–6
Battle of Rodriguez Canal, 101–7
Battle of Stono Ferry, 8
Battle of Talladega, 43–4, 52
Battle of Tallushatchee, 42–3
Battle of Villeré's Plantation, 97–101
Bean, Russell, 22, 46–7
Benton, Jesse, 36–8, 69
Benton, Thomas Hart, 36–8, 69, 181
Big Warrior, 63–4, 74–5
black battalions, 93–4, 99, 111, 120
Blount, William, 16–18, 21, 28–9, 31–3, 38–9, 42, 50, 53, 129
Bonaparte, Napoleon, 27, 79, 102, 160, 179
Bowlegs Town, 152–7

Brown, Jacob, 129–30, 174
Bush, George W., 178
Butler, Robert, 87

Calhoun, John C., 139–42, 144–5, 159–60, 162–3, 166, 168, 173
Cameron, Charles, 146–7, 158
Campbell, George, 28
Canada, 1, 68, 70
Carolina, 99, 101–3
Carroll, William, 36, 52, 94, 96, 99, 109, 111, 114
censure, 140–4, 167–72, 177
character, x–xii, 2–3, 7–26, 34–8, 42–56, 60–5, 68–9, 87–8, 99, 104–5, 117–22, 127–9, 140–1, 144, 146, 150, 156, 159–60, 166–73, 175–9
Charleston, South Carolina, 8, 10, 39
Chef Menteur, 87, 89, 95, 99, 105
Chenubbee (Chief), 150
Cherokees, 7, 13–17, 19–20, 23, 25–6, 28, 30, 57–8, 61, 66–7, 72, 131–5, 179
Chickasaws, 16–17, 27–8, 30–1, 38, 66–7, 131–5, 179
Choctaws, 27–8, 84, 111, 132, 134–5, 179
civil rights, 125, 178
Civil War, x, 178
Clay, Henry, 171–2
Claiborne, Ferdinand L, 39, 50
Claiborne, William C. C., 20, 27, 88, 91, 93
Clark, William, 130–1
Cobb, Thomas W., 171–2
Cochrane, Alexander, 80–1, 83, 85, 88–9, 94–7, 108, 148
Cockburn, George, 79
Cocke, John, 39
Cocke, William, 18, 42–3, 47, 49, 55

Coffee, John, 41–2, 44, 46–7, 49, 54, 58–60, 71, 86, 94–6, 99, 103, 110–11, 116, 118, 131–5
Colbert, George, 30
Conway, George, 19
Cook, Peter, 155
Cornwallis, Charles (1ˢᵗ Marquess Cornwallis), 10
correspondence, 28–30, 34, 35, 47–8, 59, 62, 70–1, 75–7, 94–5, 107, 140–4, 155, 160–2, 168–9
Crawford, Jane (aunt), 5
Crawford, Thomas (uncle), 10
Crawford, William H., 133, 136, 141, 174
Creek War, 37–68, 70–7, 117, 130, 133, 137, 143, 177
    peace negotiations, 70–6
    See Battle of Emuckfaw Creek; Battle of Enotachopco Creek; Battle of Horseshoe Bend; Battle of Talladega; Battle of Tallushatchee; Fort Mims massacre; Treaty of Fort Jackson
Creeks, 16–17, 23, 27–32, 37–68, 70–7, 80–1, 130–1, 133–4, 137, 145–6, 148, 153–4, 156–8, 179
    See Creek War; Duck River killings; Fort Mims massacre; Red Sticks
Crockett, Davy, 42
Cuba, 162, 166, 174

Dallas, Alexander J., 130
Daquin, Jean, 93, 111
Davie, William Richardson, 8–9
de la Croix, Dussau, 98–9
de Onís, Luis, 143, 167, 170
de Neuville, Hyde, 167

de Zúñiga, Mauicio, 136
Declaration of Independence, 8
Democratic party, x, 178
Denmark, 179
Dickinson, Charles, 37
Dinsmore, Silas, 27
Donelson, John, 17
Donelson, Samuel, 14
Dubourg, Louis Guillaume Valentin, 126–7
Duck River killings, 29–32, 38
duels, 6, 24, 36–7
Dyer, Robert H., 154

East Tennessee army, 42–3
Eaton, John H., 104, 174
Edwards, Ninian, 130–1
Eisenhower, Dwight D., 176
executive power, 180

First Seminole War, 135–63
    See Bowlegs Town; Fort St.
        Marks; Fowltown;
        Mikasukians;
Florida, xi-xii, 1–2, 16, 21, 26–7,
    33–4, 62–3, 66, 70–3, 76,
    79–85, 90, 126, 130–52,
    160–1, 166–75, 177
    East, 76, 79, 140, 143–4, 152,
        166, 170, 174
    West, 33–4, 80, 140, 143, 170,
        174
    See Adams-Onís Treaty; First
        Seminole War; Fort St.
        Marks; Pensacola; Spain
Flournoy, Thomas, 39
Floyd, John, 39, 50
Fort Barrancas, 84–5
Fort Bowyer, 80–3, 86, 121
Fort Carlos de Barrancas, 162, 166
Fort Deposit, 41, 46, 55
Fort Gadsden, 146, 148, 160, 162
Fort Jackson, 63, 67, 70–2, 79

Fort Mims massacre, 37–8, 42, 61,
    64–6
Fort Petites Coquilles, 90
Fort St. Leon, 86
Fort St. Marks, 147–52, 155–6,
    160, 166, 168–9, 171
Fort St. Philip, 81, 86, 89
Fort Scott, 138, 144–5
Fort Strother, 42, 44, 46–7, 49–57
Fort Williams, 57–8, 62–3, 65, 67
Forty-fourth (East Essex) Regiment
    of Foot (U.K.), 111–12, 114
Fowltown, 138–9
France, 27–8, 88, 102
Francis, Josiah, 63, 66, 77, 151–2,
    156, 158, 166, 179

Gadsden, James, 146, 150–1, 155,
    165
Gaines, Edmund Pendleton,
    136–40, 142, 145, 154, 156
Gaines, George, 32
Georgia, 8, 50, 67, 72, 83, 125, 134,
    138, 152
Georgia militia, 50, 63, 144, 154,
    156
Gibbs, Samuel, 111–18
Girod, Nicholas, 88
Gordon, John, 45–6, 149
Great Britain, x-xii, 1–2, 6–10, 16,
    21, 23, 28, 32–3, 35, 61, 63,
    66, 70–1, 73–4, 76–7,
    79–122, 124–7, 130–1,
    134–8, 140, 142, 146–8,
    152, 155–60, 167, 170, 175,
    177, 179
    See First Seminole War; War of
        1812
Grundy, Felix, 34, 129
Gulf of Mexico, 1, 16, 28, 76, 80,
    87, 135, 177

habeas corpus, 127–8, 178

Hall, Dominick A., 92, 127–8
Hambly, William, 157
Hampton, Wade, 68
Harrison, William Henry, 68
Hawkins, Benjamin, 27, 66–7,
    70–5, 131
Hayne, Arthur P., 86
Hays, Chris, 17
Highlanders, 115–16
Himollemico, 151–2, 156, 166
Hinds, Thomas, 96, 117
Houston, Sam, 59
Hull, William, 32

Illinois, 130
Indian Removal Act, 179
Ireland, 83

Jackson, Andrew
    appearance, 7, 12, 176–7
    childhood, x-xi, 3, 6–10, 42, 179
    education, x, 6, 178
    health, 37–8, 69, 86, 156, 166,
        173
    judgeship, 21–2, 26
    land speculator, 26, 75–6
    lawyer, 11–12, 14–15, 26
    marriage, 14
    racism, 25–6
    teenage years, 2, 8–11
    wounds, 37–8, 69
    See censure; character;
        correspondence; duels;
        manifest destiny; martial law;
        military appointments;
        military legacy; mutiny;
        national security; political roles
Jackson, Andrew (father), 5
Jackson, Jr., Andrew (adopted son),
    86, 128
Jackson, Elizabeth Hutchinson
    (mother), 5–10
Jackson, Hugh (brother), 6–8

Jackson, Lyncoya (adopted son),
    42–3, 86
Jackson, Rachel Donelson Robards
    (wife), 14, 35, 42, 48, 59, 61,
    69, 75–6, 86, 128, 166
Jackson, Robert (brother), 6–10
Jamaica, 80, 85, 89
Jefferson, Thomas, x, 26–7, 29, 125,
    129
Johnson, Richard M., 172
Jones, Thomas ap Catesby, 90, 94

Keane, John, 89, 97–101, 111,
    115–18
Kennard, Noble, 154
Kentucky, 13–14, 16, 83, 86, 94
Kentucky militia, 95, 109, 111,
    114–16, 118–19
King Ferdinand VII, 170, 173
King George, 147
King, William, 165
Knox, Henry, 19
Knoxville, Tennessee, 12, 24

Lacoste, Pierre, 93, 111
Lafitte, Jean, 90–2, 104–5
Lafitte, Pierre, 90–3
Lake Borgne
    See Battle of Lake Borgne
Lake Pontchartrain, 87, 95, 135
Lambert, John, 107, 111, 116–17,
    121
Latour, Arsène Lacarrière, 89, 101
Lavack, John, 116–17
Lawrence, William, 80–1
Lewis, William B., 34, 171–2
Lincoln, Abraham, 178
Livingston, Edward, 88, 90, 92, 121
Lockyer, Nicolas, 91, 93–4
Louaillier, Louis, 127–8
Louisiana, 16, 20–1, 26–7, 33–4,
    83, 86, 91, 102–3, 126, 143
    See Baton Rouge; New Orleans

Louisiana, 101–3, 119
Louisiana militia, 97, 99–100, 105,
    118
Louisiana Purchase, 33–4, 140, 143
Luengo, Don Francisco Caso y,
    149–52

Madison, James, 32, 70–1, 79,
    125–6, 135–6, 140
manifest destiny, 1–2, 16, 28–9,
    70–6, 132, 142, 166
Manrique, Don Matteo González,
    76–7, 82, 84–5
Marshall, George, 176
martial law, xii, 96, 127–8, 177–8
Masot, José, 149, 161–3
McCain, John, 176
McCay, Spruce, 11–12
McIntosh, William, 146, 148, 154
McKee, John, 134
McKeever, Isaac, 146, 148, 151
McKinney, Henry, 25–6
McNairy, John, 12–14
McQueen, Peter, 63, 66, 77, 153
Meriwether, David, 134
Mexico, 90, 168
Mikasukians, 148–50, 156
military appointments (militia)
    judge advocate, 17
    major general, 18–19, 23–32,
        37–50, 176
    See also U.S. Army; U.S.
        Volunteers
military legacy, 175–8
    criticism of, 105–11, 117–18
    gaze, xii, 22–3, 46–7
    heroism, 123–9, 133–4, 172
    leadership, x-xi, 2–3, 12–15, 19,
        24–5, 34–6, 43–55, 117,
        121–2, 175–7
    luck, 35, 52, 98–9, 177
    nicknames, 63, 72, 82, 127, 177
    See "Old Hickory"

tactician, xi, 35, 55
troops, 2–3, 24–6, 34–6, 38,
    41–9, 54–6, 67, 96–7, 146,
    176–7
reputation, 17–20, 27, 47, 53,
    56, 68, 123–9
strategy, xi, 25, 44, 176
willpower, 34–6, 69, 127, 177
    See censure; martial law
militia, 8, 13, 17–20, 23–32, 37–63,
    81–2, 86, 95–7, 99–100,
    105, 109, 111, 114–15, 118,
    133, 144–5, 176
    See Georgia militia; Kentucky
        militia; Louisiana militia;
        Mississippi Dragoons;
        Tennessee militia
Mississippi, 16, 27, 37, 39, 67–8,
    80–1, 90, 94, 127, 134, 136
Mississippi Dragoons, 96, 99, 117
Mississippi River, 16, 28, 67, 80–1,
    85–7, 97–8, 101, 105,
    108–12, 118, 131, 135
Missouri, 130
Mobile, Alabama, 34, 80–3, 85–9,
    121, 143
Monroe, James, 83, 88–9, 100, 107,
    109, 120, 133, 139–43, 160,
    166, 167–8, 173–4
Montgomery, Lemuel P., 59
Morgan, David, 100, 105, 109–11,
    118–19
Morgan, Gideon, 59
Mullins, Thomas, 112
mutiny, xii, 45–9, 55–6

Napoleonic Wars, 179
Nashville, Tennessee, x, 2, 12–17,
    21, 32–6, 38, 44–7, 68, 128,
    130, 135, 167
national debt, 180
national security, 1–2, 29, 67, 72–3,
    135

Native Americans, xi, 1–2, 6–7, 9,
        12–21, 23–32, 35, 37–77,
        79–80, 82–3, 85, 90–1, 125,
        130–5, 137–63, 165–70,
        176–7, 179
    early campaigns against, 15, 17,
        19–21
    and frontier communities, 13, 17
    and Jackson, 21, 23, 25–31,
        42–3, 62–7, 70–6, 132–4,
        140
    treaties with, 134–5
    See Creek War; Creeks;
        Cherokees; Chickasaws; First
        Seminole War; Mikasukians;
        Shawnees; Treaty of Fort
        Jackson; Treaty of Hopewell;
        Treaty of New York
Neamathla, 138
Negro Fort, 135–7, 146, 160, 166
New Orleans, Louisiana, 16, 27,
        32–3, 39, 80–1, 83, 85–101,
        104, 107, 126–7, 135, 146,
        161, 172, 177–8
    See Battle of New Orleans
Nicholls, Edward, 80, 82, 85, 91,
        130–1, 148
North Carolina, 11–12, 16, 63, 134,
        136
    See Waxhaws

"Old Hickory," 34–7, 44–7, 51–2,
        54–5, 57–8, 62, 68, 70–1,
        85, 93, 99–100, 109, 113,
        143, 162, 168, 173, 177
Overton, John, 14, 75

Pakenham, Michael, 89, 102–5,
        107–11, 114–18, 121
Panic of 1819, 174
Peddie, John, 96
Patterson, Daniel T., 88, 90–2, 105,
        107–10, 119

Pensacola, 34, 63, 66, 76, 80–6,
        140, 148–9, 152, 160–2,
        165, 168–9, 171–2, 177
    occupation of, 83–5, 140, 168,
        171–2, 177
Percy, William, 82
Piernas, Luis, 162
Pigot, Hugh, 80
Pinckney, Thomas, 39, 51–4, 57–8,
        63, 66–7, 70, 72, 74–5
Plauché, Jean, 94
Poindexter, George, 172
political roles
    congressman, 18–21, 27, 88
    governor, 173–4
    president, x, xii, 37, 43, 56, 174,
        178–81
    senator, 21
Portugal, 96, 179

Red Eagle (Chief)
    See William Weatherford
Red Sticks, 37–9, 44, 50–6, 61–6,
        73–7, 137–8, 146, 149,
        151–3
Reid, John, 47, 52–4, 56, 87, 102,
        106, 128
Rennie, Robert, 117–18
Rhea, John, 134, 140–1, 143, 168
Roane, Archibald, 23, 25
Roberts, Isaac, 55
Robertson, James, 27
Ross, George, 111
Ross, Robert, 102
Russell, William, 25
Russia, 33, 179

St. Marks, See Fort St. Marks
Scott, Richard W., 139, 149,
        152–3
Searcy, Bennett, 12–14
Second National Bank of the United
        States, 180

Seminoles, 137–63, 179
    See First Seminole War
Sevier, John, 19–21, 23–4
Shawnees, 29, 37
Shepherd, Richard S., 110
Smith, Daniel, 16
Smith, Harry, 114
Smyth, Alexander, 172
South Carolina, 5, 8–11, 39, 136,
    180
    See Charleston; Waxhaws
Spain, xii, 1–2, 9, 16, 26–8, 33–5,
    62–3, 66, 70–1, 73, 76,
    79–85, 88, 90–1, 96, 130,
    135–7, 139, 141–3, 147–51,
    160–3, 166–70, 174–5
    See Adams-Onís Treaty; Florida
Spanish Conspiracy, 16–17
Spencer, Robert, 96
Stephenson, James White, 6
Stokes, John, 12

Tarleton, Banastre, 8
Tatum, Howell, 88
Tecumseh, 37, 63–4, 73
Tennessee, x–xi, 12–21, 28–36, 38,
    49–50, 53–4, 67–8, 75, 83,
    86, 134, 144–5, 148, 167
    See Knoxville; Nashville;
    Tennessee militia; Tennessee
    volunteers
Tennessee militia, 17–20, 23–7, 32,
    37–62, 67–8, 94–6, 99, 105,
    109, 111, 114–16, 133
    See East Tennessee army; West
    Tennessee army
Tennessee volunteers, 143, 148,
    153–4, 167
Thirty-ninth Infantry Regiment
    (U.S.), 53–4, 57, 59, 61
Thornton, William, 97–8, 108,
    111–12, 118–19
Trail of Tears, 43, 179

Treaty with the Cherokees, 133–4
Treaty of Fort Jackson, 72–5, 130–1,
    133–4, 138, 157
Treaty of Ghent, 83, 101, 122,
    124–6, 130–1, 134, 138
Treaty of Hopewell, 28
Treaty of New York, 28
Treaty of San Ildefonso, 27

United States, x–xii, 1–2, 8, 9,
    16–17, 27, 32–3, 66, 70,
    73–7, 79–81, 83–5, 95,
    123–6, 134, 143, 158,
    166–7, 170, 175–8
    independence of, x–xii, 1–2, 8, 9,
    32, 124–5, 167, 175–6
    and military force, 83
    nationalism, 124
    See Adams-Onís Treaty; First
    Seminole War; War of 1812
U.S. Army
    brigadier general, 68
    commander of Division of the
    South, 129–30, 135
    major general, 24, 68–70, 77,
    174, 176
    military road, construction of,
    135
    commander of Seventh Military
    District, 68, 70
    See Thirty-ninth Infantry
    Regiment
U.S. Congress, 16, 18, 27, 33, 76,
    88, 125, 129, 132, 144, 160,
    169–72, 178, 180
U.S. Constitution, 16, 169, 178
U.S. House of Representatives,
    18–20, 133, 143, 160, 171–2
U.S. Senate, 18, 21, 37, 126, 133,
    160, 174
U.S. Volunteers, 32–4

Villeré, Gabriel, 97–9

Villeré, Jacques, 89, 97, 108

War of 1812, xii, 1–2, 32–7, 61, 68,
    76, 79–122, 147
  See Battle of Fort Bowyer;
    Battle of Lake Borgne;
    Battle of Villeré's Plantation;
    Battle of New Orleans;
    Creek War
Washington, George, 16, 18, 125
Waxhaws, 7–11, 14
Weatherford, William, 37, 43, 61,
    63–5
West Tennessee army, 41–62, 67–8

Whig party, 178
White, Hugh Lawson, 19–20
Wilkinson, James, 27, 34
Wilkinson, Thomas, 116
Williams, John, 54, 57
Williams, Sampson, 15
Williamson, Thomas, 154
Winchester, James, 2, 25–6, 33, 86
Woodbine, George, 130, 138,
    147–8, 155, 158
Woods, John, 55–6

Yorktown, Virginia, 10
You, Dominique, 90, 92, 106–7